Real-Resumes for Career Changers

Anne McKinney, Editor

PREP PUBLISHING

FAYETTEVILLE, NC

PREP Publishing
1110½ Hay Street
Fayetteville, NC 28305
(910) 483-6611

Cover design by Chris Pearl

Library of Congress Cataloging-in-Publication Data

Real-resumes for career changers : actual resumes and cover letters that
helped real people change their careers / Anne McKinney, editor.
      p. cm. -- (Real-resumes series)
    ISBN 1-885288-17-4
    1. Résumés (Employment) 2. Cover Letters. I. McKinney, Anne, 1948-
II. Series.

    HF5383 .R3957 2000
    808'.06665–dc21   00-037309
                                                                          CIP

Printed in the United States of America

By PREP Publishing

Business and Career Series:

RESUMES AND COVER LETTERS THAT HAVE WORKED

RESUMES AND COVER LETTERS THAT HAVE WORKED FOR MILITARY PROFESSIONALS

GOVERNMENT JOB APPLICATIONS AND FEDERAL RESUMES

COVER LETTERS THAT BLOW DOORS OPEN

LETTERS FOR SPECIAL SITUATIONS

RESUMES AND COVER LETTERS FOR MANAGERS

REAL-RESUMES FOR TEACHERS

REAL-RESUMES FOR STUDENTS

REAL-RESUMES FOR CAREER CHANGERS

REAL-RESUMES FOR SALES

REAL ESSAYS FOR COLLEGE & GRADUATE SCHOOL

Judeo-Christian Ethics Series:

SECOND TIME AROUND

BACK IN TIME

WHAT THE BIBLE SAYS ABOUT...Words that can lead to success and happiness

A GENTLE BREEZE FROM GOSSAMER WINGS

BIBLE STORIES FROM THE OLD TESTAMENT

Fiction:

KIJABE...An African Historical Saga

Table of Contents

Goal: From Self-Employment to Something Totally Different

A WORD FROM THE EDITOR:
ABOUT THE REAL-RESUMES SERIES

This book is dedicated to career changers. We hope the superior samples will help you reengineer your career so that you will find work aligned to your career interests.

Welcome to the Real-Resumes Series. The Real-Resumes Series is a series of books which have been developed based on the experiences of real job hunters and which target specialized fields or types of resumes. As the editor of the series, I have carefully selected resumes and cover letters (with names and other key data disguised, of course) which have been used successfully in real job hunts. That's what we mean by "Real-Resumes." What you see in this book are *real* resumes and cover letters which helped real people get ahead in their careers.

The Real-Resumes Series is based on the work of the country's oldest resume-preparation company known as PREP Resumes. If you would like a free information packet describing the company's resume preparation services, call 910-483-6611 or write to PREP at 1110½ Hay Street, Fayetteville, NC 28305. If you have a job hunting experience you would like to share with our staff at the Real-Resumes Series, please contact us at preppub@aol.com or visit our website at http://www.prep-pub.com.

The resumes and cover letters in this book are designed to be of most value to people already in a career change or contemplating a career change. If we could give you one word of advice about your career, here's what we would say: Manage your career and don't stumble from job to job in an incoherent pattern. Try to find work that interests you, and then identify prosperous industries which need work performed of the type you want to do. Learn early in your working life that a great resume and cover letter can blow doors open for you and help you maximize your salary.

As the editor of this book, I would like to give you some tips on how to make the best use of the information you will find here. Because you are considering a career change, you already understand the concept of managing your career for maximum enjoyment and self-fulfillment. The purpose of this book is to provide expert tools and advice so that you *can* manage your career. Inside these pages you will find resumes and cover letters that will help you find not just a job but the type of work you want to do.

Overview of the Book

Every resume and cover letter in this book actually worked. And most of the resumes and cover letters have common features: all are one-page, all are in the chronological format, and all resumes are accompanied by a companion cover letter. The book is divided into three parts. **Part One** provides some advice about job hunting. Step One begins with a discussion of why employers prefer the one-page, chronological resume. In Step Two you are introduced to the direct approach and to the proper format for a cover letter. In Step Three you learn the 14 main reasons why job hunters are not offered the jobs they want, and you learn the six key areas employers focus on when they interview you. Step Four gives nuts-and-bolts advice on how to handle the interview, send a follow-up letter after an interview, and negotiate your salary. At the end of Part One, you'll find advice about how to research and locate the companies and organizations to which you want to send your resume.

Since the cover letter plays such a critical role in a career change, **Part Two** of the book is entitled Cover Letters for Career Changers. You will learn from the experts how to format your cover letters and you will see suggested language to use in particular career-change situations. It has been said that "A picture is worth a thousand words" and, for that reason, you will see numerous examples of effective cover letters used by real individuals to change fields, functions, and industries. Part Two ends with answers to the 16 most commonly asked questions about cover letters and job hunting, and the answers are provided in the form of actual cover letters.

Parts One and Two lead up to the most important part of the book, which is Real-Resumes for Career Changers—**Part Three.** In this section you will see people in varying stages of change. Some of the individuals whose resumes and cover letters you see wanted to change the product, company, or service they were selling, managing, or representing. As Part Three evolves, you discover resumes and cover letters used by people who wanted to find a completely different type of work to do. Then there are resumes and cover letters of people who wanted a change but who probably wanted to remain in their industry. Many of you will be especially interested by the resumes and cover letters of individuals who knew they definitely wanted a career change but had no idea what they wanted to do next. Other resumes and cover letters show individuals who knew they wanted to change fields and had a pretty good idea of what they wanted to do next. Part Three ends with resumes and cover letters of folks who moved from self-employment, usually in small companies, to something totally different.

Whatever your field, and whatever your circumstances, you'll find resumes and cover letters that will "show you the ropes" in terms of successfully switching careers. Bear in mind that you can learn a lot from any of the resumes in this book. For example, if you are a professional who wants to remain in your field, you will find useful the resume of Samantha Yurko on page 105; here you will find a resume and cover letter of a cosmetics professional who wants to move into an outside sales position in her industry. You don't have to be part of the cosmetics industry to learn a lot from her resume and cover letter in terms of style and language. You will find resumes and cover letters of professionals in financial services, retailing, bookselling, cosmetics, credit card services, food products, furniture and home comfort products, industrial settings, the insurance industry, medical and pharmaceutical environments, mortgage services, the automobile industry, personnel recruiting services, the printing industry, property rentals, real estate, the computer field, telecommunications, media and advertising, wholesale food and beverages, the travel industry, and many more.

Before you proceed further, think about why you picked up this book.
- Are you dissatisfied with the type of work you are now doing?
- Would you like to change careers, change companies, or change industries?
- Are you satisfied with your industry but not with your niche or function within it?
- Do you want to transfer your skills to a new product or service?
- Even if you have excelled in your field, have you "had enough?" Would you like the stimulation of a new challenge?
- Are you aware of the importance of a great cover letter but unsure of how to write one?
- Are you preparing to launch a second career after retirement?
- Have you been downsized, or do you anticipate becoming a victim of downsizing?
- Do you need expert advice on how to plan and implement a job campaign that will open the maximum number of doors?
- Do you want to make sure you handle an interview to your maximum advantage?
- Would you like to master the techniques of negotiating salary and benefits?
- Do you want to learn the secrets and shortcuts of professional resume writers?

> The "direct approach" is the style of job hunting most likely to yield the maximum number of job interviews.

> Using references in a skillful fashion in your job hunt will inspire confidence in prospective employers and help you "close the sale" after interviews.

Using the Direct Approach

As you consider the possibility of a job hunt or career change, you need to be aware that most people end up having at least three distinctly different careers in their working lifetimes, and often those careers are different from each other. Yet people usually stumble through each job campaign, unsure of what they should be doing. Whether you find yourself voluntarily or unexpectedly in a job hunt, the direct approach is the job hunting strategy most likely to yield a full-time permanent job. The direct approach is an active, take-the-initiative style of job hunting in which you choose your next employer rather than relying on responding to ads, using employment agencies, or depending on other methods of finding jobs. You will learn how to use the direct approach in this book, and you will see that an effective cover letter is a critical ingredient in using the direct approach.

Lack of Industry Experience Not a Major Barrier to Entering New Field

"Lack of experience" is often the last reason people are not offered jobs, according to the companies who do the hiring. If you are changing careers, you will be glad to learn that experienced professionals often are selling "potential" rather than experience in a job hunt. Companies look for personal qualities that they know tend to be present in their most effective professionals, such as communication skills, initiative, persistence, organizational and time management skills, and creativity. Frequently companies are trying to discover "personality type," "talent," "ability," "aptitude," and "potential" rather than seeking actual hands-on experience, so your resume should be designed to aggressively present your accomplishments. Attitude, enthusiasm, personality, and a track record of achievements in any type of work are the primary "indicators of success" which employers are seeking, and you will see numerous examples in this book of resumes written in an all-purpose fashion so that the professional can approach various industries and companies.

The Art of Using References in a Job Hunt

You probably already know that you need to provide references during a job hunt, but you may not be sure of how and when to use references for maximum advantage. You can use references very creatively during a job hunt to call attention to your strengths and make yourself "stand out." Your references will rarely get you a job, no matter how impressive the names, but the way you use references can boost the employer's confidence in you and lead to a job offer in the least time. You should ask from three to five people, including people who have supervised you, if you can use them as a reference during your job hunt. You may not be able to ask your current boss since your job hunt is probably confidential. A common question in resume preparation is: "Do I need to put my references on my resume?" No, you don't. And even if you create a page of references at the same time that you prepare your resume, you don't need to mail your references page with the resume and cover letter. The potential employer is not interested in your references until he meets and gets interested in you, so the earliest you need to have references ready is at the first interview. An excellent attention-getting technique is to take to the first interview not just a page of references (giving names, addresses, and telephone numbers) but an actual letter of reference written by someone who knows you well and who preferably has supervised or employed you. A professional way to close the first interview is to thank the interviewer, shake his or her hand, and then say you'd like to give him or her a copy of a letter of reference from a previous employer. Hopefully you already made a good impression during the interview, but you'll "close the sale" in a dynamic fashion if you leave a letter praising you and your accomplishments. For that reason, it's a good idea to ask employers during your final weeks in a job if they will provide you with a written letter of recommendation which you can use in future job hunts. Most employers will oblige, and you will have a letter that has a useful "shelf life" of many years. Such a letter often gives the prospective employer enough confidence in his opinion of you that he may forego checking out other references and decide to offer you the job in the next few days. Whom should you ask to serve as references? References should be people who have known or supervised you in a professional, academic, or work situation. References with big titles, like school superintendent or congressman, are fine, but remind busy people when you get to the interview stage that they may be contacted soon. Make sure the busy official recognizes your name and has instant positive recall of you! If you're asked to provide references on a formal company application, you can simply transcribe names from your references list. In summary, follow this rule in using references: If you've got them, flaunt them! If you've obtained well-written letters of reference, make sure you find a polite way to push those references under the nose of the interviewer so he or she can hear someone other than you describing your strengths. Your references probably won't ever get you a job, but glowing letters of reference can give you credibility and visibility that can make you stand out among candidates with similar credentials and potential!

With regard to references, it's best to provide the names and addresses of people who have supervised you or observed you in a work situation.

The approach taken by this book is to (1) help you master the proven best techniques of conducting a job hunt and (2) show you how to stand out in a job hunt through your resume, cover letter, interviewing skills, as well as the way in which you present your references and follow up on interviews. Now, the best way to "get in the mood" for writing your own resume and cover letter is to select samples from the Table of Contents that interest you and then read them. A great resume is a "photograph," usually on one page, of an individual. If you wish to seek professional advice in preparing your resume, you may contact one of the professional writers at Professional Resume & Employment Publishing (PREP) for a brief free consultation by calling 1-910-483-6611.

Part One: Some Advice About Your Job Hunt

What if you don't know what you want to do?

Your job hunt will be more comfortable if you can figure out what type of work you want to do. But you are not alone if you have no idea what you want to do next! You may have knowledge and skills in certain areas but want to get into another type of work. What *The Wall Street Journal* has discovered in its research on careers is that most of us end up having at least three distinctly different careers in our working lives; it seems that, even if we really like a particular kind of activity, twenty years of doing it is enough for most of us and we want to move on to something else!

Figure out what interests you and you will hold the key to a successful job hunt and working career. (And be prepared for your interests to change over time!)

That's why we strongly believe that you need to spend some time figuring out *what interests you* rather than taking an inventory of the skills you have. You may have skills that you simply don't want to use, but if you can build your career on the things that interest you, you will be more likely to be happy and satisfied in your job. Realize, too, that interests can change over time; the activities that interest you now may not be the ones that interested you years ago. For example, some professionals may decide that they've had enough of retail sales and want a job selling another product or service, even though they have earned a reputation for being an excellent retail manager. We strongly believe that interests rather than skills should be the determining factor in deciding what types of jobs you want to apply for and what directions you explore in your job hunt. Obviously one cannot be a lawyer without a law degree or a secretary without secretarial skills; but a professional can embark on a next career as a financial consultant, property manager, plant manager, production supervisor, retail manager, or other occupation if he/she has a strong interest in that type of work and can provide a resume that clearly demonstrates past excellent performance in *any* field and *potential* to excel in another field. As you will see later in this book, "lack of exact experience" is the last reason why people are turned down for the jobs they apply for.

"Lack of exact experience" is the last reason people are turned down for the jobs for which they apply.

How can you have a resume prepared if you don't know what you want to do?

You may be wondering how you can have a resume prepared if you don't know what you want to do next. The approach to resume writing which PREP, the country's oldest resume-preparation company, has used successfully for many years is to develop an "all-purpose" resume that translates your skills, experience, and accomplishments into language employers can understand. What most people need in a job hunt is a versatile resume that will allow them to apply for numerous types of jobs. For example, you may want to apply for a job in pharmaceutical sales but you may also want to have a resume that will be versatile enough for you to apply for jobs in the construction, financial services, or automotive industries.

Based on 20 years of serving job hunters, we at PREP have found that **an all-purpose resume** and **specific cover letters tailored to specific fields** is often your best approach to job hunting rather than trying to create different resumes for different occupational areas. Usually, you will not even need more than one "all-purpose" cover letter, although the cover letter rather than the resume is the place to communicate your interest in a narrow or specific field. An all-purpose resume and cover letter that translate your experience and accomplishments into plain English are the tools that will maximize the number of doors which open for you while permitting you to "fish" in the widest range of job areas.

Your resume will provide the script for your job interview.

When you get down to it, your resume has a simple job to do: Its purpose is to blow as many doors open as possible and to make as many people as possible want to meet you. So a well-written resume that really "sells" you is a key that will create opportunities for you in a job hunt.

This statistic explains why: The typical newspaper advertisement for a job opening receives more than 245 replies. And normally only 10 or 12 will be invited to an interview.

But here's another purpose of the resume: it provides the "script" the employer uses when he interviews you. If your resume has been written in such a way that your strengths and achievements are revealed, that's what you'll end up talking about at the job interview. Since the resume will govern what you get asked about at your interviews, you can't overestimate the importance of making sure your resume makes you look and sound as good as you are.

Your resume is the "script" for your job interviews. Make sure you put on your resume what you want to talk about or be asked about at the job interview.

So what is a "good" resume?

Very literally, your resume should motivate the person reading it to dial the phone number you have put on the resume. (If you are relocating, that's one reason you should think about putting a local phone contact number on your resume, if possible, when your contact address is several states away; employers are much more likely to dial a local telephone number than a long-distance number when they're looking for potential employees.)

If you have a resume already, look at it objectively. Is it a limp, colorless "laundry list" of your job titles and duties? Or does it "paint a picture" of your skills, abilities, and accomplishments in a way that would make someone want to meet you? Can people understand what you're saying?

The one-page resume in chronological format is the format preferred by most employers.

How long should your resume be?

One page, maybe two. Usually only people in the academic community have a resume (which they usually call a *curriculum vitae*) longer than one or two pages. Remember that your resume is almost always accompanied by a cover letter, and a potential employer does not want to read more than two or three pages about a total stranger in order to decide if he wants to meet that person! Besides, don't forget that the more you tell someone about yourself, the more opportunity you are providing for the employer to screen you out at the "first-cut" stage. A resume should be concise and exciting and designed to make the reader want to meet you in person!

Should resumes be functional or chronological?

Employers almost always prefer a chronological resume; in other words, an employer will find a resume easier to read if it is immediately apparent what your current or most recent job is, what you did before that, and so forth, in reverse chronological order. A resume that goes back in detail for the last ten years of employment will generally satisfy the employer's curiosity about your background. Employment more than ten years old can be shown even more briefly in an "Other Experience" section at the end of your "Experience" section. Remember that your intention is not to tell everything you've done but to "hit the high points" and especially impress the employer with what you learned, contributed, or accomplished in each job you describe.

Once you get your resume, what do you do with it?

You will be using your resume to answer ads, as a tool to use in talking with friends and relatives about your job search, and, most importantly, in using the "direct approach" described in this book.

When you mail your resume, always send a "cover letter."

A "cover letter," sometimes called a "resume letter" or "letter of interest," is a letter that accompanies and introduces your resume. Your cover letter is a way of personalizing the resume by sending it to the specific person you think you might want to work for at each company. Your cover letter should contain a few highlights from your resume—just enough to make someone want to meet you. Cover letters should always be typed or word processed on a computer—never handwritten.

Never mail or fax your resume without a cover letter.

1. Learn the art of answering ads.

There is an "art," part of which can be learned, in using your "bestselling" resume to reply to advertisements.

Sometimes an exciting job lurks behind a boring ad that someone dictated in a hurry, so reply to any ad that interests you. Don't worry that you aren't "25 years old with an MBA" like the ad asks for. Employers will always make compromises in their requirements if they think you're the "best fit" overall.

What about ads that ask for "salary requirements?"

What if the ad you're answering asks for "salary requirements?" The first rule is to avoid committing yourself in writing at that point to a specific salary. You don't want to "lock yourself in."

What if the ad asks for your "salary requirements?"

There are two ways to handle the ad that asks for "salary requirements."

First, you can ignore that part of the ad and accompany your resume with a cover letter that focuses on "selling" you, your abilities, and even some of your philosophy about work or your field. You may include a sentence in your cover letter like this: "I can provide excellent personal and professional references at your request, and I would be delighted to share the private details of my salary history with you in person."

Second, if you feel you must give some kind of number, just state a range in your cover letter that includes your medical, dental, other benefits, and expected bonuses. You might state, for example, "My current compensation, including benefits and bonuses, is in the range of $30,000-$40,000."

Analyze the ad and "tailor" yourself to it.

When you're replying to ads, a finely-tailored cover letter is an important tool in getting your resume noticed and read. On the next page is a cover letter which has been "tailored to fit" a specific ad. Notice the "art" used by PREP writers of analyzing the ad's main requirements and then writing the letter so that the person's background, work habits, and interests seem "tailor-made" to the company's needs. Use this cover letter as a model when you prepare your own reply to ads.

Date

Mr. Arthur Wise
Chamber of Commerce of the U.S.
9439 Goshen Lane
Dallas, TX 22105

Dear Mr. Wise:

I would appreciate an opportunity to show you in person, soon, that I am the energetic, dynamic individual you are looking for as your State Sales Manager for the Chamber of Commerce in Texas.

Here are just three reasons why I believe I am the effective young professional you seek:

- *I myself am "sold" on the Chamber of Commerce* and have long been an admirer of its goal of forming a cohesive business organization to promote the well-being of communities and promote business vigor. As someone better known that I put it long ago, "the business of America is business." I wholeheartedly believe that the Chamber's efforts to unite, solidify, and mobilize American business can be an important key in unlocking the international competitiveness and domestic vitality of our economy. I am eager to contribute to that effort.

- *I am a proven salesperson* with a demonstrated ability to "prospect" and produce sales. In my current job as a sales representative, I contact more than 150 business professionals per week and won my company's annual award for outstanding sales performance.

- *I enjoy traveling and am eager to assist in the growth of Texas and vicinity.* I am fortunate to have the natural energy, industry, and enthusiasm required to put in the long hours necessary for effective sales performance.

You will find me, I am certain, a friendly, good-natured person whom you would be proud to call part of the Chamber's "team." Although I have worked primarily in profit-making environments, I am confident that I could enthusiastically and gracefully transition my skills into a trade association environment. I would enjoy the opportunity to share my proven sales techniques and extensive knowledge with other junior sales professionals in a management and development position.

I hope you will call or write me soon to suggest a convenient time when we might meet to discuss your needs further and how I might serve them.

Yours sincerely,

Your Name

Employers are trying to identify the individual who wants the job they are filling. Don't be afraid to express your enthusiasm in the cover letter!

2. Talk to friends and relatives.

Don't be shy about telling your friends and relatives the kind of job you're looking for. Looking for the job you want involves using your network of contacts, so tell people what you're looking for. They may be able to make introductions and help set up interviews.

About 25% of all interviews are set up through "who you know," so don't ignore this approach.

3. Finally, and most importantly, use the "direct approach."

More than 50% of all job interviews are set up by the "direct approach." That means you actually send a resume and a cover letter to a company you think might be interesting to work for.

The "direct approach" is a strategy in which you choose your next employer.

To whom do you write?

In general, you should write directly to the *exact name* of the person who would be hiring you: say, the vice-president of marketing or data processing. If you're in doubt about to whom to address the letter, address it to the president by name and he or she will make sure it gets forwarded to the right person within the company who has hiring authority in your area.

How do you find the names of potential employers?

You're not alone if you feel that the biggest problem in your job search is finding the right names at the companies you want to contact. But you can usually figure out the names of companies you want to approach by deciding first if your job hunt is primarily geography-driven or industry-driven.

In a **geography-driven job hunt,** you could select a list of, say, 50 companies you want to contact **by location** from the lists that the U.S. Chambers of Commerce publish yearly of their "major area employers." There are hundreds of local Chambers of Commerce across America, and most of them will have an 800 number which you can find through 1-800-555-1212. If you and your family think Atlanta, Dallas, Ft. Lauderdale, and Virginia Beach might be nice places to live, for example, you could contact the Chamber of Commerce in those cities and ask how you can obtain a copy of their list of major employers. Your nearest library will have the book which lists the addresses of all chambers.

In an **industry-driven job hunt,** and if you are willing to relocate, you will be identifying the companies which you find most attractive in the industry in which you want to work. When you select a list of companies to contact **by industry,** you can find the right person to write and the address of firms by industrial category in *Standard and Poor's, Moody's,* and other excellent books in public libraries. Many Web sites also provide contact information.

Many people feel it's a good investment to actually call the company to either find out or double-check the name of the person to whom they want to send a resume and cover letter. It's important to do as much as you feasibly can to assure that the letter gets to the right person in the company.

At the end of Part One, you will find some advice about how to conduct library research and how to locate organizations to which you could send your resume.

What's the correct way to follow up on a resume you send?

There is a polite way to be aggressively interested in a company during your job hunt. It is ideal to end the cover letter accompanying your resume by saying, "I hope you'll welcome my call next week when I try to arrange a brief meeting at your convenience to discuss your current and future needs and how I might serve them." Keep it low key, and just ask for a "brief meeting," not an interview. Employers want people who show a determined interest in working with them, so don't be shy about following up on the resume and cover letter you've mailed.

STEP THREE: Preparing for Interviews

It pays to be aware of the 14 most common pitfalls for job hunters.

But a resume and cover letter by themselves can't get you the job you want. You need to "prep" yourself before the interview. Step Three in your job campaign is "Preparing for Interviews." First, let's look at interviewing from the company's point of view.

What are the biggest "turnoffs" for companies?

One of the ways to help yourself perform well at an interview is to look at the main reasons why companies *don't* hire the people they interview, according to companies that do the interviewing.

Notice that "lack of appropriate background" (or lack of experience) is the *last* reason for not being offered the job.

The 14 Most Common Reasons Job Hunters Are Not Offered Jobs *(according to the companies who do the interviewing and hiring):*

1. Low level of accomplishment
2. Poor attitude, lack of self-confidence
3. Lack of goals/objectives
4. Lack of enthusiasm
5. Lack of interest in the company's business
6. Inability to sell or express yourself
7. Unrealistic salary demands
8. Poor appearance
9. Lack of maturity, no leadership potential
10. Lack of extracurricular activities
11. Lack of preparation for the interview, no knowledge about company
12. Objecting to travel
13. Excessive interest in security and benefits
14. Inappropriate background

Department of Labor studies have proven that smart, "prepared" job hunters can increase their beginning salary while getting a job in *half* the time it normally takes. (4½ months is the average national length of a job search.) Here, from PREP, are some questions that can prepare you to find a job faster.

Are you in the "right" frame of mind?

It seems unfair that we have to look for a job just when we're lowest in morale. Don't worry *too* much if you're nervous before interviews. You're supposed to be a little nervous, especially if the job means a lot to you. But the best way to kill unnecessary fears about job hunting is through 1) making sure you have a great resume and 2) preparing yourself for the interview. Here are three main areas you need to think about before each interview.

Do you know what the company does?

Don't walk into an interview giving the impression that, "If this is Tuesday, this must be General Motors."

Find out before the interview what the company's main product or service is. Where is the company heading? Is it in a "growth" or declining industry? (Answers to these questions may influence whether or not you want to work there!)

Research the company before you go to interviews.

Information about what the company does is in annual reports as well as newspaper and magazine articles. Just visit your nearest library and ask the reference librarian to guide you to materials on the company. Internet searches will yield valuable information. At the end of Part One you will find many suggestions about how to research companies.

Do you know what you want to do for the company?

Before the interview, try to decide how you see yourself fitting into the company. Remember, "lack of exact background" the company wants is usually the last reason people are not offered jobs.

Understand before you go to each interview that the burden will be on you to "sell" the interviewer on why you're the best person for the job and the company.

How will you answer the critical interview questions?

Put yourself in the interviewer's position and think about the questions you're most likely to be asked. Here are some of the most commonly asked interview questions:

Anticipate the questions you will be asked at the interview, and prepare your responses in advance.

Q: *"What are your greatest strengths?"*
A: Don't say you've never thought about it! Go into an interview knowing the three main impressions you want to leave about yourself, such as "I'm hard-working, loyal, and an imaginative cost-cutter."

Q: *"What are your greatest weaknesses?"*
A: Don't confess that you're lazy or have trouble meeting deadlines! Confessing that you tend to be a "workaholic" or "tend to be a perfectionist and sometimes get frustrated when others don't share my high standards" will make your prospective employer see a "weakness" that he likes. Name a weakness that your interviewer will perceive as a strength.

Q: *"What are your long-range goals?"*
A: If you're interviewing with Microsoft, don't say you want to work for IBM in five years! Say your long-range goal is to be *with* the company, contributing to its goals and success.

Q: "What motivates you to do your best work?"
A: Don't get dollar signs in your eyes here! "A challenge" is not a bad answer, but it's a little cliched. Saying something like "troubleshooting" or "solving a tough problem" is more interesting and specific. Give an example if you can.

Q: "What do you know about this company?"

A: Don't say you never heard of it until they asked you to the interview! Name an interesting, positive thing you learned about the company recently from your research. Remember, company executives can sometimes feel rather "maternal" about the company they serve. Don't get onto a negative area of the company if you can think of positive facts you can bring up. Of course, if you learned in your research that the company's sales seem to be taking a nose-dive, or that the company president is being prosecuted for taking bribes, you might politely ask your interviewer to tell you something that could help you better understand what you've been reading. Those are the kinds of company facts that can help you determine whether you want to work there or not.

Q: "Why should I hire you?"

A: "I'm unemployed and available" is the wrong answer here! Get back to your strengths and say that you believe the organization could benefit by a loyal, hard-working cost-cutter like yourself.

In conclusion, you should decide in advance, before you go to the interview, how you will answer each of these commonly asked questions. Have some practice interviews with a friend to role-play and build your confidence.

STEP FOUR: Handling the Interview and Negotiating Salary

Now you're ready for Step Four: actually handling the interview successfully and effectively. Remember, the purpose of an interview is to get a job offer.

Eight "do's" for the interview

According to leading U.S. companies, there are eight key areas in interviewing success. You can fail at an interview if you mishandle just one area.

1. Do wear appropriate clothes.
   You can never go wrong by wearing a suit to an interview.

2. Do be well groomed.
   Don't overlook the obvious things like having clean hair, clothes, and fingernails for the interview.

3. Do give a firm handshake.
   You'll have to shake hands twice in most interviews: first, before you sit down, and second, when you leave the interview. Limp handshakes turn most people off.

4. Do smile and show a sense of humor.
   Interviewers are looking for people who would be nice to work with, so don't be so somber that you don't smile. In fact, research shows that people who smile at interviews are perceived as more intelligent. So, smile!

5. Do be enthusiastic.
   Employers say they are "turned off" by lifeless, unenthusiastic job hunters who show no special interest in that company. The best way to show some enthusiasm for the employer's operation is to find out about the business beforehand.

> Go to an interview prepared to tell the company why it should hire you.

> A smile at an interview makes the employer perceive of you as intelligent!

6. Do show you are flexible and adaptable.

An employer is looking for someone who can contribute to his organization in a flexible, adaptable way. No matter what skills and training you have, employers know every new employee must go through initiation and training on the company's turf. Certainly show pride in your past accomplishments in a specific, factual way ("I saved my last employer $50.00 a week by a new cost-cutting measure I developed"). But don't come across as though there's nothing about the job you couldn't easily handle.

7. Do ask intelligent questions about the employer's business.

An employer is hiring someone because of certain business needs. Show interest in those needs. Asking questions to get a better idea of the employer's needs will help you "stand out" from other candidates interviewing for the job.

8. Do "take charge" when the interviewer "falls down" on the job.

Go into every interview knowing the three or four points about yourself you want the interviewer to remember. And be prepared to take an active part in leading the discussion if the interviewer's "canned approach" does not permit you to display your "strong suit." You can't always depend on the interviewer's asking you the "right" questions so you can stress your strengths and accomplishments.

Employers are seeking people with good attitudes whom they can train and coach to do things their way.

An important "don't": Don't ask questions about salary or benefits at the first interview.

Employers don't take warmly to people who look at their organization as just a place to satisfy salary and benefit needs. Don't risk making a negative impression by appearing greedy or self-serving. The place to discuss salary and benefits is normally at the second interview, and the employer will bring it up. Then you can ask questions without appearing excessively interested in what the organization can do for you.

"Sell yourself" before talking salary

Make sure you've "sold" yourself before talking salary. First show you're the "best fit" for the employer and then you'll be in a stronger position from which to negotiate salary.

Interviewers sometimes throw out a salary figure at the first interview to see if you'll accept it. Don't commit yourself. You may be able to negotiate a better deal later on. Get back to finding out more about the job. This lets the interviewer know you're interested primarily in the job and not the salary.

Now…negotiating your salary

You must avoid stating a "salary requirement" in your initial cover letter, and you must avoid even appearing **interested** in salary before you are offered the job.

Don't appear excessively interested in salary and benefits at the interview.

Never bring up the subject of salary yourself. Employers say there's no way you can avoid looking greedy if you bring up the issue of salary and benefits before the company has identified you as its "best fit."

When the company brings up salary, it may say something like this: "Well, Mary, we think you'd make a good candidate for this job. What kind of salary are we talking about?"

Never name a number here, either. Give the ball back to the interviewer. Act as though you hadn't given the subject of salary much thought and respond something like this: "Ah, Mr. Jones, salary. . .well, I wonder if you'd be kind enough to tell me what salary you had in mind when you advertised the job?" Or ... "What is the range you have in mind?"

Don't worry, if the interviewer names a figure that you think is too low, you can say so without turning down the job or locking yourself into a rigid position. The point here is to negotiate for yourself as well as you can. You might reply to a number named by the interviewer that you think is low by saying something like this: "Well, Mr. Lee, the job interests me very much, and I think I'd certainly enjoy working with you. But, frankly, I was thinking of something a little higher than that." That leaves the ball in your interviewer's court again, and you haven't turned down the job, either, in case it turns out that the interviewer can't increase the offer and you still want the job.

Salary negotiation can be tricky.

Last, send a follow-up letter.

Finally, send a letter right after the interview telling your interviewer you enjoyed the meeting and are certain (if you are) you are the "best fit" for the job. The people interviewing you will probably have an attitude described as either "professionally loyal" to their companies or "maternal and proprietary" if the interviewer also owns the company. In either case, they are looking for people who want to work for *that* company in particular. The follow-up letter you send might be just the deciding factor in your favor if the employer is trying to choose between you and someone else.

Sample follow-up letters are shown in the next section. Be sure to modify the model letter according to your particular skills and interview situation.

A follow-up letter can help the employer choose between you and another qualified candidate.

Researching companies and locating employers

Figuring out the names of the organizations to which you want to mail your resume is part of any highly successful job campaign. Don't depend on only answering the ads you read in printed or electronic form, waiting for the ideal job to appear in **newspapers or magazines,** many of which are published online. If you are geographically oriented and need to find work in a particular city or town, check out the Sunday advertisements in the classified sections which suit you best, such as "administrative" or "professional" or "technical." Also aggressively research possible employers. Here is some information which you can use in researching the names of organizations for which you might be interested in working.

In electronic and printed form, most libraries have a variety of information available on various organizations throughout the U.S. and worldwide. If your local library has computers, you will probably have access to a vast network of information. Many printed materials might be available only for use in the reference room of the library, but some items may be checked out. Listed below are some of the major sources to look for, but be sure and check at the reference desk to see if there are any resources available in a printed or online form related to the specific types of companies you wish to investigate.

The Worldwide Chamber of Commerce Directory

Most chambers of commerce annually produce a "list of major employers" for their market area (or city). Usually the list includes the name, address, and telephone number of the employer along with information about the number of people employed, kinds of products and services produced, and a person to contact about employment. You can obtain the "list of major employers" in the city where you want to work by writing to that chamber. There is usually a small charge.

The *Worldwide Chamber of Commerce Directory* is an alphabetical listing of American and foreign chambers of commerce. It includes:

    All U.S. Chambers of Commerce (with addresses and phone numbers)
    American Chambers of Commerce abroad
    Canadian Chambers of Commerce
    Foreign Chambers of Commerce in principal cities worldwide
    Foreign Embassies and Consulates in the U.S.
    U.S. Consulates and Embassies throughout the world

Standard and Poor's Register of Corporations, Directors, and Executives

Standard and Poor's produce three volumes annually with information concerning over 77,000 American corporations. They are:

Volume 1—**Corporations.** Here is an alphabetical listing of a variety of information for each of over 77,000 companies, including:
- name of company, address, telephone number
- names, titles, and functions of several key officers
- name of accounting firm, primary bank, and law firm
- stock exchange, description of products or services
- annual sales, number of employees
- division names and functions, subsidiary listings

Volume 2—**Directors and Executives.** This volume lists alphabetically over 70,000 officers, directors, partners, etc. by name. Information on each executive includes:
- principal business affiliation
- business address, residence address, year of birth
- college and year of graduation, fraternal affiliation

Volume 3—**Index.**

Moody's Manuals

Moody's Manuals provide information about companies traded on the New York and American Stock Exchanges and over the counter. They include:

Moody's Industrial Manual

Here, Moody's discusses detailed information on companies traded on the New York, American, and regional stock exchanges. The companies are listed alphabetically. Basic information about company addresses, phone numbers, and the names of key officers is available for each company listed. In addition, detailed information about the financial and operating data for each company is available. There are three levels of detail provided:

Complete Coverage. Companies in this section have the following information:
- *financial information* for the past 7 years (income accounts, balance sheets, financial and operating data).
- *detailed description of the company's business* including a complete list of subsidiaries and office and property sites.
- *capital structure information,* which includes details on capital stock and long-term debt, with bond and preferred stock ratings and 2 years of stock and bond price ranges.
- *extensive presentation of the company's last annual report.*

Full Measure Coverage. Information on companies in this section includes:
- *financial information for the past 7 years* (income accounts, balance sheets, financial and operating data).
- *detailed description of company's business,* with a complete list of subsidiaries and plant and property locations.
- *capital structure information,* with details on capital stock and long term debt, with bond and preferred stock ratings and 2 years of stock and bond price changes.

Comprehensive Coverage. Information on companies in this section includes:
- *5 years of financial information* on income accounts, balance sheets, and financial and operating ratios.
- *detailed description of company's business,* including subsidiaries.
- *concise capital structure information,* including capital stock and long term debts, bond and preferred stock ratings.

Moody's OTC Manual
Here is information on U.S. firms which are unlisted on national and regional stock exchanges. There are three levels of coverage: complete, full measure, and comprehensive (same as described above). Other Moody's manuals include: *Moody's Public Utility Manual, Moody's Municipal and Government Manual,* and *Moody's Bank and Finance Manual.*

Dun's Million Dollar Directory
Three separate listings (alphabetical, geographic, and by products) of over 120,000 U.S. firms. There are three volumes:
Volume 1—The 45,000 largest companies, net worth over $500,000.
Volume 2—The 37,000 next largest companies.
Volume 3—The 37,000 next largest companies.

U.S. industrial directories
Ask your librarian to guide you to your library's collection of industrial directories. Almost every state produces a manufacturing directory, for example, and many libraries maintain complete collections of these directories. You may find information on products and the addresses and telephone numbers of industrial companies.

Thomas' Register of Manufacturers
16 volumes of information about manufacturing companies.
Volumes 1-8—Alphabetical listing by product.
Volumes 9-10—Alphabetical listing of manufacturing company names, addresses, telephone numbers, and local offices.
Volumes 11-16—Alphabetical company catalog information.

Information About Foreign Companies
If you'd like your next job to be overseas or with an international company, you can find much helpful information in the library. You approach these companies in the same way as you would approach U.S.-based companies.

Directory of Foreign Manufacturers in the U.S.
Alphabetical listing of U.S. manufacturing companies which are owned and operated by parent foreign firms. The information provided includes the name and address of the U.S. firm, the name and address of the foreign parent firm, and the products produced.

Directory of American Firms Operating in Foreign Countries
Alphabetical listing of the names, addresses, chief officers, products, and country operated in of U.S. firms abroad.

International Firms Directory
This lists foreign corporations.

Hoover's Handbook of World Business
This lists corporations in Asia and Europe.

Principal International Businesses
This is a comprehensive directory of international businesses.

Information Available From The Internet
Information about companies is also available through the Internet. You can use all the search engines to help you in your search for company information and company website addresses. It is not the purpose of this book to recommend websites by name, but you can type in "jobs" or "employment" or "careers" as a key word using any search engine and you will be introduced to organizations that will allow you to post your resume online. You can also usually find an organization's website by typing in the following website addresses, just substituting the name of the company you want to find, such as "Dell," for "organizationname":

  http://www.organizationname.com
  http://www.organizationname.org
  http://www.organizationname.net

However, sometimes finding what you are looking for takes trial and error. For example, if you wanted to find Hewlett Packard's website, you would find it either by typing in "Hewlett Packard" as a key word or by typing in http://www.HP.com. Not all website addresses are perfectly obvious, straightforward, or intuitive, but the search engines usually perform in an excellent fashion when you type in key words in a trial-and-error "surfing" or fact-finding mode.

Many people are aware of the importance of having a great resume, but most people in a job hunt don't realize just how important a cover letter can be. The purpose of the cover letter, sometimes called a **"letter of interest,"** is to introduce your resume to prospective employers.

"A Picture Is Worth a Thousand Words."

As a way of illustrating how important the cover letter can be, we have chosen to show you on the next two pages the cover letter and resume of a young person seeking her first job in the teaching field. If the employer received only her resume without a cover letter, this promising young teacher would look like a cook and restaurant worker! A busy principal would probably not be motivated to dial her telephone number to suggest an interview time. In her case, the cover letter is probably more important than the resume she has been asked to submit. What the cover letter allows her to do is to explain that she worked as a cook, closing manager, and cashier full time while going back to school to earn her college degree. This puts her work experience in a different perspective.

The cover letter is the critical ingredient in a job hunt such as Marcia Vivero's because the cover letter allows her to say a lot of things that just don't "fit" on the resume. For example, she can emphasize her commitment to the teaching profession and stress her talent for teaching mathematics to people who find the subject difficult.

One of the things that sets her apart from other new graduates in her field is that she is a mature professional who, at age 27, is accustomed to a demanding work schedule. She's no "old lady" but she is five years older and wiser than the typical 22-year-old college graduate. In the high-stress profession which high school teaching is often considered to be, many principals will perceive of her age and experience as a positive factor.

Although the general rule is that women do not mention how many children they have in their resume and cover letter, there are exceptions to every rule, and Ms. Vivero breaks that rule for a good reason. She points out that she is a wife and mother and would bring to the classroom an in-depth understanding of the learning styles of children.

Finally, the cover letter gives her a chance to stress the outstanding character and personal values which she feels will be a positive influence on the high school students to whom she wishes to teach mathematics.

You will see on the next two pages that the cover letter gives you a chance to "get personal" with the person to whom you are writing whereas the resume is a more formal document. Even if the employer doesn't request a cover letter, we believe that it is *always* in your best interest to send a cover letter with your resume. The aim of this book is to show you examples of cover letters designed to blow doors open so that you can develop your own cover letters and increase the number of interviews you have.

A cover letter is an essential part of a career change.

Please do not attempt to implement a career change without a cover letter such as the ones you see in Part Two and in Part Three of this book. A cover letter is the first impression of you, and you can influence the way an employer views you by the language and style of your letter.

Your cover letter and resume are "companion" documents.

Date

Exact Name of Principal
Exact Title
School Name
School Address
City, State Zip

**New graduate
seeking her first job
in the teaching field**

Although this cover
letter has a very
"personal" tone, it has
been written so that Ms.
Vivero can send it to
principals at all the high
schools in her area. If
there is a school where
she particularly wants to
work, she would be wise
to get the exact name of
the principal so
she can address the
letter to him or her by
name and title.
Otherwise, she can
duplicate this "Dear Sir
or Madam" letter, date
and sign it, and send it
to principals at the
schools where she might
want to seek
employment.

Dear Exact Name: (or Dear Principal if you don't know the Exact Name)

With the enclosed resume, I would like to introduce myself and initiate the process of being considered for a position as a Mathematics Teacher in your high school.

As you will see from my resume, I recently graduated from the University of Rhode Island with a B.S. degree in Mathematics which I earned **magna cum laude**. I am especially proud of graduating with honors since I was combining a rigorous academic curriculum with a demanding work schedule which involved handling a variety of managerial, accounting, and customer service responsibilities.

Although I graduated in May 2000 with my B.S. degree, I am 27 years old and offer considerable experience in working with children of all ages. Since I am a wife and mother, I would bring to the classroom much understanding of the learning styles of children. I feel I would be skilled in classroom behavior management, and I would offer a maturity which younger college graduates might not have. I am a responsible individual known for my well-organized work habits and disciplined style.

I am deeply committed to a career in the teaching profession, and I intend in my spare time to earn my Master's degree in Mathematics and then a Ph.D. I am a highly motivated hard worker, and I feel my own strong values could be an inspiration to high school students. Although I have earned my degree in Mathematics with high honors, I am fully aware of how difficult mathematics is for many people, and I excel in translating abstract concepts into understandable language.

If you can use a vibrant young teaching professional who could enhance the fine reputation of your school, I hope you will contact me to suggest a time when I could make myself available for a personal interview. I can provide outstanding personal and professional references.

Sincerely,

Marcia Vivero

MARCIA VIVERO

1110½ Hay Street, Providence, RI 28305

(910) 483-6611 • preppub@aol.com

OBJECTIVE

To contribute to a high school that can use a dedicated mathematics teacher who is attuned to the varied learning abilities and styles which students bring to the classroom.

EDUCATION

Earned B.S. degree in **Mathematics,** University of Rhode Island, Providence, RI, May 2000.
- Graduated **Magna Cum Laude** with a GPA of 3.754.
- Received the Certificate of Excellence and was named to the Chancellor's List.
- Excelled academically while working part-time to finance my college education.

Graduated from Eastern Senior High School, Pawtucket, RI, 1990.
- Participated in track and intramural sports.

EXPERIENCE

CLOSING MANAGER, COOK, CASHIER. Chuck's Chicken & Barbecue, Providence, RI (1997-present).
- Was singled out to handle a variety of management responsibilities, and became known for my trustworthiness and cheerful disposition while simultaneously earning my college degree **with honors.**
- Refined my interpersonal skills working with all types of customers and with other employees.
- Trained other employees; assigned tasks to junior employees and supervised their work.
- Expertly operated a cash register, and was known for my accuracy in handling large amounts of cash; trained other employees to use the register.
- As Closing Manager, was responsible for closing the store at the end of the business day; accounted for financial transactions and oversaw end-of-the-day maintenance and security matters.
- Was frequently commended for my gracious style of dealing with the public and for my courteous approach to customer service.

COMPUTER OPERATOR/CLERICAL AIDE. Clear Lake Elementary School, Pawtucket, RI (summer 1990).
- In the summer after my high school graduation, excelled in an office position handling numerous responsibilities related to record keeping for students in summer school.
- Operated a computer in order to input data and maintain records.
- Filed and typed as needed.
- Was known for my attention to detail and accuracy when handling large volumes of work under tight deadlines.

PERSONAL

Have aspirations to earn my Master's degree in Mathematics, and believe I could be a great asset to the teaching profession. Can provide outstanding references. Have taught in Bible School Programs. Believe all students can learn, and am skilled at communicating difficult mathematics concepts to students who find math difficult.

Date

**Addressing the
Cover Letter:** Get the
exact name of the
person to whom you are
writing. This makes your
approach personal.

Exact Name of Person
Exact Title of Person
Company Name
Address
City, State Zip

Dear Sir or Madam:

First Paragraph: This
explains why you are
writing.

With the enclosed resume, I would like to make you aware of my strong desire to become a part of your teaching staff.

Second Paragraph:
You have a chance to
talk about whatever
you feel is your most
distinguishing feature.

As you will see from my resume, I recently earned my Bachelor of Science in Education (B.S.E.) degree at the University of Georgia. Since it has always been my childhood dream to become a teacher, my college graduation was an especially meaningful event in my life.

Third Paragraph: You
bring up your next most
distinguishing qualities
and try to
sell yourself.

As you will see from my resume, I recently completed a teaching internship as a first grade student teacher, and I successfully assumed all the duties of a first grade teacher. During those two months, under the guidance of an experienced educator, I wrote and completed my own professional growth and development plan, and I also planned and implemented a classroom and behavior management program.

Fourth Paragraph:
Here you have another
opportunity to reveal
qualities or
achievements which will
impress your future
employer.

In my previous two-month internship as a kindergarten student teacher, I performed with distinction in planning and implementing creative lessons, communicating with teaching professionals and parents, and working with the children. You will notice from my resume that I have expressed my true love for children through my summer and part-time jobs while in college. For four years, I was a nanny for a professional family and in that capacity I cared for three triplet newborns as well as two older children. It is an understatement to say that I refined my time management skills in that part-time job!

Final Paragraph: She
asks the employer to
contact her. Make sure
your reader knows
what the "next step" is.

If you can use a highly motivated young professional with unlimited personal initiative as well as strong personal qualities of dependability and trustworthiness, I hope you will contact me to suggest a time when we might meet to discuss your needs. I can provide excellent personal and professional references, and I am eager to apply my strong teaching skills and true love for children in an academic institution which emphasizes hard work and a commitment to the highest learning goals.

Sincerely,

**Alternate Final
Paragraph:** It's more
aggressive (but not too
aggressive) to let the
employer know that
you will be calling him
or her. Don't be afraid
to be persistent.
Employers are looking
for people who know
what they want to do.

Melanie Thompson

Alternate final paragraph:
I hope you will welcome my call soon when I contact you to try to arrange a brief meeting to discuss your needs and how my talents might help you. I appreciate whatever time you could give me in the process of exploring your needs.

Date

Exact Name of Person
Title or Position
Name of Company
Address (number and street)
Address (city, state, and zip)

Dear Exact Name of Person: (or Dear Sir or Madam if answering a blind ad)

I would appreciate an opportunity to talk with you soon about how I could contribute to your organization through my proven accounts management, customer service, and public relations skills.

You will see from my resume that I began working when I was 16 years old; I continued working for the same company while earning my Bachelor of Business Administration degree. After college graduation, the university where I earned my degree recruited me for a job in its admissions office, and I excelled in handling a wide variety of administrative and public relations tasks.

Most recently I have worked full time as an Account Representative while going to school at nights and on the weekends to earn my M.B.A., which I received recently. I have been handling key accounts worth more than $2 million annually for my employer and am being groomed for rapid promotion into a higher management position.

I have, however, decided to explore career opportunities outside my current firm. I am seeking an employer who can use a highly motivated individual with strong communication, sales, customer service, and public relations skills. Because I earned both my undergraduate and graduate degrees while excelling in demanding professional positions, I have acquired excellent organizational and time management skills which permit me to maximize my own productivity.

If you can use a self-starter who could rapidly become a valuable part of your organization, I hope you will contact me to suggest a time when we might meet to discuss your needs and how I might serve them. I can provide outstanding references.

Sincerely,

Louise Patton

cc: Thomas Crane

Sample Cover Letters for Career Changers

The cover letters in this section are written for people who need a very creative and resourceful cover letter. These cover letters are designed to accompany resumes of individuals trying to embark on a course of employment which is different from what they have been doing most recently.

Career-change cover letters are designed to help you find employment in a new field or industry. In this type of cover letter, you must "make sense" of yourself to the prospective employer. Otherwise, the prospective employer may look at your resume and ask himself, "Why is an air traffic controller writing to me about this marketing job?" The career-change cover letter is the employer's first impression of you and can explain why you are approaching him or her.

If you don't know what you want to do next, it's best to make your cover letter "all purpose."
In a job hunt, the all-purpose cover letter can be a time saver because it can serve as a "standard" or "model" or "template" which you can use each time you send out your resume. You may wish to modify it from time to time, but the all-purpose cover letter is there, already written, often in your computer, when you see an ad you want to answer or when you identify an employer whom you wish to contact in order to explore suitable opportunities for someone of your skills and abilities. The all-purpose cover letter can be used for employers in your current field or for employers in other industries.

When you are seeking your first job in a new field, use language that makes you "look" and "sound" as though you would be a credit to the profession you are trying to enter.
Most people know the frustration of not having any experience in the field in which they are seeking employment. There are particular techniques that should be used when writing a cover letter to try to obtain the first job in one's field. This type of cover letter "builds a bridge" to a new field. Ms. Vivero's cover letter, which was used as an example on page 18, is an example of this type of cover letter. Ms. Vivero is entering a new field after completing a degree program, but a career change may happen at any age and stage in one's life. Sometimes you just get tired of doing something you've done effectively for many years and feel that a change is needed in order to retain your enthusiasm and interest. For example, you will see one resume in this book of a sales professional who no longer wants to work in the tobacco industry. You will see another resume of a self-employed manager who sold his company and ended up with a "noncompete" clause which forced him to find a new industry home. But whether the job hunter is young or mature, the career-change cover letter must reach out personally to prospective employers and explain why the prospective employer's business is of interest. That's what *anyone* in a career change must do: reach out personally to the potential employer and make the employer believe that you are serious about your desire to make a career change, not just "having a bad day."

Exact Name of Person
Title or Position
Name of Company
Address (number and street)
Address (city, state, and zip)

Dear Exact Name of Person: (or Sir or Madam if answering a blind ad)

With the enclosed resume, I would like to express my interest in exploring employment opportunities with your organization and make you aware of my versatile skills and abilities which could complement your goals.

As you will see from my enclosed resume, I earned my B.S. from Michigan State University where I maintained a 3.5 GPA. During my senior year I worked as many as 50 hours a week as a Research Assistant and Tutor in the university's chemistry lab.

In my most recent job as a middle school science and math teacher, I refined my communication, organizational, and time management skills while organizing and directing numerous projects. On my own initiative, I planned the school's first science fair as well as a Christmas play and a musical. Earlier while serving in the U.S. Army for four years, I was handpicked for supervisory positions ahead of my peers and commended for my effective leadership style.

Both my management experience in the military and my teaching experience have helped me refine my verbal and written communication skills. I am highly regarded for my ability to persuade, motivate, and lead, and I am certain I could utilize those skills and talents in order to positively impact a company's bottom line.

If you can use a proven performer with an ability to work well with others, I hope you will contact me to suggest a time when we might talk to discuss your needs. Single and available for worldwide relocation, I would cheerfully travel as frequently as your needs require. I can provide excellent references at the appropriate time.

Sincerely,

Julie M. Vogel

CAREER-CHANGE COVER LETTERS

Changing careers from teaching

This career-change letter emphasizes the communication skills and versatility of a young professional with teaching experience as well as a distinguished military record. Lack of experience in a particular field is not a main reason why employers choose not to interview applicants. Employers are looking for a track record of accomplishment in whatever you have done so far.

Date

Director of Human Resources
Princeton Community College
2200 Airport Road
Princeton, NY 20233

**CAREER-CHANGE
COVER LETTERS**

**Changing Careers from
government to the
academic community**
In this letter, a city
engineer is attempting
to make a career
change from
government to the
academic
environment. He has
some part-time
teaching experience in
addition to experience
in training others as a
military officer. Every
employer knows that
attitude is a critical
factor in job
performance, so this
individual is stressing
his strong desire to
share his vast
experience and
technical knowledge
with others in what for
him will be a second
career.

Dear Sir or Madam:

With the enclosed resume describing my qualifications and experience, I would like to respond to your advertisement for a Civil Engineering Technology Instructor.

As you will see from my resume, I offer skills and experience that would be of great value to your students. After earning a B.S. in Civil Engineering and then completing one year of graduate studies, I served as a U.S. Army Engineer Officer and was handpicked as the Chief of the Master Planning Branch at a large military base. Most recently I have excelled as a Staff Engineer with the City of Albany. Although I am held in high regard by my colleagues and am considered a valuable asset of the city, I enjoy teaching and would relish the opportunity to share my vast experience with students at the beginning of their careers.

You will also see from my resume that my teaching credentials are top-notch. For the past 10 years, I have served as an adjunct instructor with Albany Technical Community College and have taught courses including Surveying, Topographic Surveying and Aerial Photography, Astronomical Calculations and State Plane Coordinates, Highway Surveying, and Construction Staking and Layout.

I am conversant with the latest thinking in my field as continuous professional development has been a routine throughout my career. My current job requires that I remain abreast of environmental issues such as wetlands and erosion control, and I have attended numerous review courses at New York State University and Columbia.

You would find me in person to be a congenial individual who takes much pleasure in sharing my technical knowledge. It would certainly be a pleasure to talk with you in person to discuss how my unique background could benefit your academic program and enhance the Civil Engineering career path of your undergraduates. I hope you will contact me to suggest a time when we might meet in person to discuss your needs and how I might serve them. Thank you in advance for your time.

Yours sincerely,

Jason Bessemer

Date

Exact Name of Person
Exact Title of Person
Exact Name of Organization
Address
City, State Zip

Dear Exact Name: (or Dear Sir or Madam if answering a blind ad)

With the enclosed resume, I would like to make you aware of my interest in utilizing my outstanding sales, marketing, communication, and management skills for the benefit of your organization.

Although I most recently have been working in the aviation field and am excelling in my current position, I have decided to embark on a radical career change. I have a strong desire to work in a professional position in which I can combine my extroverted personality and "natural" sales ability with my customer relations and problem-solving ability.

My recent experience in airport management, air traffic control, and in piloting advanced attack aircraft may not appear relevant to your needs, but my stable work history also includes several jobs which, I believe, illustrate my versatility. In one job I excelled as a juvenile counselor and thoroughly enjoyed the experience of providing a strong role model for troubled youth labeled as "uncontrollable." In another job in Florida I was part of the movie-making industry as I worked as a double for Mel Gibson. (During college, I also worked as a professional model.) A gourmet cook, I grew up in an Italian family which was in the restaurant business so I learned customer service at a young age!

In my current job involved in overseeing people and key areas related to airport management at one of the military's busiest traffic hubs, I am continually using my problem-solving and decision-making skills. I am confident that my management ability, resourcefulness, and ability to relate effectively to others are qualities which could transfer to any field. In one of my jobs in the aviation industry, I managed a $3.5 million budget with outstanding results, and I offer a strong bottom-line orientation.

If you can use a highly motivated self-starter known for unlimited personal initiative and a creative problem-solving style, I hope you will contact me to suggest a time when we might meet to discuss your needs. I am single and would relocate and travel extensively as your needs require, and I can provide outstanding references at the appropriate time. Thank you in advance for your consideration.

Yours sincerely,

Mason Jensen

CAREER-CHANGE COVER LETTERS

Changing Careers from air traffic control to a sales or marketing role
In this letter, an Air Traffic Controller is seeking to change fields and move from aviation into an industry which can utilize his strong sales, marketing, and communication skills. Notice how he tries to make the employer understand why someone with his specialized technical background is approaching companies that need generalists and communicators. In a career change, experienced professionals often must sell their personality and potential more than their actual work experience in order to "blow the door open."

Date

Exact Name of Person
Exact Title of Person
Exact Address
City, State Zip

**Changing Careers with a
cover letter that
emphasizes financial
knowledge**
In this letter, a young
person completing his
bachelor's degree
reaches out to
employers in various
fields. He emphasizes
his track record of
accomplishment with
his current employer.
Although this is an all-
purpose cover letter,
Mr. Ferdinand is mostly
interested in
accounting, financial, or
management activities,
so there is a subtle
emphasis on his skills
and interests in those
functional areas within
this all-purpose
framework.

Dear Sir or Madam:

With the enclosed resume, I would like to acquaint you with the considerable accounting, financial, and management skills I could put to work for your organization.

As you can see from the enclosed resume, I am continuing to excel in a "track record" of promotion with a food industry corporation. I began with the company as an assistant manager, was promoted to store manager, and then advanced to my present position as supervisor overseeing multiple stores in five cities.

While utilizing my strong communication and problem-solving skills in guiding store managers at 11 locations throughout New Hampshire, I am continuously involved in financial analysis and budget preparation. You will see from my resume that I hold an A.A.S. degree in Accounting, and I am completing my Bachelor's degree. I have learned from practical work experience as well as formal courses in program analysis, auditing, budget preparation, and quantitative analysis.

My computer operation skills are highly refined. I offer proficiency with numerous popular software products including Lotus 1-2-3 and offer the ability to troubleshoot and repair various types of equipment problems. While previously serving my country for two years in the U.S. Army, I received extensive training in computer operations and telecommunications operations/repair.

You would find me in person to be a dynamic young professional who prides myself on my ability to rapidly become a contributing member of any team. I can provide outstanding personal and professional references at the appropriate time, and I hope I will have the opportunity to meet with you in person to discuss your needs and how I might meet them.

Sincerely,

Terrell A. Ferdinand

Date

Exact Name of Person
Title or Position
Name of Company
Address (number and street)
Address (city, state, and zip)

Dear Exact Name of Person: (or Sir or Madam if answering a blind ad)

With the enclosed resume, I would like to make you aware of my interest in putting my considerable management and communication skills to work for your organization.

As you will see from my resume, I am pursuing a Master's in Public Administration (M.P.A.) degree at the University of Texas at San Antonio while excelling in my full-time job as an executive with Parke-Davis Pharmaceutical Division. It is my strong desire to transfer my considerable skills into the public sector, and I feel I can make major contributions to a government organization through my strategic thinking skills, management ability, as well as my highly effective approach in training, developing, and managing other employees.

You will notice that I have thus far excelled in a track record of achievement as a sales and marketing executive. I am certain that the planning, organizing, problem-solving, decision-making, and negotiating skills which I utilize daily in my job could be effectively utilized in the public sector. In my prior position with Smith Boyle, Inc., I worked extensively with government officials while servicing up to 700 commercial and government accounts in Utah cities. I am well acquainted with government purchasing procedures and with the steps involved in government decision making.

I can provide outstanding personal and professional references at the appropriate time, and I can assure you that you would find me in person to be a poised communicator who would take pride in contributing to your organizational goals. I hope you will contact me if you feel my considerable management and communication skills could be helpful to you.

Thank you in advance for your time.

Sincerely,

Danny Flanders

Date

Exact Name of Person
Exact Title
Exact Name of Company
Address
City, State Zip

**CAREER-CHANGE
COVER LETTERS**

**Changing Careers from retail
to management in a new
industry**
This letter holds the key
to this individual's
intense desire to become
employed in a sector
other than retail.
Although he has a
background as an
accomplished retail
manager, he desires a
change. Remember that
in a career-change
situation, your approach
simply has to "make
sense" to prospective
employers and they
must feel that you are
genuinely interested in
leaving the industry you
know best—not just
"having a bad day."

Dear Exact Name of Person: (or Dear Sir or Madam if answering a blind ad)

With the enclosed resume, I would like to make you aware of the considerable skills I feel I could offer your organization.

As you will see from my resume, I have excelled in a track record of advancement with the Macy's organization, where I started as a management trainee and advanced into a senior management position in charge of 25 individuals. After earning my undergraduate degree in Business Administration with a minor in Economics, I was attracted to the Macy's organization because of its tradition of regarding its managers as profit centers and treating them essentially as entrepreneurs. While hiring and supervising personnel, I handled general management responsibilities including preparing business plans four times a year, reviewing progress monthly toward goals, and performing extensive community relations and public relations. For example, I was active in the Chamber of Commerce.

Although I was excelling in my job and held in high regard, I made the decision to resign from Macy's for two reasons: first, I wanted to spend a few weeks caring full-time for my widowed mother, who had undergone a serious operation, and second, I had decided that I wished to pursue a career outside retailing. I left on excellent terms and can provide outstanding personal and professional references within the Macy's organization including from my immediate supervisor, Crawford McFarland, who would gladly welcome me back at any time.

I feel certain that I could make valuable contributions to your organization through the diversified management experience I have gained as a Senior Manager at Macy's. Although I am only 34 years old, I have controlled buying decisions of more than $5 million annually while refining my skills in prospecting, customer service, public relations, financial forecasting and financial analysis, and budgeting.

I am single and would cheerfully travel as your needs require. If you feel that my skills and background might be of interest to you, I hope you will contact me to suggest a time when we might meet in person. I am a hard worker and have become an excellent problem solver and negotiator. Thank you in advance for your consideration of my skills.

Sincerely yours,

Christopher Jarvis

Date

Exact Name of Person
Title or Position
Name of Company
Address (number and street)
Address (city, state, and zip)

Dear Exact Name of Person: (or Dear Sir or Madam if answering a blind ad)

I would appreciate an opportunity to talk with you soon about how I could contribute to your organization through my education in finance and my reputation as a hardworking, knowledgeable, and dedicated professional.

As you will see from my enclosed resume, I recently received my Bachelor of Business Administration (B.B.A.) degree with a concentration in Finance from The University of Colorado at Boulder, where I funded my college education by working full time. I am especially proud that I excelled academically while simultaneously advancing in jobs which required expertise in managing human and material resources.

The majority of my experience with the retail giant Buy Mart has been in inventory control and support activities, but I have been given opportunities to demonstrate my finance and accounting knowledge. Selected for a six-month assignment as a Billing and Data Processing Supervisor, I was involved in conducting complex audits which required strong analytical and problem-solving skills.

Although I have established a track record of accomplishments in supervisory positions since the age of 20 with this national retailer, I am exploring employment opportunities which will allow me to apply my education in finance.

If you can use a self-confident and self-motivated individual who is persistent and assertive, I hope you will contact me to suggest a time when we might meet to discuss your needs and how I might help you. Thank you in advance for your time.

Sincerely,

Gisela Myshka

Alternate last paragraph:
I hope you will welcome my call soon to try to arrange a brief meeting to discuss your needs. Thank you in advance for your time.

CAREER-CHANGE COVER LETTERS

Changing Careers from managing people to managing finances
In this letter, an individual with a newly minted degree in finance is attempting to move away from responsibilities for managing people to responsibilities for managing finances. With this letter, she will be able to approach controllers of large companies while also exploring financial planning and financial consulting careers with organizations such as Solomon Smith Barney. She may also approach nonprofit organizations since they often like their top managers to be skilled in financial management.

Date

Exact Name of Person
Title or Position
Name of Company
Address (number and street)
Address (city, state, and zip)

**CAREER-CHANGE
COVER LETTERS**

**Changing Careers into the
pharmaceutical sales field**
In this letter, a grocery
store manager is
seeking to transfer her
strong bottom-line
orientation and
impressive
accomplishments in
boosting sales and
profit into a new
industry. She is
primarily interested in
the pharmaceutical
industry, and the letter
is designed to acquaint
pharmaceutical
companies with her
knowledge of the
territory she would be
covering as well as
with her fine personal
and professional
reputation. She is
hoping that the
company will be willing
to train a highly
motivated producer
who has excelled in
another industry.

Dear Exact Name of Person: (or Dear Sir or Madam if answering a blind ad)

I would appreciate an opportunity to talk with you soon about how I could contribute to your organization through my excellent sales, communication, and customer service skills. I am responding to your advertisement for a Pharmaceutical Sales Representative. I am very knowledgeable of the Dallas, TX, area and offer an outstanding personal and professional reputation in the community.

As you will see from my enclosed resume, I have been highly successful in sales and operations management with a major corporation. Beginning as a Customer Service Manager, I was promoted to manage stores with increasing sales volumes of $7 million, $8.5 million, and $11.5 million annually. In my current position, I have raised total sales by 20%, and profit levels by 25% through my aggressive sales orientation.

Although I am held in high regard by my employer and can provide outstanding references at the appropriate time, I have decided that I would like to apply my sales, customer service, and communication skills within the pharmaceutical sales field. I am certain that my sales ability and strong bottom-line orientation would be ideally suited to pharmaceutical sales. As a store manager, I have become very familiar with a wide range of pharmaceutical products as I have provided oversight of store merchandising, vendor relations, and product mix. I interact with pharmacists and other healthcare professionals with regard to the range of pharmaceutical products carried by the store.

With a B.S.B.A. degree, I possess an educational background which complements my sales and management experience. My highly developed communication skills, assertive personality, and time-management ability have allowed me to effectively manage as many as 100 employees. I offer a reputation as a forceful yet tactful salesperson who is able to present ideas as well as products in a powerful and convincing fashion.

I can assure you that this is a very deliberate attempt on my part to transition into the pharmaceutical sales field, and I hope you will call or write me soon to arrange a brief meeting to discuss your current and future needs and how I might serve them. Thank you in advance for your time.

Sincerely,

Gloria Pena

Date

Exact Name of Person
Exact Title
Exact Name of Company
Address
City, State Zip

Dear Sir or Madam:

With the enclosed resume describing my qualifications and experience, I would like to initiate the process of applying for a position as a Flight Attendant with your airline.

First Aid Knowledge

As you will see from my resume, I am knowledgeable of first aid procedures through my medical and scientific training in the area of anesthesiology.

Fluency in French

An American citizen, I am fluent in French. I have traveled extensively throughout the U.S. as well as in Germany, Greece, France, and the Caribbean. Although I became an American citizen at age 13, I was raised in the South of France in Gandrage.

Modeling Background

During my junior and senior years of high school, I was a part-time model for both a department store and for a meat packing plant which featured me on television commercials. After high school, the Wilhelmina Agency in New York recommended me for a runway modeling job in Paris because of my modeling ability and fluency in French.

Customer Relations and Management Experience

Most recently I have excelled as a small business manager, and I am skilled in dealing with the public, resolving problems in a gracious manner, and managing my time for maximum efficiency and profitability. I have developed my current customer base largely through word of mouth because of the excellent services I provide as well as my public relations skills. You will see from my resume that I have also worked as a hostess and waitress in the Hilton Hotel in Chicago, where I frequently served celebrity customers in an upscale restaurant/bar catering to the affluent.

Please send me information about the Flight Attendant career field with your airline, and I would be delighted to make myself available for a personal interview at the appropriate time. I can provide excellent personal and professional references.

Yours sincerely,

Angela Hapsburg

Date

Exact Name of Person
Exact Title
Exact Name of Company
Address
City, State Zip

CAREER-CHANGE
COVER LETTERS

Changing Careers from
social services to the
academic environment
Changing careers from
social services to
academic administration
is the purpose of this
cover letter. Although
Ms. Bustier has enjoyed
her work in human
services, she is
interested in obtaining
her Ph.D. and feels that
she would be better able
to pursue this goal if she
were transplanted to an
academic institution.
What she is marketing to
academic institutions is
her managerial
resourcefulness and
expertise in staff
development.

Dear Sir or Madam:

With the enclosed resume, I would like to make you aware of the background in program management and staff development which I could put to work for your organization.

While excelling in the track record of advancement which you will see summarized on my resume, I have applied my strong organizational skills in implementing new programs, organizing conferences and seminars, training and counseling professional-level employees, and transforming ideas into operational realities. On numerous occasions, I have developed effective formats for formal written documents which have been described as "models."

In my current position, I have served as a Program Manager for the state of South Carolina while spearheading the development of new housing options and employment opportunities for the developmentally disabled and mentally impaired. With a reputation as a vibrant and persuasive communicator, I routinely interface with legislators, state and federal officials, as well as with local program managers. It has often been my responsibility to take a new law and make sure it is efficiently and resourcefully implemented at the local level while assuring compliance with federal and state guidelines. I am continuously involved in teaching and training others—not only the professionals whom I directly supervise but also professionals regionally and locally who turn to me for advice and assistance in problem solving.

I feel confident that my resourceful leadership, expertise in staff training and staff development, and pragmatic approach to operations management and service operations delivery could be valuable to your organization. If you feel you could use my considerable experience in initiating new programs, making existing programs work better, and establishing effective working relationships, I hope you will contact me to suggest a time when we might meet to discuss your needs and how I might serve them. I can provide outstanding personal and professional references at the appropriate time.

Yours sincerely,

Elaine Bustier

In this section you will find answers to common questions about cover letters. Lots of "oddball" situations come up in job hunting, and you will find the answers to many of those questions in this section. In this section you will find out how to phrase the answers to delicate questions such as questions about salary.

Question 1: What is the "direct approach?"

Question 2: How do I address a letter to an ad that provides names and addresses?

Question 3: What's the best way to answer a "blind ad?"

Question 4: How do I respond to a recruiter or headhunter who has approached me?

Question 5: How do I apply for internal openings?

Question 6: How do I ask for consideration for multiple job openings?

Question 7: How do I e-mail or fax my resume and cover letter?

Question 8: If I want to "drop a name" in a cover letter, what's the best way?

Question 9: If I'm relocating soon, how do I say that in the cover letter?

Question 10: If I've recently relocated, what do I say in the cover letter?

Question 11: What if I want to reopen a door that I closed previously?

Question 12: What if they ask for salary requirements?

Question 13: What if they ask for salary history?

Question 14: How do I make it clear that I want my approach to be confidential?

Question 15: How do I write a follow-up letter after an interview?

Question 16: How do I resign—gracefully?

Exact Name of Person
Title or Position
Name of Company
Address (number and street)
Address (city, state, and zip)

THE
DIRECT APPROACH

Question 1: What is the
"direct approach?"
You need to master the
technique of using the
"direct approach" in
your job hunt. By
using the direct
approach, you create
an all-purpose letter,
such as the one on this
page, which you can
send to numerous
employers introducing
yourself and your
resume. The direct
approach is a
proactive, aggressive
approach to a job
campaign, and it sure
beats waiting around
until the "ideal job"
appears in the
newspaper (and 200
other people see it,
too). Figure out the
employers you wish to
approach either (1) by
geographical area or
(2) by industry and
directly approach them
expressing your
interest in their
company. Believe it or
not, most people get
their jobs through the
direct approach!

Dear Exact Name of Person: (or Dear Sir or Madam if answering a blind ad)

I would appreciate an opportunity to talk with you soon about how I could contribute to your organization through my extensive expertise in the financial field including my recent experience as a Financial Consultant.

As you will see from my resume, I hold the Series 7, Series 63, Series 24, and Series 65 licenses and am a Registered Member of numerous exchanges and associations of securities dealers. In 2000 I left a Wall Street firm to relocate to the South, where my wife and her family live. Since 2000 I have been working for Merrill Lynch, and after my training and licensing, I established 364 accounts and produced $5 million in managed money in my first six-month period of production. Although I am excelling in my job and have been offered a branch management position in another state, I wish to remain in the Norfolk area. Since I am not under contract with Merrill Lynch, I am exploring suitable opportunities with area firms.

Much of my rapid success as a Financial Consultant stems from my background in nearly all aspects of finance, credit, and collections, in addition to my entrepreneurial background. As Managing Director, I owned and managed a lead-based company for Dun & Bradstreet. Subsequent to that, I worked with Wall Street firms in New York City until I met my wife and she decided she wanted us to relocate to Norfolk to be near her family. I offer an extensive background in working with high net worth individuals.

I can provide outstanding personal and professional references, and I would be delighted to make myself available at your convenience for a personal interview. Thank you in advance for your professional courtesies and consideration.

Yours sincerely,

Elias Johnson III

Date

Ms. Myrtle McConnell
Clark Management, Inc.
Post Office Box 82
Virginia Beach, VA 34098

Dear Ms. McConnell:

I am writing to express my interest in the position of Manager of the Virginia Beach Resort and Tennis Club which was advertised in the *Virginia Beach Gazette* of Monday, December 18, 2000. With the enclosed resume, I would like to introduce you to my proven supervisory and guest services skills along with my track record of success as Owner/Operator and General Manager of a number of establishments.

In my most recent position in the hospitality industry, I purchased a 150-seat restaurant and 50-seat lounge from the O'Brien's chain. I changed the restaurant's name and developed a new, expanded menu while implementing higher levels of guest service. I directed the work of the front end, bar, and kitchen managers, overseeing a staff of 25 employees. In my previous position at Kasey's in Virginia Beach, we dealt with a large client base of repeat customers, arranging reservations at local golf courses as well as serving their dining needs.

For the past year, I have excelled as Business Manager of ABC Construction, helping my brother to set up his commercial contracting business. Now that his business is up and running, I am very interested in returning to the hospitality industry, and my wife and I are considering relocation to the Virginia Beach area. I feel that my strong management background and proven skills in customer service, staff development, and training would make me a valuable addition to your operation.

When we meet in person, you will see that I am a congenial professional and avid tennis player with extensive management experience that could make me an ideal candidate for this position. I offer an outstanding reputation in our industry and can provide excellent references at the appropriate time.

Yours sincerely,

Bill Adams

ANSWERING ADS

Question 2: How do I respond to an ad that provides the name and address?
It's easy enough to reply to an ad when you have the name and address of the person you're writing to, but there's more to this question than meets the eye. Read the ad carefully and tailor your letter as precisely to the ad as possible. Notice the sentence in the last paragraph where Mr. Adams mentions that he's a tennis player. He is picking up on the fact that the ad is for a tennis resort, and he is making his reader aware that he plays the game and understands the passion of the club's customers.

P.O. Box 66
Dallas, TX 90345

ANSWERING ADS

**Question 3: What's the
best way to answer a
"blind ad?"**

"To whom it may
concern" or "Dear Sir
or Madam" is the
proper salutation for a
letter responding to a
"blind ad" or an ad
which does not reveal
the company name or
the name of the
person to whom you
are writing. Sometimes
companies don't put
their name in the ad
because they don't
want their competitors
to know they are
hiring. Sometimes
companies don't give
their name because
they think it might
encourage telephone
calls about the job.

To whom it may concern:

With the enclosed resume, I would like to respond to your advertisement in the *Dallas Chronicle* for a Management Trainee and make you aware of the considerable office, sales, and management abilities I could put to work for you.

As you will see from my resume, I am skilled in all aspects of office activities and am proficient with WordPerfect and the Windows programs including Word, Excel, and Access. I am a very cheerful and adaptable person, as has been demonstrated by my ability to adapt rapidly and become quickly productive while working in long-term and short-term temporary assignments for major corporations, small businesses, and utility companies. I am skilled at operating a multiline switchboard system.

A resourceful and enthusiastic individual, I have always found ways to contribute to increased efficiency in all of my jobs. For example, in one job with an electrical supply company, I developed ideas which resulted in increased efficiency in supply parts ordering. In another job with a prominent retailer, I was named Sales Representative of the Month and was credited with playing a key role in increasing repeat business through my customer service and sales skills.

You will also see that I offer proven management skills and personal initiative. In one of my first professional positions, I was promoted rapidly by a children's entertainment company to responsibilities which involved traveling to conventions to book shows and negotiate contracts. The youngest person ever promoted to vice president, I am still a member of the Board of Directors of that company and am respected for my business insights and marketing instincts.

If you can use a versatile young professional known for an excellent attitude as well as superior work habits including reliability, dependability, and honesty, I hope you will contact me to suggest a time when we might meet to discuss your needs. I can assure you in advance that I could rapidly become an asset to your organization.

Sincerely,

Simone Guardado

Date

Mr. John Smith
XYZ Management Recruiters
Address (number and street)
Address (city, state, and zip)

Dear Mr. Smith:

After reviewing the materials you sent me regarding the Des Moines Public Schools Superintendency, I believe that my professional and personal attributes are complementary to the needs of the school system.

In my current position as Superintendent of Fort Leavenworth Schools, I am entrusted with serving 5,700 students and supervising a staff of 660. The challenges in this district serving military dependents have been many and varied. With the cooperation of the staff and the greater school community, we have been successful in securing outstanding financial support from both the Department of Defense and Congress. As a result, we were able to open a new elementary school and expand five existing schools.

As Superintendent in Huntsville, AL, and at Fort Leavenworth, I provided the impetus for expansion of technology in the instructional program. During this past year, one of Fort Leavenworth's elementary schools was chosen as a testbed site for President Clinton's Technology Initiative (PTI). This pilot project will afford our students and staff an opportunity to share innovative programs and instructional strategies.

Believing that mutual cooperation from internal and external sources is critical for success, I am known for my ability to forge strong alliances and partnerships with community organizations. While serving as Superintendent in Huntsville, I was instrumental in forming a regional school and business alliance (SABA) which developed partnerships with the business community. Serving as Director on several boards has also provided me with opportunities to gain community support for school programs. Indeed, any professional accomplishments I have achieved during my career have been attained through the combined efforts of many people. If I were to be selected as Superintendent, I would work diligently to gain local, state, and national support in order to move the Des Moines Public Schools forward.

Thank you for your interest in my qualifications, and I look forward to talking with you soon about the next step you suggest in my formally applying for the position as Superintendent of the Des Moines School System.

Yours sincerely,

Andrew J. Foster

RESPONDING TO RECRUITERS

Question 4: How do I respond to a recruiter or "headhunter" who has approached me?
Don't take any shortcuts when responding to a recruiter who has approached you to see if you might be interested in a new situation. In Mr. Foster's case, he has been approached by a management recruiting firm handling the search for a school superintendent of a major school district. He makes sure the recruiter understands him professionally and philosophically by developing a cover letter that fully markets his interest and background. As always, make sure your cover letter "sells" you!

Date

Exact Name of Person
Title or Position
Name of Company
Address (number and street)
Address (city, state, and zip)

**APPLYING FOR
INTERNAL OPENINGS**

**Question 5: How do I
apply for internal
openings?**
We recommend
sacrificing no formality
when applying for
internal promotions. As
you see from this
cover letter, you still
need to "sell" your
interest and
qualifications, even
when the insiders
know you.

Dear Exact Name of Person: (or Dear Sir or Madam if answering a blind ad)

With the enclosed resume, I would like to make you aware of my interest in the position of **Financial Management Analyst II with the Vermont Department of Revenue.** As you will see from my enclosed resume, I offer a background as a seasoned accounting professional with exceptional analytical, communication, and organizational skills. In my current job, I perform essentially as a Financial Management Analyst in my role as a Field Auditor and Revenue Officer with the Vermont Department of Revenue.

With the Department of Revenue, I have advanced in a track record of increasing responsibilities. In my current position as a Field Auditor, I analyze financial reports of businesses and individuals, reconciling various general ledgers as well as investment and checking accounts in order to accurately determine tax liability. Earlier as a Revenue Officer, I consulted with taxpayers to assist them in determining the validity of deductions and calculating the amount of individual income tax owed. In both of these positions, I trained my coworkers, sharing my extensive knowledge of Internal Revenue Service and Vermont Department of Revenue codes and laws while educating department personnel on correct procedures related to professional auditing and collections.

I hold an Associate of Applied Science degree in Accounting from Central Berkshire Community College and a Bachelor of Science in Business Administration from the University of Oregon at Portland.

Please favorably consider my application for this internal opening, and please also consider my history of dedicated service to the Vermont Department of Revenue. I feel certain that I could excel in this job and could be a valuable asset to the department.

Sincerely,

Kevin Strafford

Date

Exact Name of Person
Title or Position
Name of Company
Address (number and street)
Address (city, state, and zip)

Dear Exact Name of Person: (or Sir or Madam if answering a blind ad)

SEEKING MULTIPLE JOB CONSIDERATION

With the enclosed resume, I would like to make you aware of the considerable skills I could put to work for the Baltimore Family Health System. Although I would like you to consider me for any situation where my versatile skills could be of value to you, I am particularly interested in the following positions:

> Access Coordinator
> Assistant Practice Manager
> Network Analyst II (Information Systems)
> Account Analyst

You will see that I offer skills compatible with those and other business office positions. I hold a B.A. in Finance and have acquired experience in internal business auditing activities, payroll calculation and administration, computer operations, and office management. I have worked for only two companies and have been promoted to increasing responsibilities in both organizations because of my initiative, productivity, and office skills. Even in high school, I began working for Camelot Music and was promoted to Assistant Manager for a store with $1.5 million in annual sales and 15 employees. In my current job, I handle a variety of internal auditing procedures, troubleshoot accounting problems, and handle liaison with the home office. I am proficient in utilizing numerous software programs including Excel, Lotus, and many others.

With a reputation as a congenial individual with outstanding customer service and public relations skills, I can provide outstanding personal and professional references at the appropriate time. Although I am excelling in my current position and am highly regarded by my employer, it is my desire to work in a medical environment.

If you can use an energetic and highly motivated hard worker who offers versatile skills and abilities, I hope you will contact me to suggest a time when we might meet to discuss your needs and how I might serve them. Thank you in advance for your time.

Yours sincerely,

Holly M. Vargo

Question 6: How do I request consideration for multiple job openings in the organization?
This individual knows the organization she wants to work for; she just isn't sure what job she wants within the organization! In such a situation, you can plainly state in the first paragraph of your cover letter that you wish to be considered for multiple job openings by name. The employer will probably be glad to learn of your versatility.

Date

BY FAX TO: Human Resources Department
910-483-2439
Reference Job Code XYZ 9034

**E-MAILING OR FAXING
YOUR RESUME AND
COVER LETTER**

**Question 7: How do I
e-mail or fax my resume?**
The answer is: always
with a cover letter.
When you fax your
resume and the cover
letter introducing your
resume, we
recommend that you
put the fax number on
the top of the letter. In
this way you identify to
the receiver how you
contacted them
(remember, they may
be receiving dozens of
other resumes and
cover letters), and you
also have a record of
the fax number on the
top of your copy of the
letter. Never send any
type of
correspondence in
business without dating
it.

Dear Sir or Madam:

With the enclosed resume, I would like to make you aware of my interest in employment as a Pharmaceutical Healthcare Representative with Johnson & Johnson. I believe you are aware that Walter Freeman, one of your Healthcare Representatives, has recommended that I talk with you because he feels that I could excel in the position as Pharmaceutical Healthcare Representative.

As you will see from my enclosed resume, I offer proven marketing and sales skills along with a reputation as a highly motivated individual with exceptional problem-solving abilities. Shortly after joining my current firm as a Mortgage Loan Specialist, I was named Outstanding Loan Officer of the month through my achievement in generating more than $20,000 in fees.

I believe much of my professional success so far has been due to my highly motivated nature and creative approach to my job. For example, when I began working for my current employer, I developed and implemented the concept of a postcard that communicated a message which the consumer found intriguing. The concept has been so successful that it has been one of the main sources of advertisements in our office and the concept has been imitated by other offices in the company.

In addition to my track record of excelling in the highly competitive financial services field, I gained valuable sales experience in earlier jobs selling copying equipment and sleep systems. I have also applied my strong leadership and sales ability in the human services field, when I worked in adult probation services. I am very proud of the fact that many troubled individuals with whom I worked told me that my ability to inspire and motivate them was the key to their becoming productive citizens.

If you can use a creative and motivated self-starter who could enhance your goals for market share and profitability, I hope you will contact me to suggest a time when we could meet in person to discuss your needs and goals and how I could meet them. I can provide strong personal and professional references at the appropriate time.

Yours sincerely,

Cheri Garcia

Date

Exact Name of Person
Title or Position
Name of Company
Address (number and street)
Address (city, state, and zip)

Dear Exact Name of Person: (or Sir or Madam if answering a blind ad)

With the enclosed resume, I would like to make you aware of my interest in joining your organization in some capacity which could utilize my extensive experience related to consumer lending, credit, and collections. I am responding to your recent advertisement for a Loan Processor. I am somewhat familiar with your organization because I had the pleasure of working by telephone last year with several of your employees on matters related to skip tracing, and I was impressed with the professionalism of your personnel. Ms. Lenette Wilson, in particular, was especially helpful to me and gave me an outstanding impression of your organization.

My family and I have recently relocated to Little Rock from El Paso, TX, where I excelled in a track record of achievement as a Collections Officer. I began working for the Ft. Bliss Credit Union as a Teller, was quickly named "Teller of the Quarter," and then was promoted to handle complex responsibilities related to collections. I received numerous Customer Service Awards and achieved an extremely low delinquency rate on repossessed vehicles while maintaining the lowest possible ratios related to bankruptcies and written-off loans. I am skilled in every aspect of collections.

In addition to excelling as a Collections Officer, I became knowledgeable of consumer lending and banking while handling money orders, bank checks, IRA withdrawals, travelers checks, savings bonds, coin exchanges, night deposit posting, handling the closing of members' accounts, filing members' open-account cards, processing returned checks, as well as processing and filming checks to National Credit Union Headquarters.

If you can use a hard-working young professional who offers a reputation as a thorough, persistent, and highly motivated individual, I hope you will contact me to suggest a time when we might meet to discuss your needs and goals and how I could help you achieve them. I would be delighted to discuss the private details of my salary history with you in person, and I can provide outstanding personal and professional references.

Sincerely,

Athena Zibart

NAME DROPPING

Question 8: If I want to "drop a name" in a letter, what's the best way?
It's nice to play the "who you know" game socially and in business, and it can help you get in the door for interviews, too. If a current employee has recommended that you write to the organization, or if you have worked with members of the organization on some project, you can "drop a name" gracefully. In so doing, you will add warmth to a cover letter that will exude a very personalized tone.

Date

Exact Name of Person
Title or Position
Name of Company
Address (number and street)
Address (city, state, and zip)

RELOCATING SOON

Question 9: If I'm relocating soon, how do I say that?
Employers are nosy people! If they receive a resume from someone whose last (or current) job was in another town or state, they wonder why you've relocated. Go ahead and satisfy their curiosity in the cover letter you send in advance of your arrival in town.

Dear Exact Name of Person: (or Sir or Madam if answering a blind ad)

With the enclosed resume, I would like to initiate the process of being considered for employment within your organization. Because of family ties, I am in the process of relocating to the Houston area by a target date of December 5. Although I already have a Houston address which is shown on my resume, it is my brother's home and I would prefer your contacting me at the e-mail address shown on my resume or at my current telephone number if you wish to talk with me prior to December 5th.

Since graduating from the University of North Carolina at Chapel Hill, I have a track record of rapid promotion with a corporation headquartered in Miami Beach. I began as an Assistant Branch Manager and Head Buyer, was cross-trained as a Sales Representative, and have been promoted to my current position in which I manage the selling process related to 3,500 different products. In that capacity, I am entrusted with the responsibility for nearly $15 million in annual expenditures, and I maintain excellent working relationships with more than 150 vendors of name-brand consumer products sold through chain and convenience stores.

In my job, rapid change is a daily reality, and I have become accustomed to working in an environment in which I must make rapid decisions while weighing factors including forecasted consumer demand, distribution patterns, inventory turnover patterns, and vendor capacity and character. I have earned a reputation as a persuasive communicator and savvy negotiator with an aggressive bottom-line orientation.

If you can use my versatile experience in sales, purchasing, distribution, and operations management, I hope you will contact me to suggest a time when we might meet to discuss your needs and how I might serve them. I can provide excellent personal and professional references, and I assure you in advance that I am a hard worker who is accustomed to being measured according to ambitious goals for profitability in a highly competitive marketplace.

Yours sincerely,

Dale P. Jensen

Date

Exact Name of Person
Title or Position
Name of Company
Address (number and street)
Address (city, state, and zip)

Dear Exact Name of Person: (or Sir or Madam if answering a blind ad)

With the enclosed resume, I would like to make you aware of my background in accounts management, personnel supervision, and customer service as well as my strong organizational, interpersonal, and communication skills. My husband and I have relocated back to Rochester, where our respective families are from.

While recently completing my Bachelor of Science degree, I excelled academically and was named to the Dean's List seven times. Prior to earning my degree, I excelled in both military and civilian environments.

In one job in North Carolina, I began as a Receptionist answering a 30-line phone system for a 1100-employee company which provided on-line computer services. I rapidly advanced to Accounts Manager and Shift Supervisor, which placed me in charge of eight people. In that job I made hundreds of decisions daily which involved committing the company's technical resources. In addition to dispatching technicians and managing liaison with companies such as The Bank of Chicago, United Carolina Bank, and Stein Mart, I was authorized to commit company resources valued at up to $500,000.

With my husband's retirement, we are eager to replant our roots in New York, and I am seeking employment with a company that can use a highly motivated hard worker who is known for excellent decision-making, problem-solving, and organizational skills. If you can use a resourceful and versatile individual with administrative and computer skills, I hope you will contact me to suggest a time when we can discuss your present and future needs and how I might meet them. I can provide outstanding personal and professional references, and I thank you in advance for your time and consideration.

Sincerely,

Antoinette Pardue

Date

Exact Name of Person
Title or Position
Name of Company
Address (number and street)
Address (city, state, and zip)

REOPENING A DOOR

Dear Exact Name of Person: (or Sir or Madam if answering a blind ad)

Question 11: What if I want to reopen a door I closed previously?
Employers can get their feelings hurt if you turn down a job they offer you. This lady had pulled out of the last round of interviews for a job with a newspaper, and months later she realized she'd made a mistake. This letter accompanying her resume reopened the door for her and led to an offer (and acceptance) of a job.

As I hope you will recall, several months ago I interviewed with you for a position involving responsibility for advertising sales with the *Hartford News and Observer*. I very much appreciated your many kindnesses to me during the interviewing process.

During the time when I was interviewing with you for a position, my current employer approached me and asked if I would take on a special project which involved performing outside sales for the business. Since I had worked at Cross Roads Chrysler-Buick for five years and was very familiar with the customer base and with the company's style of doing business, he wanted me in particular to take on the project and I felt, because of his business circumstances at the time, that I had a personal and moral obligation to serve the company in that role.

For that reason I was unable to follow through with the final stage of becoming an employee of the *Hartford News and Observer*.

That project has now been completed and I feel I have loyally completed my obligation to the company in that regard. I would like to ask that you reconsider me for an advertising sales position with the *Hartford News and Observer*. I can provide outstanding personal and professional references, including from my current employer, and I can assure you that I would offer the *Hartford News and Observer* the same loyalty as I have consistently shown to my current employer.

My resume is enclosed to refresh your memory about my skills and professional qualifications. You may also recall that we first became acquainted years ago when I was attending St. Joseph's Episcopal Church.

I have a high opinion of you and of the *Hartford News and Observer* and I hope you will consider me for any position within your company which requires a positive, highly motivated individual with a proven track record of excellent performance in sales and customer service. Thank you again for your past courtesies, and I hope you will welcome my call soon when I try to contact you to see if you have needs I could fill. Best wishes for the holiday season and the New Year.

Yours sincerely,

Samantha Griggers

Date

Exact Name of Person
Title or Position
Name of Company
Address (number and street)
Address (city, state, and zip)

Dear Exact Name of Person: (or Sir or Madam if answering a blind ad)

I would like to make you aware of my strong interest in the position of Training and Development Manager advertised in the *Houston Chronicle*. As you will see, I have a track record of success as an experienced instructor and training program developer as well as proven skills in employee supervision, staff development, and production management.

As you will see, I have excelled as an instructor, course developer, and technical writer. Training and counseling junior personnel have always been key responsibilities.

With a versatile background which includes experience in the telecommunications field as well as aircraft and vehicle maintenance, I have been involved in most areas of operations to include logistics, planning and scheduling, and safety as well as in heavy equipment operations. I offer a reputation as a skilled communicator who has been especially effective in providing instruction in individual and group situations. I am especially proud of the associate's degree I earned while excelling in my full-time job.

With regard to my salary requirements, I would be delighted to discuss the private details of my salary history with you in person. I can assure you that I can provide excellent references at the appropriate time.

If you can use an experienced professional who is dedicated to setting and achieving high standards in all areas of performance, I hope you will contact me to suggest a time when we might meet to discuss your needs. I am confident that I could become an asset to Dickinson Associates.

Sincerely,

Chico Flores, Jr.

WHEN THEY ASK FOR SALARY REQUIREMENTS

Question 12: What if they ask for salary requirements?
It's not in your best interests to provide your salary requirements in response to an ad. It's better to discuss that subject in person with the employer, and always let the employer bring the subject up. If the employer brings up salary, he or she is probably interested in you and you'll be able to negotiate your best package. See the fourth paragraph for the exact wording in handling this delicate matter.

Date

Exact Name of Person
Title or Position
Name of Company
Address (number and street)
Address (city, state, and zip)

WHEN THEY ASK FOR SALARY HISTORY

Question 13: What if they ask for salary history?
You may be asked to provide your salary history in writing, but be sure to add in everything so that the prospective employer receives a fair picture of your total compensation. Please note that we recommend that you handle a request for salary history as it is handled in the letter on the previous page rather than by providing the intimate details of your salary history in a letter.

Dear Exact Name of Person: (or Sir or Madam if answering a blind ad)

I would like to take this opportunity to thank you for considering me for the job on June 4 as a Sales Representative for Proctor & Gamble, Inc.

I enjoyed meeting with you and being able to learn more about the company. I believe that Proctor & Gamble has a quality product line and I would be honored to represent these products.

I would also like to thank you for considering my busy schedule as a State Probation and Parole Officer and allowing me to come back for the second interview in the same afternoon. I am an extremely reliable and dependable professional, and I appreciated your professional courtesies in helping me be away from my current job as little as possible.

In response to your question about my salary history, I am currently making in the neighborhood of $35,000 with a raise anticipated within two months that could take me to close to $40,000. I enjoy a full benefits package with my current employer.

I am very interested in the position we discussed, and I can provide exceptionally strong personal and professional references at the appropriate time. Thank you for talking with me and helping me learn more about your fine company, and I hope to hear from you soon.

Sincerely,

Kim Chiang

Date

Exact Name of Person
Title or Position
Name of Company
Address (number and street)
Address (city, state, and zip)

Dear Exact Name of Person: (or Sir or Madam if answering a blind ad)

WHEN CONFIDENTIALITY MATTERS

Question 14: How do I make it clear that I want my approach to be confidential?
Here's another example of the wording to use when you want to stress that you wish your approach to be confidential.

With the enclosed resume, I would like to make you aware of my interest in the possibility of putting my strong management, production operations, and sales background to work for your company. Please treat my inquiry as highly confidential at this point. Although I can provide outstanding personal and professional references at the appropriate time, I do not wish my current employer to be aware of my interest in your company.

As you will see from my enclosed resume, I have been in the multipurpose concrete applications business my entire working life. I began in entry-level positions with Fabrico Concrete in New Orleans and was promoted to Plant Manager and Sales Manager. Then I joined Alfred Wright and Son, Inc. in Lafayette, LA, where I tripled production and transformed that company into an attractive acquisition candidate which caught the attention of Handy Concrete. When Handy Concrete Company bought Alfred Wright in 1996, I became a Division Manager and in 1998 was promoted to Regional Manager.

In my current position I manage operations at 10 divisions while supervising three Division Managers and overseeing activities of 85 people at 10 locations. I also supervise four sales and customer service professionals in addition to preparing budgets for each of the 10 divisions.

If you can use a professional with versatile management skills transferable to any industry, I hope you will contact me to suggest a time when we might meet. Should you have ambitious goals in either the production management or sales area, I feel certain that my experience could be useful.

Sincerely,

Eugene H. Dubois, Jr.

Date

Exact Name of Person
Title or Position
Name of Company
Address (number and street)
Address (city, state, and zip)

FOLLOW-UP LETTER

Dear Exact Name of Person: (or Sir or Madam if answering a blind ad)

Question 15: How do I write a follow-up letter after an interview?
Notice the last paragraph. A follow-up letter is an excellent opportunity to send your requests for reimbursement for any out-of-pocket expenses you incurred in connection with the interview.

I want you to know how much I enjoyed talking with you in Sioux Falls on Friday, January 12th.

I am intensely interested in working with you to develop retail applications in the convenience store industry. I believe you are aware that I performed essentially that job for the construction industry in a previous position. With Newcombe Computer Systems, I rose from System Programmer to Director of Development as I transformed a failing operation into an efficient and profitable business.

In my current job as Vice President of Management Information Systems (MIS), I played a key role in making many changes within FashionPlus, a major retail chain, which made the company an acquisition target. Now that we are a part of a larger retail company, I am directing network systems development for this vastly larger organization. I understand your company's growth goals, as you explained them to me, and I feel I could become a valuable part of your strategic planning and implementation process.

One of my strengths is that I have a vast knowledge of many different areas, ranging from accounting systems and accounting development, to user interface, to putting together specifications, to the continual troubleshooting of problems and refinement of systems. It has been my responsibility to sit with technical experts in all functional areas and be able to assure the attainment of specific goals in their area of operation. I am confident that I could apply my expertise related to UNIX, NT, and programming within your industry, and I am skilled at establishing effective working relationships at all levels.

Thank you for giving me so much of your time and for letting me become better acquainted with your needs. I am enclosing a copy of my mileage statement (423 miles) and a copy of the hotel statement. I believe I could become a valuable member of your management team.

Sincerely,

James W. White

Date

Exact Name of Person
Title or Position
Name of Company
Address (number and street)
Address (city, state, and zip)

Dear Exact Name of Person:

It is with genuine sadness and many mixed feelings that I must inform you that I will be resigning from my position at Cranford, Sweeney & Co., CPAs, effective July 26.

The firm of Hill, Gilbert & Wilkins in Spokane, also a public accounting firm, has offered me a position as a CPA at a salary of nearly $50,000 annually, and I feel it is a time in my life when I must move on.

Leaving the firm of Cranford, Sweeney & Co., CPAs, is very difficult for me professionally and emotionally. After I passed the CPA Exam, you gave me my first job in the public accounting field, and I have thoroughly enjoyed the family atmosphere coupled with the professional style of both you and Mr. Cranford. You have taught me so much about how to solve problems, how to work more efficiently, and how to handle difficult clients. I am deeply grateful for your encouragement, professional mentoring, and strong personal example.

Although the decision to leave Cranford, Sweeney & Co., CPAs, is difficult, I really feel that I have no choice. As a single parent who provides full financial support of my daughter, I am driven by the desire to provide a gracious standard of living for my small family. I will be placing her in a Christian school in Spokane so that she can continue learning in the same Christian environment as she has had in Tacoma.

I hope you know that I have always given 110% to your firm in terms of my financial knowledge, intelligence, and problem-solving ability, and I hope you feel that I have made contributions to its reputation. I feel I am separating more from a family than from an employer, and I felt I wanted to put this information in writing to you as a first step because getting the words out verbally would be a difficult emotional experience for me.

Thank you from the bottom of my heart for all you have done for me professionally and personally.

Yours sincerely,

Elizabeth J. Ritchie

Question 16: How do I resign—gracefully?
Here's an example of a letter that will be an emotional experience for the people receiving it as it was for the person who signed it. Employers are often not happy when you leave them, so a great letter of resignation can ease the hurt.

Date

TO: John Smith
    Elaine Bryant
    Meredith Kleinfield

**ANOTHER LETTER OF
LEAVE TAKING**

**Question 16: How do I
resign — gracefully?**
A letter of resignation
can be a highly
emotional experience,
both for the person
sending it and for the
individuals receiving it.
It gives you a formal
opportunity to declare
your last day on the
job and to thank
appropriate people.

Dear Friends and Valued Colleagues:

It is with much sadness as well as with great personal affection for all of you that I wish to inform you that I will be leaving the Ford Motor Company. My final departure date can be worked out according to your wishes, but I would suggest Wednesday, December 20, 2000.

A sales position has become available at *The Schofield Gazette* and I believe the hours of employment will be better suited to my needs as a single parent.

Because I have been employed with Ford Motor Company since 1995, I feel as though I am "leaving home," and in that nostalgic frame of mind, it is my desire to tell you how much I have appreciated your training me, helping me, and giving me opportunities to try new things and gain new skills. I am very truly grateful to you, and I hope you know that I always gave my best effort.

I can assure you that I will continue to be a highly productive source of referrals for you even when I am gone, because I believe wholeheartedly in the products and the product line we all have represented. If I can ever help any of you individually in any way, too, please let me know.

In the meantime, please accept my sincere thanks for all the kindnesses and professional courtesies you have shown me.

Yours sincerely,

Mary Anne Murphy

In this section, you will find resumes and cover letters of people who have successfully changed careers. If you have picked up this book, you probably have been thinking about making a change in your career. In this book you will find numerous "case studies" of people who have used their resume and cover letter to build bridges to new careers. A good place to start in using this book is to look at the Table of Contents. You are not expected to "find yourself" in the Table of Contents, but you will find more than 100 "case studies" of real people who have succeeded in changing their work situation in ways that range from very dramatic to relatively minor.

The resumes of career changers must "build bridges."

If you have never worked in a field or industry before, you do not have the same kind of credibility as others who have been working in the field. Your resume and cover letter are extremely important in a career-change situation, since you must persuade the reader to take a chance on someone who is "untested." The language of the cover letter and resume must appeal to a broad range of individuals, most of whom will not be familiar with the "lingo" of your current field. In most cases, you will need to "translate" what you've been doing into understandable language.

How to use this book...

By deliberate design, this book has been developed as a manageable size so that its owner will have time to look over all of the resumes and cover letters. Visit the Table of Contents and you will find the resumes and cover letters of real people who changed careers.

- If you are not satisfied with the industry you're in, Ken Soifer's resume on page 113 will show you an example of a resume and cover letter of someone who moved on from the furniture industry. George Louik's resume and cover letter on page 133 show a professional transitioning from the textile industry.

- Want to see an example of a young probation officer who wants out of the public sector and into a profit-making corporation? See the resume and cover letter of Cynthia Willis on page 154 and 155.

- Is your goal **finding a new product or service to sell, represent, or market?** The resumes and cover letters on pages 56-77 will interest you in particular.

- If your goal is **finding a completely different type of work to do**, you will enjoy looking over the resumes and cover letters on pages 78-103.

- Are you **seeking a change but trying to stay in the same industry?** The resumes and cover letters on pages 104-115 will interest you.

- If you are **changing fields but have no idea what you want to do next,** the resumes and cover letters on pages 116-133 will provide helpful insights.

- If you are **changing fields but have a pretty good idea what you want to do next,** you will probably be interested in the language and look of the resumes and cover letters on pages 134-163.

Now let's start with a resume that shows a radical career change: **from motherhood** and working at home full-time for more than 15 years to a new career as a flight attendant with a major airline!

A word from the editor:

The resumes and cover letters in this book have been carefully selected. Regardless of whether you are making a major change in your career, such as finding a completely different type of work to do, or a slight change in your career, such as finding a new product or service to sell, you will find "kindred souls" in this book. All these people changed their lives and improved their job satisfaction by changing careers. The techniques you see in these resumes and cover letters will help you in your own career-change efforts.

GOAL: Finding a New Career After Motherhood

Date

**Full-Time Homemaker to
Airline Travel Attendant**

Exact Name of Person
Exact Title
Exact Name of Company
Address
City, State, Zip

Dear Exact Name of Person (or Dear Sir or Madam if answering a blind ad):

I would appreciate an opportunity to talk with you soon about how I could contribute to your organization through my proven ability to serve the public and "bring out the best in people." I am interested in becoming a flight attendant for your airline.

Both in high school and in college, I was fortunate enough to be the recipient of many honors ranging from winning the pageant in my high school to becoming elected class president on my college campus. I am known as a self-starter with a high energy level and a true concern for others.

As you will see from my resume, I have excelled in jobs as a financial consultant and account executive/sales representative. During the period of that employment, however, I have pursued and excelled in studies related to travel, tourism, computer reservations, and the travel agent field. Through the extensive experience described on my resume, I have become a "professional traveler" and I am positive I have all the natural ingredients and acquired skills necessary to excel as a flight attendant.

You would find me to be a gracious and polished person who would enhance the image and reputation of any organization. I can provide outstanding personal and professional references, and I am willing to travel and relocate according to your needs.

I hope you will write or call me soon to let me know what the "next step" is with regard to my goal of joining your airline as a flight attendant. Thank you in advance for your help in this matter, and I look forward to hearing from you.

Sincerely,

Florence Martin

**Full-Time Homemaker to
Airline Travel Attendant**

For some time, this devoted wife and mother made plans to make a career in the travel industry, once her children were out of the home. This cover letter and resume was used to approach numerous airlines. All she had to do was address each one personally to the appropriate person at each airline with the hiring authority for flight attendants. On the basis of this letter and resume, she became a flight attendant with a major airline.
Note: This is a very creative resume designed to make her look and sound as though she is a natural "fit" with the travel industry. If she were trying to re-enter the financial services field and resume the type of work she did 15 years ago, her resume would be written in an entirely different fashion.

FLORENCE MARTIN

1110½ Hay Street, Fayetteville, NC 28305 • preppub@aol.com • (910) 483-6611

OBJECTIVE

I want to contribute to an organization that can use a dynamic self-starter with a strong service orientation and proven public relations skills along with a love of teamwork and travel; I am willing to relocate.

LIFESAVING SKILLS

CPR Certified; knowledgeable of first aid.
Am on a community lifesaver team.

TRAVEL

Offer a natural talent for establishing rapport with others and have become knowledgeable about other cultures through traveling to places including:

New York City, NY	Islands of Oahu and Maui, HI	Toronto, Canada
Washington, DC	San Juan and Dorado, PR	Richmond, VA
Lake Tahoe, NV	Orlando and Miami, FL	France
San Francisco, CA	Acapulco, Mexico	Switzerland
Atlanta, GA	New Orleans, LA	Omaha, NE

HIGHLIGHTS

Physical Appearance: Was selected as "Miss Autryville High School" over 350 other contestants; have judged beauty pageants and was chosen as official chaperone for the Queen of the Azalea Festival on visits to resorts and special events such as the Cotton Bowl.

Intellect: Was named a Marshall in my college studies based on academic achievements.

Leadership: Was voted Class President of my college campus because of my leadership ability.

Service to Others: Have become respected for my reputation as a "doer" and "giver" through volunteering my time to help others in organizations that include Meals on Wheels, United Way, and Junior League as well as my church, garden club, and the local hospital.

EXPERIENCE

ACCOUNT EXECUTIVE. Madison Avenue Communications, Autryville, SC (2000-present). In a part-time job for this communications company with diversified advertising, publishing, and public relations interests, played a key role in creating and publishing *The Autryville Newcomer's Guide for 2001,* a publication with a 25,000-person distribution that is the "bible" for area newcomers and travelers.

- After extensive analysis and research, produced a comprehensive profile of educational, cultural, religious, and business activities.
- Used my strong sales skills and public relations ability to sell advertising in the publication to businesses and other organizations.

Previous experience: Prior to working inside the home full-time while my children were at home, excelled in these positions:

FINANCIAL CONSULTANT. Optimum Planning Resources, Inc., Autryville, NC. After completing a rigorous course of study, earned my license to sell life, accident, and health insurance; worked with professionals from every field to create sound investment and insurance portfolios.

- Assisted many people in reducing their taxes and expanding their wealth.
- Analyzed risk tolerance of clients and made recommendations for repositioning assets.

BANK TELLER. Autryville National Bank, Autryville, NC. Was rapidly promoted to train other tellers while earning respect for my outstanding customer service skills.

PERSONAL

Excellent references on request. Outstanding reputation. In my spare time, enjoy dancing and aerobics. Am in excellent physical condition.

Date

Exact Name of Person
Exact Title
Exact Name of Company
Address
City, State, Zip

**Full-Time Homemaker to
Office Professional**

After devoting herself to
duties associated with
being a wife and mother,
this talented woman is
trying to reenter the job
market. Notice how she
tells the prospective
employer "straight out"
what she has been
doing. She explains her
recent period of
employment in a way
that a reasonable
employer will
understand.

Dear Exact Name of Person (or Dear Sir or Madam if answering a blind ad):

With the enclosed resume, I would like to make you aware of my interest in exploring part-time employment with your organization.

As you will see from my resume, I have acquired a variety of data entry and customer service skills while working in a banking environment for one employer, Atlanta Citizens Bank. After 20 years with the bank, I resigned from Atlanta Citizens in 1998 when my husband received a promotion with the Prudential Company and we relocated from Atlanta to Dallas.

We have settled into our new house in Dallas, and I am eager to resume my professional career on a part-time basis. I am a reliable hard worker with skills in numerous areas, and I can provide outstanding references from both of the branch managers with whom I worked.

You will notice from my resume that I excelled in a track record of promotion at the bank, where I began as a Savings Clerk, was promoted to Customer Service Clerk and Senior Customer Service Clerk, and then to Financial Services Representative. I played a key role in helping the bank implement numerous changes related to automation and internal restructuring over the years, and I became known as a gracious and reliable professional. I am accustomed to working in an environment in which attention to detail and accuracy at all times is required.

If you can use a versatile and dependable professional in a part-time role, I hope you will call me soon to suggest a time when we might meet and discuss your organization's needs and how I could help meet them.

Sincerely,

Brandy Sullivan

BRANDY SULLIVAN

1110½ Hay Street, Fayetteville, NC 28305 • preppub@aol.com • (910) 483-6611

OBJECTIVE   To benefit an organization that can use an experienced office professional with superior communication skills and outstanding references who offers a background related to data entry and computer operations, customer service and sales, and accounting and collections.

EDUCATION   Completed numerous professional development and technical training programs sponsored by Atlanta Citizens Bank which provided training related to:

customer service	operations management
loan processing	legal issues and regulatory matters
sales	data entry and computer operations

COMPUTERS   Familiar with Microsoft Programs and the Windows operating system; have utilized numerous customized banking and financial programs.

EXPERIENCE   **Until I resigned in 1998 when my husband was promoted and we moved from Atlanta to Dallas, I worked for one employer for 20 years and I excelled in the following track record of advancement to increasing responsibilities: Atlanta Citizens Bank.**
- Can provide outstanding references from both the Branch Managers for whom I worked:
  Fortuna McDonald   910-483-6611
  Terry Bradshaw   910-483-6611

1996-98: FINANCIAL SERVICES REPRESENTATIVE. Handled new accounts and established loans for consumer goods; was given the authority to authorize unsecured loans up to $30,000 based on prescribed formulas and guidelines.
- Became skilled at making judgments about character and credit worthiness.
- Was involved in collection during special projects as requested by branch managers.
- Input new account data for loans and performed data entry; performed audit checks.
- Handled an extensive volume of correspondence.
- Was recognized for superior leadership skills and quality performance as well as for my strong oral communication skills.
- Played a role in implementing new efficiencies and new computer applications; my opinion was sought by reengineering personnel with respect to how changes would affect customer service and client relations.
- Frequently trained new customer service personnel; prepared internal control reports which accumulated data related to cash control, balancing of vaults, and other matters.
- Became known for my flexibility and willingness to work wherever I was needed; worked well with employees and branch managers at branches of different sizes.

1986-96: SENIOR CUSTOMER SERVICE REPRESENTATIVE. After being promoted to this position, trained new Customer Service Representatives.

1979-86: CUSTOMER SERVICE REPRESENTATIVE. Handled new accounts and established accounts related to checking, saving, Certificates of Deposit (CDs), and IRAs.

1978-79: SAVINGS CLERK. In my first job in the bank, specialized in serving customers of savings accounts.
- Opened new accounts, resolved customer problems; was promoted based on my ability to make sound decisions and interact with the public in a gracious manner.

PERSONAL   Enjoy reading in my spare time. Physically fit. Excellent references.

GOAL: Finding a New Product or Service to Sell

Date

Exact Name of Person
Exact Title
Exact Name of Company
Address
City, State, Zip

Account Sales

Dear Exact Name of Person (or Dear Sir or Madam if answering a blind ad):

In a gracious way, this professional is announcing his desire to become a part of an organization which will use him in sales or sales management roles. Here's a tip about employers: they like people who know what they want to do, because if you are in a job doing what you want to do, you are more likely to excel—and make money for the company.

With the enclosed resume, I would like to make you aware of my desire to seek employment with your organization and to contribute to your success through my strong sales skills.

As you will see from my resume, I am currently servicing 75 accounts and prospecting for new ones for a company which provides direct mail services.

In my prior work experience, I excelled in a track record of accomplishment as a military professional working for the famed "Special Operations Command," which is headquartered at the nation's largest U.S. military base. I was entrusted with a Top Secret security clearance, and I was handpicked for jobs which required an outstanding communicator who could "sell" ideas and concepts. In one position, I worked as the "right arm" for a three-star general and I was constantly involved in coordinating with the media and high-ranking VIPs including the Secretary of State and the Vice President of the U.S.

In another job, I managed three people while managing a budget of up to $1 million used for engineering projects. I was authorized to purchase up to $5,000 on a government credit card without approval.

My computer skills are very strong, and I have prepared numerous slide show presentations using PowerPoint. I am proficient in utilizing Microsoft Office, Excel, PowerPoint, Windows, WordPerfect, Lotus, and Word, and I offer a proven ability to rapidly master any type of software application.

If you can use a disciplined hard worker with a proven ability to contribute to the bottom line while satisfying customers and assuring the delivery of quality services, I hope you will contact me to suggest a time when we might meet to discuss your needs. Thank you in advance for your time.

Sincerely,

Wes T. Sevier

WES T. SEVIER

1110½ Hay Street, Fayetteville, NC 28305 • preppub@aol.com • (910) 483-6611

OBJECTIVE	To contribute to an organization that can use an articulate professional with exceptional communication and organizational skills who offers strong computer proficiency and a track record of excellence in executive-level liaison, operations management, and administration.
EDUCATION	**College:** Completed nearly two years of college course work towards a **Bachelor of Science** in **Business Administration**, Washington State University, Seattle, WA; will complete my degree in my spare time in the evenings while working full-time. **Professional Development:** As a military professional, completed extensive technical and management training including the Mid-Level Manager's Course, Primary Leadership Development Course, and the Administrative Specialist Course.
COMPUTERS	Proficient with many of the most popular computer operating systems and software, including Windows, Microsoft Office, including Word, Excel, Access, and PowerPoint; Lotus 1-2-3; and Harvard Graphics, among others.
EXPERIENCE	**SALES MANAGER.** Mountain Money Mailer, Olympia, WA (1998-present). Service 75 existing accounts and prospect for new business; promote sales of advertising space in the direct mail "Money Mailer" marketing tool on behalf of a local radio station.

- Develop a strong rapport with clients from diverse backgrounds, calling on local businesses to encourage them to place advertising or coupons in the "Money Mailer."
- Am an Ambassador for the city's Chamber of Commerce and am extensively involved in public relations and business liaison.

While serving with the U.S. Army, was promoted ahead of my peers and individually selected for highly sensitive positions of responsibility:

1997-1998: **SUPERVISOR.** Ft. Lewis, WA. Supervised and trained up to 60 employees while overseeing all operational aspects of the Special Operations Command mail room; held accountable for three vehicles and numerous pieces of mail handling equipment.

1994-1996: **OFFICE MANAGER.** Ft. Lewis, WA. Managed the engineering office for Special Operations Command, monitoring budgetary compliance, inventory control, and record keeping as well as reviewing all correspondence and personnel actions.

- Effectively managed an annual budget of up to $1 million dollars for engineering projects, verifying engineering requirements for pending work orders.
- Supervised three individuals; maintained records and prepared reports accurately and under deadlines.

1992-1994: **GENERAL'S AIDE & EXECUTIVE ASSISTANT.** Ft. Lewis, WA. Was handpicked for this high-visibility job as the "right arm" to a 3-star general; was selected because of my outstanding previous work performance as well as my reputation for impeccable manners and poise when dealing with others.

- Assisted the General and his staff on all matters pertaining to protocol, diplomacy, and customs; coordinated hotel and travel arrangements for worldwide itineraries.
- Assisted in developing itineraries for all VIPs to the headquarters; constantly interacted with the media and VIPs, including the Vice President of the U.S., the Secretary of State, and Ambassadors who visited the General.

PERSONAL	Excellent references on request. Outstanding reputation. Held a Top Secret clearance.

GOAL: Finding a New Product or Service to Sell

Date

Exact Name of Person
Title or Position
Name of Company
Address (no., street)
Address (city, state, zip)

Agricultural Sales

Dear Exact Name of Person: (or Dear Sir or Madam if answering a blind ad.)

Sometimes the Objective on a resume emphasizes personal qualities, as this one does. Since his job titles are nearly identical in each of his three jobs, he has a chance to reveal something about his strong personal characteristics in his Objective. Remember that a great resume helps an employer "get to know you."

I would appreciate an opportunity to show you soon in person that I am the young, energetic, dynamic salesperson you are looking for.

As you can see from my resume, I am a proven professional with a demonstrated ability to "prospect" and produce sales. Under my direction, The Tobacco Warehouse was able to maintain a sales volume of $3.5 million despite a depressed agricultural economy. As a salesman and warehouse supervisor with Industrial Agricultural Cooperative, I increased sales from $500,000 to $1.5 million in two years. I have earned a reputation for my dedication and hard work in addition to a sincere concern for the customers I serve. Although I have established an excellent reputation in the industry and can provide outstanding references from my employer, I have decided to transfer my sales skills from agricultural and tobacco products to another industry.

I feel certain you would find me to be a well-organized, reliable professional with a genuine customer service orientation. I pride myself on my ability to make "cold calls" and relate to people at all levels of any organization, from the mail clerk to the president. I can provide excellent personal and professional references.

I hope you will welcome my call soon to arrange a brief meeting at your convenience to discuss your current and future needs and how I might serve them. Thank you in advance for your time.

Sincerely yours,

Larry McPhail

Alternate last paragraph:
I hope you will call or write me soon to suggest a time convenient for us to meet and discuss your current and future needs and how I might best serve them. Thank you in advance for your time.

LARRY MCPHAIL

1110½ Hay Street, Fayetteville, NC 28305 • preppub@aol.com • (910) 483-6611

OBJECTIVE

To offer my leadership, problem-solving ability, and public relations skills to an organization that can use a hard-working young professional who is known for unquestioned integrity, unflagging enthusiasm, and tireless dedication to excellence.

EXPERIENCE

SALES MANAGER. The Agricultural Market, Inc., Marietta, GA (1995-present). Applied my financial expertise and excellent public relations/communication skills to contribute to the "bottom line" of this agricultural chemical and fertilizer manufacturer.
- Performed "cold calls" within a 30-mile sales territory; established and maintained approximately 175-200 accounts with dealers and individual customers.
- Ensured timely delivery of products and services.
- Billed customers and collected on delinquent accounts.
- Supervised three employees in administration/distribution.

SALES SUPERVISOR. The Tobacco Warehouse, Graceland, KY (1990-1995). Built "from scratch" this successful tobacco sales and distribution center with sales totaling $3.5 million even though the agricultural economy was at a low point.
- As co-owner, managed all administrative and financial aspects of operations.
- Hired, supervised, and trained 12 employees, including floor workers, secretaries, and bookkeepers.
- Developed and maintained a loyal customer network of local farmers.
- Organized and conducted auctions to sell the product to tobacco companies.

SALESMAN and **WAREHOUSE SUPERVISOR**. Industrial Agricultural Cooperative, Lexington, KY (1986-90). Excelled in a variety of roles because of my versatile management skills.
- Was accountable for warehouse inventory; determined product line and ordered fertilizers and agricultural chemicals.
- Performed collections and made bank deposits.
- Astutely managed finances and purchasing, meeting the company's budget goals each year.
- Through exceptional customer service to approximately 200 accounts, was able to increase sales from $500,000 to $1.5 million in two years.

SALESMAN. Best Seed Co., Raleigh, NC (1986). Applied my top-notch customer service skills to introduce this company's cotton seed line to 12 distributors throughout the state.

SPECIALIZED TRAINING

Attended more than 36 hours of instruction on pesticides 1990-present at Georgia State University, Kentucky University, and North Carolina State University.
Completed extensive training related to sales and customer service.

PERSONAL

Am a hard worker with a high energy level. Enjoy the challenge of motivating a team of employees while contributing to my organization's "bottom line" and serving customers.

GOAL: Finding a New Product or Service to Sell

Date

Exact Name of Person
Title or Position
Name of Company
Address (number and street)
Address (city, state, and zip)

All-Purpose Sales

This young manager is using her cover letter and resume to formally apply for a variety of sales positions. She has succeeded in (1) owning and managing her own company and in (2) working for a large corporation, and she has decided that she prefers specializing in marketing and sales in a large corporate environment rather than running a small business.

Dear Sir or Madam:

With the enclosed resume, I would like to make you aware of the considerable sales, management, and marketing skills I could offer your organization.

As you will see from my resume, I have excelled most recently in managing a women's clothing store which has closed its doors after 25 years due to intensive pressure from the name-brand retailers in the malls. As General Manager, I hired and trained employees, handled accounts payable and receivable, and coordinated with a variety of vendors while handling the buying function.

In my previous position as Marketing Director and Events Coordinator with Towertech Corporation, I was involved in a wide range of management and marketing activities and was credited with playing a key role in the rapid growth of this multi-million-dollar company. I managed up to 10 branch managers while developing and coordinating advertising, marketing, and special events.

In a prior job with WGJX Broadcasting as an Advertising Consultant, I created effective advertising and became skilled in cold-calling business owners to sell them on radio advertising. While working with Towertech Corporation and WGJX Broadcasting, I was active with community organizations including the Chamber of Commerce.

If you can use a vibrant and hard-working professional with versatile sales and marketing skills, I hope you will contact me to suggest a time when we could meet to discuss your needs and how I might meet them. I feel certain that I could make valuable contributions to your organization through my diversified marketing and management experience as well as through my creativity, aggressive sales skills, and highly positive personal attitude. I can provide excellent references at the appropriate time.

Sincerely yours,

Leslie R. Miller

LESLIE R. MILLER

1110½ Hay Street, Fayetteville, NC 28305   •   preppub@aol.com   •   (910) 483-6611

OBJECTIVE

To contribute to an organization that can use an experienced manager who offers a background in managing retail and marketing operations, buying and controlling inventory, supervising and managing personnel, as well as in handling public relations.

EDUCATION

GENERAL MANAGER. Belle's Boutique, Inc., Raleigh, NC (1997-present). In charge of all areas of operation as the General Manager of this high-end women's fashion store.
- Interview, hire, and train all employees; manage three people.
- Prepare business plans four times a year and review goal accomplishments monthly.
- Handle accounts payable and accounts receivable; reconcile invoices.
- Reconcile daily, weekly, and monthly receipts with actual deposits; handle all liaison with the bank.
- Make buying decisions and order inventory; coordinate with vendors and perform extensive liaison with suppliers and manufacturers who act as vendors.
- Purchase and distribute the full line of beauty control makeup products; create innovative and effective sales and marketing strategies.

MARKETING DIRECTOR & EVENTS COORDINATOR. Towertech Corp., Raleigh, NC (1991-96). Joined one of the state's fastest-growing companies with sales of $18 million annually; played a key role in its impressive growth to well over $22 million; utilized my previous advertising sales and copywriting experience to create effective advertising and marketing concepts.
- Developed a newsletter of current events which acquainted the business community and employees with Towertech's business strategy and successes.
- Assumed a variety of management roles within this fast-growing company; managed 10 branch managers located throughout southeast North Carolina.
- Created and managed special events which celebrated company milestones and which established excellent public relations.
- Designed and directed innovative marketing activities; handled the development of co-op advertising for all branches and assisted the branches in developing their budgets.
- Became skilled in identifying the strengths and talents of key personnel in order to effectively delegate appropriate activities to them.
- Traveled extensively to coordinate with branch managers and others.
- Became known for my enthusiastic and outgoing personality, and learned that a positive attitude is essential in developing an attitude of teamwork.

ADVERTISING CONSULTANT. WGJX Broadcasting, Raleigh, NC (1987-90). While working with this popular radio station, excelled in numerous roles including working as an on-air personality in the News/Talk format.
- Prepared proposals for advertising plans and established projected budgets and goals for local businesses; became skilled in cold-calling companies.
- Performed on live remotes to promote products.
- Wrote effective advertising copy including jingles which became memorable.

EDUCATION

Completed extensive training related to marketing, management, sales, and other areas sponsored by employers including Towertech and WGJX Broadcasting.

PERSONAL

Can provide excellent personal and professional references. Am highly creative and enjoy new challenges. Enjoy the challenge of representing a quality product or service.

GOAL: Finding a New Product or Service to Sell

Date

Exact Name of Person
Title or Position
Name of Company
Address (number and street)
Address (city, state, and zip)

All-Purpose Sales

Although he doesn't reveal this fact in his cover letter or resume, this entrepreneur lost his zest for his business when two of his employees were killed on the job. He is seeking a sales position in a large company.

Dear Exact Name of Person: (or Dear Sir or Madam if answering a blind ad.)

With the enclosed resume, I would like to introduce you to the proven leadership ability, management skills, and sales/marketing experience which I could put to work for your organization.

Through my strong sales and management skills, I built a business "from scratch" which rapidly grew into a profitable venture grossing more than $2 million last year. I am a very hard-working individual and am highly confident in my ability to sell any type of service or product to any type of individual or organization.

You will see from my resume that I offer a proven ability to prospect not only for new customers and new accounts but also for new business opportunities and new niches, markets, and segments in which to position a product and grow market share. After I established a residential landscaping business, I rapidly identified new sales opportunities and became a major force in the wholesale and retail sod brokerage business. Through my ability to deal with people and establish strong personal relationships, I became a respected individual who was often called in on complex commercial projects after a low bidder or initial contractor had botched the job. I am experienced in negotiating large commercial projects.

Although I am a very successful businessman who is effective in hiring and retaining quality employees, I have decided that I wish to become involved full-time in sales and marketing, since I feel that is where my strongest abilities lie.

If you can use a dedicated person with an outstanding personal and professional reputation to enhance your growth and profitability, I hope you will give me a call to suggest a time when we might meet to discuss your needs and how I might help you. Thank you in advance for your time.

Sincerely,

William Goldman

WILLIAM GOLDMAN

1110½ Hay Street, Fayetteville, NC 28305 • preppub@aol.com • (910) 483-6611

OBJECTIVE

To contribute to an organization which can use a motivated professional with exceptionally strong sales, leadership, stress management, and customer relations skills along with proven abilities related to managing operations, boosting profitability, and solving problems.

EXPERIENCE

PRESIDENT & SALES MANAGER. Quality Turf, Inc., Virginia Beach, VA (1990-2000). With only a pickup truck and an aggressive sales orientation, started "from scratch" a business which grew from $54,000 in gross revenue in its first year to over $2 million last year; started out by providing residential landscaping services and then expanded and diversified into other areas as I gained knowledge, experience, and a reputation for reliability and quality.

- Once established in residential landscaping, identified an opportunity for statewide sod sales; became a broker and eventually serviced customers from Atlanta to Washington, DC while providing quality sod and grading services to prominent golf courses.
- As a large sod wholesaler and retailer, achieved an 80% market share in the Virginia Beach market; serviced most landscapers and gardeners.
- Negotiated numerous multimillion-dollar contracts for services provided to organizations such as AT&T, the City of Virginia Beach, privately owned golf courses, Target Stores, Home Depot Stores, and large construction companies.
- Expanded the company into the tree surgery business, and personally completed extensive formal training which resulted in my becoming a Certified Arborist (tree surgeon); became a member of the International Society of Arboculture.
- Acquired a million-dollar inventory of pickup trucks, dump trucks, tractors, fork lifts, front-end loaders, tree chippers, and other equipment.
- Employed up to 40 people including three crew foremen while always acting as General Sales Manager and negotiating all commercial contracts.
- Gained extensive experience in bidding on government and commercial contracts; on numerous occasions was called in on a job after a low bidder had mishandled and often abandoned the project.

COMMUNICATIONS TECHNICIAN. U.S. Army, Ft. Bragg, NC (1987-90). Received an Honorable Discharge and several medals for exceptional performance while serving my country as a Radio Technician.

FOREMAN. Bekins Moving and Storage, Phoenix, AZ (1985-87). In my first job after high school, began working for one of the world's largest moving and storage companies, and became the company's youngest-ever full-time employee and youngest-ever foreman.

- Supervised 30 individuals involved in moving office and industrial goods.

EDUCATION

Completed extensive management and technical training sponsored by the U.S. Army. Excelled in numerous executive development programs related to sales and marketing, effective communications, and operations management.

PERSONAL

Am a highly motivated hard worker who excels in communicating with others. In sales situations, have always sold my strengths rather than my competitor's weaknesses. Believe that establishing a personal relationship based on trust is the key to sales success. Have a visionary approach to business; am able to troubleshoot problems before they arise.

GOAL: Finding a New Product or Service to Sell

Exact Name of Person
Exact Title
Exact Name of Company
Address
City, State, Zip

Automobile Rental Sales

Notice the aggressive
and dynamic first
sentence of this cover
letter. What employer
couldn't use an
employee who could
improve sales and
profitability? Also notice
the similar nature of the
Objective on his resume.
It is specific without
"nailing him down" to a
particular industry. (He is
actually seeking a
change from automobile
rental sales.)

Dear Exact Name of Person (or Dear Sir or Madam if answering a blind ad):

Can you use a dynamic young professional with a proven ability to boost market share, achieve exceptionally high customer satisfaction levels, develop new sales opportunities, and boost profitability?

I have been excelling with Dollar Rent-A-Car in positions of increasing responsibility. In my most recent position as Regional Manager for the city of Utica, NY, I supervised 105 personnel in a region with annual sales of $8.8 million dollars. Earlier, as Area Manager for the western region of St. Louis, I launched the highly successful start-up of this new region, which quickly grew to six locations employing 49 personnel. By designing and implementing innovative and effective marketing plans, our sales increased 47% per year over a three-year period and the region achieved annual sales of $4.8 million.

As Branch Manager, I was responsible for opening a new office, which became the first location in the Southeast region to reach a monthly net profit of $40,000. Despite being a newly launched branch with a new manager and staff, we were one of the top five branches in the region for total sales. I was promoted to this position after excelling as a Management Trainee in a branch where I had the highest inside sales of any management trainee in the region, and I was promoted to Assistant Manager after only six months with Dollar.

If you can use a confident, self-motivated management professional with strong supervisory, communication, and organizational skills, I hope you will contact me to suggest a time when we might meet in person. I can provide outstanding references.

Sincerely,

Scott T. Sears

SCOTT T. SEARS

1110½ Hay Street, Fayetteville, NC 28305   •   preppub@aol.com   •   (910) 483-6611

OBJECTIVE

To benefit an organization that can use an articulate, results-oriented professional with exceptional sales and management skills who offers a background in managing multiunit operations as well as a track record of success in territory development and management.

EDUCATION

Associate of Applied Science, Marketing, Utica Technical College, Utica, NY, 1998. Completed three years of college coursework towards a Bachelor of Science in Marketing, University of Kentucky, Lexington, KY.

EXPERIENCE

With Dollar Rent-A-Car, have excelled and been promoted to positions of increasing responsibility by the largest automotive rental and leasing company in North America, with sales of $5.2 billion annually:

1997-present: **REGIONAL MANAGER.** Utica, NY. Promoted from Area Manager for St. Louis, oversee all aspects of operations in this region with multimillion-dollar annual sales; provided valuable leadership in quickly turning around an unprofitable operation and showing a profit in only eight months.
- Planned and executed the expansion of branch offices from five locations to 14.
- Supervise 105 personnel including two area managers, a corporate recruiter, one sales manager, one corporate sales manager, one trainer, and an administrative assistant.
- Developed and launched new pricing, rebate, and incentive programs, increasing sales more than 23% annually, from $3.9 million to $8.8 million annually; increased net profits from $420 thousand to $2.1 million over a 3½ year period.
- Serve as Director of Human Resources, conducting final interviews on all potential employees and determining labor needs and personnel budgets for 14 branch offices.
- Provided strong leadership to a young management team with diverse backgrounds during corporate restructuring, instilling them with pride in their accomplishments and a positive attitude during this difficult transitional period.
- Worked with office personnel to ensure the highest levels of customer service; our customer service scores went from below the company average to the top 5% of all regions.

1993-1997: **AREA MANAGER.** St. Louis, MO. Launched the start-up and managed all aspects of the western region of St. Louis as part of the Midwest Expansion Team; the new region overcame the costs associated with start-up and turned a profit in its first year.
- Interviewed, hired, and trained all new employees in a team that eventually grew to 49 employees at six locations; through my efforts in personnel development, nine of my hires were promoted to Branch Manager.
- Designed and implemented innovative marketing plans, achieving average growth of 47% per year over three years, and annual sales of $4.8 million.
- Achieved customer service scores in the top 10% of the entire company.

1991-1993: **BRANCH MANAGER.** Charlotte, NC. Managed the start-up of a new branch office, directing the marketing and sales strategies, training employees in the presentation of company products and services, and performing administrative tasks.
- Created, developed, and maintained strong relationships with insurance companies, auto dealerships and autobody repair shops to ensure a large base for referral customers.
- Became the first branch office in the southeast to achieve a net profit of $40,000 in one month; strong revenues placed our branch in the top five in the region.
- In my first position as a Management Trainee, was promoted after six months.

PERSONAL

Outstanding personal and professional references are available upon request.

GOAL: Finding a New Product or Service to Sell

Date

Exact Name of Person
Exact Title
Exact Name of Company
Address
City, State, Zip

Dear Sir or Madam:

With the enclosed resume, I would like to formally initiate the process of being considered for a position within your organization which can use my exceptionally strong sales, marketing, communication, and management skills.

As you will see from my resume, since earning my B.S. degree in Business Administration with a Marketing major, I have excelled in both sales and customer service. In my most recent job as a District Sales Manager, I traveled frequently while prospecting for new accounts and establishing outstanding relationships with insurance adjustors and car dealers throughout the state.

I am familiar with numerous types of software and offer a proven ability to rapidly master new programs.

After graduating with my college degree, I was promoted to increasing levels of responsibility related to customer service by a bank in Williamsville. I enjoy dealing with people and have often been commended for my gracious manners and positive approach to solving customer problems. While with First Bank, I received two awards recognizing my exceptional communication and customer service skills.

If you can use a highly motivated young professional with a strong bottom-line orientation, I hope you will contact me to suggest a time when we might meet to discuss your business needs and how I might serve them. Thank you in advance for your time.

Yours sincerely,

Marilyn P. Hall

MARILYN P. HALL

1110½ Hay Street, Fayetteville, NC 28305　　•　　preppub@aol.com　　•　　(910) 483-6611

OBJECTIVE　　To benefit an organization that can use a hard-working young professional with outstanding sales, communication, customer service, marketing, and management skills.

EDUCATION　　**B.S., Business Administration and Marketing,** Middlebury College, Middlebury, VT, 1995. Graduated from Smith High School, Williamsville, VT, 1990.
- Was co-captain of the Cheerleading Squad.

TECHNICAL SKILLS　　**Computers:** Familiar with WordPerfect 6.0, 5.2, 5.1; Microsoft Word; Lotus; Windows.
- Offer a proven ability to rapidly master new software.

Other: Experienced in using E-Mail, 10-key, PBX Phone, copiers, fax machines, and office equipment.

EXPERIENCE　　**DISTRICT SALES MANAGER.** Enterprise Rent-A-Car, Middlebury, VT (1997-present). Travel frequently while prospecting for and managing sales within a large territory in Vermont which includes Middlebury and which ranges from Norwich, to Wilmington, to Williamsville.
- Aggressively prospect for new accounts; acquired excellent prospecting skills.
- Target primarily insurance adjustors and car dealerships in my sales strategies; establish long-term accounts through which customers can secure rental cars while their own automobiles are being repaired.
- Have become known for my ability to provide excellent customer service; maintain rapport with a team of professionals within the parent organization so that the promises I make will be reliably delivered.
- Maintain extensive paperwork related to sales calls; schedule meetings and sales calls and maintain travel records.
- Have been commended by company officials as a highly self motivated individual with outstanding communication and interpersonal skills.

CUSTOMER SERVICE REPRESENTATIVE. First Bank, Williamsville, VT (1995-97). Began with First Bank as a Teller in 1995 and was promoted into a customer service position in 1996; worked extensively on the telephone and in person while assisting customers.
- Received the bank's **Communicator Award** for outstanding achievements in customer service and superior communication skills.
- Was awarded a **Quality Certificate** for consistently high-quality production.
- Fielded customer requests for information or problem solving, and directed customers to appropriate bank personnel.
- Was gradually cross-trained to promote the bank's products and services, and refined my skills in presenting financial services.
- As a Teller, was entrusted with safeguarding the vault while also assisting customers with banking transactions.

Other experience: Worked 30 hours per week while financing my college education:
FASHION CONSULTANT. Filenes, Middlebury, VT (1994-95). Assisted customers of Filenes' fashion merchandise and haute couture.
CUSTOMER SERVICE REPRESENTATIVE. Schenker, Middlebury, VT (1992-94). Refined my communication skills while operating a busy telephone switchboard.
- Cordially assisted customers with complaints and questions about returns.
- Was frequently complemented for my gracious telephone manners.

PERSONAL　　Have volunteered my time with the American Heart Association and Habitat for Humanity.

GOAL: Finding a New Product or Service to Sell

Date

Exact Name of Person
Title or Position
Name of Company
Address (number and street)
Address (city, state, and zip)

Automobile Sales in Career Transition to Other Types of Sales

Employers often feel that skills are transferable to other industries. For example, if an individual excels at the sale of automobiles, it is likely that person could succeed in selling other products or services. Mr. McAteer is attempting to change industries and utilize his sales skills for the benefit of a company such as UPS or FedEx, where he can use his transportation industry knowledge while functioning in an inside sales role.

Dear Sir or Madam:

With the enclosed resume, I would like to express my strong interest in exploring career opportunities with your organization and introduce you to my proven customer service, communication, and sales skills.

As you will see from my resume, I have had a successful sales career with companies in Knoxville, including my current employer, Walsh Auto Sales. Through my experience as a Sales Manager and Sales Representative, I have developed the proven ability to quickly build rapport with customers from different backgrounds.

During my tenure as Manager of Metro Pawn & Loan, I utilized my strong organizational and sales abilities to increase profits at the Wilton Road location by an average of $1500 per month while insuring the security and accountability of over $200,000 worth of inventory. I excelled in the role of Sales Manager as I trained more than 10 associates in techniques including overcoming objections and closing the sale.

Although I am highly regarded by my present employer and can provide excellent personal and professional references at the appropriate time, I have decided that I would like to express my sales abilities and communication skills in another industry.

If you can use a highly motivated, detail-oriented individual with a commitment to providing the highest possible levels of customer service, I hope you will contact me to suggest a time when we might meet to discuss your needs. I can assure you that I have an excellent reputation and could quickly become a valuable asset to your organization.

Yours sincerely,

Samuel R. McAteer

SAMUEL R. MCATEER
1110½ Hay Street, Fayetteville, NC 28305 • preppub@aol.com • (910) 483-6611

OBJECTIVE	To benefit an organization that can use an energetic, self-motivated individual with strong sales, sales management, organizational, communication, and customer service skills.

EXPERIENCE	**SALES MANAGER.** Walsh Auto Sales, Knoxville, TN (1998-present). Supervise one salesperson while overseeing the operation of this busy used car lot.

- Quickly build rapport with customers and assist them with the selection and purchase of a pre-owned vehicle.
- Communicate verbally and in writing with outside agencies, such as insurance companies, lending institutions, and advertising representatives.
- Complete customer contracts and perform credit checks on potential customers.
- Maintain existing accounts and carry out collection actions on past-due accounts.
- Open and close the lot, ensuring the security of all vehicles and money.

STORE MANAGER. Metro Pawn & Loan, Knoxville, TN (1997-1998). Hired as an Assistant Manager Trainee, was quickly promoted to Manager of my own location.

- Supervised a staff of 6-10 employees and performed all employee evaluations; trained the staff in sales techniques.
- Increased sales by an average of $1500 per month; personally set new sales records.
- Interviewed, hired, and trained all new associates.
- Opened and closed the store, completing all operational paperwork and making bank deposits and change orders.
- Responsible for an inventory of more than $200,000.
- Ordered merchandise and supplies.

ASSISTANT MANAGER. King Pawn & Loan, Nashville, TN (1996-1997). Assisted the manager in the operation of this busy retail pawn shop; hired as a trainee and was promoted to Assistant Manager in two months.

- Opened and closed the store; made bank deposits.
- Supervised up to 10 employees.
- Named **Salesperson of the Month** on several different occasions.
- Assisted customers in the selection and purchase of merchandise; responsible for maintaining a certain level of sales each month.

AUTOMOTIVE SALES CONSULTANT. Reid Olds-Nissan, Knoxville, TN (1993-1996). Assisted customers in the selection and purchase of a new or pre-owned vehicle; demonstrated the features and selling points of the vehicle; offered a demonstration drive.

- Assisted customers in filling out loan applications and other necessary paperwork to purchase a vehicle.
- Followed up with customers after the sale; ensuring their satisfaction and obtaining referrals to friends and family members.

Other experience: Proudly served my country for three years as an infantryman at Fort Bragg, NC.

COMPUTERS	Familiar with the following computer software: Windows, Microsoft Word, Excel, Publisher, Works, PowerPoint, and Expedia.

PERSONAL	Excellent personal and professional references are available upon request.

GOAL: Finding a New Product or Service to Sell

Date

Exact Name of Person
Exact Title
Exact Name of Company
Address
City, State, Zip

Business Equipment Sales in Pursuit of Another Product to Sell

This aggressive professional offers proven sales skills, and he loves sales. His goal now is to find another product or service to sell other than copier equipment. Notice the numerous achievements shown on his resume. Notice, too, that the cover letter does not emphasize "copiers" or the product line he has been selling but rather "sells" him and his abilities.

Dear Exact Name of Person: (or Dear Sir or Madam if answering a blind ad):

With the enclosed resume, I would like to make you aware of my interest in exploring sales opportunities within your company. Although I am excelling in my current position and am held in the highest regard, I am exploring other options.

A graduate of Arizona State University, I am highly skilled in utilizing all Microsoft applications, and I am adept at creating PowerPoint presentations on a laptop computer. After graduating from Arizona State University with a degree in History, I went to work in sales for a company in California, and I quickly discovered that my strong communication and problem-solving skills were highly effective in sales and marketing situations. As a Territory Manager and Sales Associate, I established the company's largest-ever national account which generated business for the company in 48 states. I was awarded numerous honors because of my success in exceeding quotas.

I was recruited for my current job in 1998 as a Major Accounts Manager and Sales Representative, and in less than a year I have transformed an unproductive territory in what was considered a "secondary market" into one of the top territories in the nation. I am currently ranked #5 among 1,000 sales representatives in the U.S. and I have won numerous awards in 1999, including a trip to Hawaii awarded to only 10 people in the company. I was named Company Sales Representative of the Month in January, March, and August 2000 for achieving the highest sales among my peers.

In my current job I call on major accounts including hospitals, and have established a strong network of contacts. I am skilled at utilizing every type of sales tool and technique including cold calling, networking through friends and referrals, and developing superior written proposals. I am a highly self-motivated individual who is satisfied with producing no less than the highest-quality results in any project I take on. I have thoroughly enjoyed applying my intellect and intelligence in the sales field, because I have discovered that sales is all about solving problems for people and companies.

If you can use a polished go-getter who would thrive on whatever challenge you place in my path, I hope you will welcome my call soon when I try to arrange a brief meeting to discuss your goals and how my background might serve your needs. I can provide outstanding references at the appropriate time.

Sincerely,

Jacob R. Dixon

JACOB R. DIXON

1110½ Hay Street, Fayetteville, NC 28305 • preppub@aol.com • (910) 483-6611

OBJECTIVE

To benefit an organization that can use an aggressive young sales professional and highly effective communicator with the proven ability to exceed ambitious goals while maximizing profitability and assuring the highest level of customer service, support, and satisfaction.

EDUCATION

Bachelor of Arts in History, Arizona State University, Phoenix, AZ, 1995.
Studied abroad through the Arizona State University program in Valencia, Spain, 1993-94.
Numerous courses related to sales including Solution Selling II, and Advance System Selling.

COMPUTERS

Highly computer proficient with all Microsoft applications; am skilled in creating PowerPoint presentations for customers on a laptop computer; work with Microsoft and Novell Computer Networks in the process of installing new products and add-ons to computer networks.

EXPERIENCE

MAJOR ACCOUNTS MANAGER & SALES REPRESENTATIVE. Effective Business Solutions, Scottsdale, AZ (1998-present). Took an unproductive territory in what is considered a "secondary market" and have transformed it into one of the top territories in the nation in only one year.

- Am **ranked #5 among nearly 1,000 U.S. corporate sales representatives**, and am currently the top sales producer in my area after only a short time with the company.
- Have exceeded year-to-date quota by 155% of which $393,000 (or 98%) was new business.
- Have already won the **National Sales Award for 2000**, a trip to Hawaii awarded to only 10 people nationwide; previously won a trip to Colorado, and was one of only 15 reps to win that trip based on second quarter sales.
- After only nine months with the company, received the prestigious **Century Club Gold Level Ring Award**, an award recognizing $200,000 in sales which normally takes an individual 1 ½ years to achieve.
- Named **Company Sales Representative of the Month in January, March, and August 2000**, for producing the highest monthly sales of all reps.
- Call on hospitals and other institutional buyers as well as businesses of all sizes while prospecting for new business and establishing highly profitable new accounts; have established a network of contacts within the medical community and hospitals.
- Call on large companies in 18 counties in Arizona; have increased market share dramatically and have significantly grown the customer base while consistently exceeding my sales quota of $33,333/month.

TERRITORY MANAGER & SALES ASSOCIATE. Better Business Information Systems, Inc., San Francisco, CA (1996-98). Prospected for new customers in eight zip code areas while servicing 400 existing accounts; became skilled in utilizing every sales tool and technique including cold calling, writing proposals, and networking through friends and referrals.

- **Established the company's largest-ever national account.**
- Exceeded year-to-date sales goals by $178,000 (218% of quota).
- Was the recipient of the **Century Club Award** for exceeding $100,000 in sales, May 1998; was awarded the President's Club Vacation for excellence in work performance, March 1998; was named a member of the **President's Club** in 1996, 1997, and 1998; received the **Nifty-Fifty Award** for exceeding $50,000 in sales for May, April, and January 1998 as well as October and April, 1997.
- Was **Salesman of the Month**, May 1998 as well as December and April 1997.

PERSONAL

Thrive on the challenge of solving customer problems. Highly motivated self starter.

GOAL: Finding a New Product or Service to Sell

Date

Exact Name of Person
Exact Title
Exact Name of Organization
Address
City, State Zip

Dear Exact Name: (or Dear Sir or Madam)

With the enclosed resume, I would like to make you aware of my strong interest in the job of Pharmaceutical Sales Representative. It has been my goal for some time to enter the field of pharmaceutical sales, and I believe you will see from my resume that I offer skills and experience which could make me very successful in the job.

In my current job as Unit Business Manager with Proctor & Gamble, I am excelling in an outside sales position which involves calling on the buyers for chains and retail stores and military accounts in a territory which covers 35 counties in Virginia. My territory includes 100 retail stores, 9 indirect headquarters, and three military retail commissaries. Because of my persistence and initiative, I have been responsible for numerous accomplishments including achieving the distribution of **all** new items in **all** stores; increasing the facings for **all** Proctor & Gamble brands in **all** stores. I have also achieved "gold standard placement" for **all** Proctor & Gamble brands while achieving the suggested retail price for **all** Proctor & Gamble brands in **all** accounts.

Most of my success in my current job has been due to my enthusiastic attention to detail as well as my relentless pursuit of the highest goals. Especially in my military accounts, I had to compete against strongly entrenched competitors who had been in the business for more than 20 years. Persistence and relentless marketing paid off, and I have succeeded in obtaining more than my fair share of shelf space for Proctor & Gamble despite stiff competition and strongly entrenched traditions.

In my previous job as a National Account Representative with American Careers, I achieved 130% of my sales goal in my first full year while also being honored as "Job Fair Coordinator of the Year" for my efforts in planning and coordinating the Houston job fair.

I hope you will contact me to suggest a time when we might meet to discuss your needs and goals and how I might help you achieve them. I can provide excellent references and I thank you in advance for your time.

Yours sincerely,

Sharron A. Howard

SHARRON ANN HOWARD

1110½ Hay Street, Fayetteville, NC 28305 • preppub@aol.com • (910) 483-6611

OBJECTIVE

To apply my sales and communication abilities to an organization in need of a mature young sales professional who offers a talent for training and teaching others as well as a reputation as a creative thinker and good listener with a high level of enthusiasm and energy.

EDUCATION

Bachelor's degree, Elementary Education, the College of Fairfax, Fairfax, VA, 1996.

EXPERIENCE

UNIT BUSINESS MANAGER (OUTSIDE SALES). Proctor & Gamble, Arlington, VA (1999-present). Am excelling in an outside sales position which involves calling on the buyers for grocery store chains and their retail stores in a territory which covers 35 counties in Virginia; my territory includes 100 retail stores, 9 indirect headquarters calls for grocery store chains, and three military commissaries.
- Plan and organize my time and schedule appointments for maximum profitability.
- When calling on retailers, maintain vigilant control of pricing, missing items, opportunities to sell newly approved products, correct implementation of planogram and stock rotation, and problems or opportunities created by competitive activity.
- When calling on indirect headquarters, am skilled in presenting new items, negotiating where that item would be placed in the appropriate category, developing pricing, ensuring a full share of shelf on planograms, and coordinating promotions with appropriate retail reductions.
- When calling on military accounts, am responsible for managing vendor stockers at each account; as a Unit Business Manager, am responsible for hiring my own vendor stockers and paying them according to how many cases they stock on the shelves. Develop incentives to encourage vendor stockers to stock as many cases as possible.
- Have excelled in selling to military accounts despite the overwhelming competition, and have succeeded in obtaining more than my fair share of shelf space even though I was competing against two competitors who had been in the business for more than 20 years.

Accomplishments:
- Achieved distribution of all new items in all stores.
- Increased facings for all Proctor & Gamble brands in all stores.
- Achieved gold standard placement for all Proctor & Gamble brands.
- Achieved suggested retail price for all Proctor & Gamble brands in all accounts.

NATIONAL ACCOUNT REPRESENTATIVE. American Careers, Arlington, VA (1997-99). Achieved 130% of my sales goal my first full year and excelled in maintaining existing accounts and establishing new ones through my strong communication skills and professional approach.
- Achieved the honor of "Job Fair Coordinator of the Year" for my efforts in planning and coordinating the Houston job fair within my first six months with the company.
- Was consistently ranked in the company's "top ten" sales professionals.

SALES REPRESENTATIVE. The Fairfax Times, Fairfax, VA (1994-95). Learned to use my persuasiveness and sales abilities while informing customers of the cost of subscriptions.

SALES REPRESENTATIVE. The Puppet Barn, Fairfax, VA (1995). Refined my sales skills working independently by setting up a booth and making attractive displays and then demonstrating different puppets for sale.

PERSONAL

Highly self motivated, resourceful, and well organized with strong bottom-line focus.

GOAL: Finding a New Product or Service to Sell

Date

Exact Name of Person
Title or Position
Name of Company
Address (number and street)
Address (city, state, and zip)

Dear Sir or Madam:

With the enclosed resume, I would like to make you aware of my background as an articulate professional with exceptional communication and organizational skills who offers a track record of accomplishments in sales and customer service.

Currently in an inside sales position with Mason-Build, Inc., I work with general contractors and builders from Metairie to Baton Rouge while handling sales and providing outstanding customer service. An outgoing person, I have natural sales ability which I have refined through 10 years of sales experience, and I have developed a strong rapport with residential and commercial customers. I am skilled at estimating jobs for concrete masonry and my extensive knowledge of construction and building supply allow me to work closely with general contractors and home builders, preparing cost estimates for concrete masonry units and related building supplies.

In an earlier position as a furniture sales representative for Heilig-Meyers Furniture, I further polished my selling skills while assisting customers with the selection and purchase of home furnishings and accessories. My outstanding customer service abilities allowed me to quickly build a solid base of repeat and referral clients, and I always exceeded the sales quotas set by my supervisors.

Although I am highly regarded by my present employer, I am interested in exploring opportunities with your company. Please, however, do not contact my current employer until after we talk.

If you can use an experienced sales and customer service professional who offers exceptional communication and organizational skills, I hope you will contact me. I can assure you in advance that I have an excellent reputation and would quickly become an asset to your organization. I can provide excellent references from all previous employers as well as from Mason-Build, Inc.

Sincerely,

Hannah J. Colvin

HANNAH J. COLVIN

1110½ Hay Street, Fayetteville, NC 28305 • preppub@aol.com • (910) 483-6611

OBJECTIVE

To benefit an organization that can use an articulate, enthusiastic sales professional with an outgoing personality as well as exceptional communication and organizational skills who offers a proven ability to establish and maintain effective working relationships.

EDUCATION

Completed college computer courses at Morton Community College, Metairie, LA. Graduated from Pine Forest High School, Baton Rouge, LA, 1984. Business subjects studied included Basic Business, Typing, and Office Machines.

EXPERIENCE

INSIDE SALES REPRESENTATIVE and **CUSTOMER SERVICE REPRESENTATIVE.** Mason-Build, Inc., Baton Rouge, LA (1998-present). For this concrete masonry company, estimate commercial and residential jobs and provide exceptional customer service and sales support.
- Have established relationships with builders including Castle Construction and Talcott-Bern as well as other companies doing business from Metairie to Baton Rouge.
- Develop rapport with clients, ascertaining their needs and estimating the cost of concrete masonry units and related building supplies.
- Work closely with general contractors, subcontractors, and home builders, utilizing my extensive knowledge of construction and building supplies to provide assistance.

FURNITURE SALES REPRESENTATIVE. Heilig-Meyers Furniture Co., Baton Rouge, LA (1997-1998). Assisted customers in the selection and purchase of home furnishings and accessories as a salesperson for this local retail furniture outlet.
- Consistently exceeded all sales quotas.
- Built a strong base of repeat and referral customers based on my natural sales ability and exceptional customer service skills.

SALES ASSISTANT & CUSTOMER SERVICE REPRESENTATIVE. Williams Products Company, Baton Rouge, LA (1989-1997). Assisted the sales, dispatch, and production operations while performing customer service and receptionist duties for this local manufacturer and supplier of masonry products.
- Provided job estimates over the phone to business and residential customers, as well as acquiring dodge reports from the Internet and assisting with certifications.
- Created, updated, and maintained files for all new and existing accounts.
- Reviewed all invoices on outbound shipments and keyed contract hauler freight data into the computer; developed a template in Lotus 1-2-3 to record this data.
- Produced daily production reports, processed payroll, and coordinated safety committee activities for the production department.

SHIPPING AND RECEIVING CLERK. Lee Furniture, Metairie, LA (1986-1988). Verified invoices against purchase orders to ensure accuracy; performed data entry of invoices and purchase orders on an IBM S/36 mainframe computer.
- Assisted store supervisors while also maintaining and updating purchase order files.

AFFILIATIONS

Former member, American Business Women's Association, Baton Rouge, LA.

PERSONAL

Received the Parent in Education Award, Edwards Elementary School, Baton Rouge, LA. Can provide excellent personal and professional references.

GOAL: Finding a New Product or Service to Sell

Date

Exact Name of Person
Title or Position
Name of Company
Address (number and street)
Address (city, state and zip)

Dear Sir or Madam:

With the enclosed resume, I would like to make you aware of my background as an experienced sales professional with exceptional communication skills, natural leadership ability, and a strong bottom-line orientation which I could put to work for your company.

As you will see from my resume, I earned a Bachelor of Science degree in Health and Physical Education from Mount Laurel College in Mount Laurel, NJ.

I have recently excelled in outside sales environments in which I serviced existing accounts and developed new business. I am skilled at building a solid customer base through prospecting as well as through networking with repeat and referral customers. My natural sales ability and strong focus on ensuring customer satisfaction while maintaining bottom-line profitability have led to record-breaking sales for my employers. I have refined my public relations skills and built a strong network of contacts within the medical, legal, and professional communities while representing the company at Chamber of Commerce events.

Although I am highly regarded by my present employer and can provide excellent personal and professional references at the appropriate time, I am interested in selectively exploring opportunities within the health systems field because that is most related to my undergraduate education. I feel that my natural salesmanship and strong network of personal contacts within the community would make me a valuable asset to the area, and I am extremely knowledgeable of the Fair Lawn community.

If you can use a confident, articulate professional whose abilities have been proven in a variety of challenging sales and management environments, I hope you will contact me. I can provide excellent references and I would enjoy the opportunity to talk with you in person about your needs.

Sincerely,

Robert W. Doyle

ROBERT W. DOYLE

1110½ Hay Street, Fayetteville, NC 2830   •   preppub@aol.com   •   (910) 483-6611

OBJECTIVE   To benefit an organization that can use an articulate, experienced sales professional with strong written and verbal communication skills who offers exceptional natural sales ability as well as a track record of excellence in sales and management environments.

EDUCATION &   **Bachelor of Science degree, Health & Physical Education**, Mount Laurel College, NJ.
TRAINING   Completed the Stephen Covey **7 Habits of Highly Effective People** course sponsored by Mobile Communications, Inc.
Completed Professional Selling Skills course sponsored by Mobile Communications, Inc.
Completed Introduction to Computers, Bowden Technical Institute.

EXPERIENCE   **ACCOUNT EXECUTIVE.** Mobile Communications, Inc., Fair Lawn, NJ (1999-present). Call on new and established commercial accounts throughout Fair Lawn and the surrounding area, presenting the line of products and digital mobile telephone services offered by Mobile Communications, Inc.
- Service and maintain existing accounts, calling on dissatisfied customers to trouble-shoot and resolve customer service complaints.
- Quickly developed a solid customer base, partly through utilizing the network of repeat and referral customers I have built in my years of sales experience in the Fair Lawn market.

OUTSIDE SALES REPRESENTATIVE & PUBLIC RELATIONS REPRESENTATIVE. Eastman Glass Co., Fair Lawn, NJ (1995-99). Serving as the only sales representative for three offices in New Jersey, contributed to record-breaking sales figures from 1996-1999.
- Consistently increased and maintained customer base by quickly responding to customer needs and developing innovative and effective marketing strategies designed to enhance sales and increase customer confidence and loyalty.
- Refined public relations skills and built a strong network of contacts within the medical, legal, and professional communities while representing the company at Chamber of Commerce events as well as at events that we sponsored, such as golf tournaments.

ASSISTANT TO THE BRANCH MANAGER and **SALESMAN**. Granby Toys Corp., Fair Lawn, NJ (1989-94). As a key member of a highly successful team for a branch that was consistently one of the two top locations since the corporation's opening, handled a variety of operational activities.
- Assumed the duties and responsibilities of the Branch Manager and Warehouse Manager in their absence; assumed other management tasks.
- Developed marketing strategies and ensured exceptional customer service, increasing sales and maintaining our existing customer base.
- Recruited, interviewed, hired and trained personnel.
- Earned numerous awards, including the 1989 Most Improved Branch Award and the 1992 President's Award for the best overall branch.

MANAGER. Dodd's Toys, Wholesale Division, Teaneck, NJ (1986-89). Directed and supervised a full-time staff of five employees while managing a $500,000 inventory and achieving a successful operating profit; attained total sales of over $1.3 million in 1988.

PERSONAL   Maintain a positive attitude. Highly motivated by new challenges. Known as a "winner by nature." Possess innovative ideas and the ability to transform concepts into realities.

GOAL: Finding a Completely Different Type of Work to Do

Date

Exact Name of Person
Exact Title
Exact Name of Company
Address
City, State, Zip

**Banking Services
Transitioning to High-Tech
Sales**

Dear Exact Name of Person (or Dear Sir or Madam if answering a blind ad):

There are some things you can learn from this cover letter and resume. When you read the cover letter, you will see that this young woman has figured out what interests her the most careerwise, and she is taking careful aim at companies which will stimulate her technological interests and offer her an opportunity to become involved in a business which is focused on creating quality hardware or software products. She would be most happy, she thinks, if she were involved in training customers, selling quality products, or communicating in a high-tech business.

With the enclosed resume, I would like to make you aware of my desire to utilize and expand my knowledge of computer software and business applications within an organization that can use my enthusiastic personality, sales and marketing background, as well as my strong desire to work in an environment on the forefront of technology.

I am proficient with a wide range of computer software, including most versions of Microsoft Word, Excel, and PowerPoint, as well as Publisher, DragonDictate, and Website Developer. In my current position, I utilize numerous software packages to compile data and produce reports, newsletters, and other documents for distribution to 30 branch offices. I want to stress that **on my own initiative** and in my spare time I have mastered these software programs and utilized them for the benefit of my employer. I have also trained others in software operation, which allowed branch managers whom I instructed to achieve maximum productivity from their use of the Mobius computer report system.

Through my rapid advancement with Bank of New York, I have been afforded the opportunity to achieve a degree of success rare for a young professional. While I am highly regarded by my present employer and can provide excellent references at the appropriate time, I feel that my strong software knowledge and excellent communication skills would be of great value to an organization with a strong technological orientation.

If you can use a highly motivated young professional whose personality and technical knowledge could surely enhance your organization, I hope you will contact me to suggest a time when we might meet to discuss your needs and how I might meet them. Thank you in advance for your time.

Sincerely,

Vivian E. Perdue

VIVIAN E. PERDUE

1110½ Hay Street, Fayetteville, NC 28305 • preppub@aol.com • (910) 483-6611

OBJECTIVE

To utilize my knowledge of computer software and business applications within an organization that can use a highly motivated young professional with strong communication, sales, customer service, and technical support skills.

COMPUTERS

Proficient in the operation of a wide range of computer software including the following:
- Word Processing—Microsoft Word for Windows, Word for Windows, Access.
- Spreadsheet —Microsoft Excel, Excel, and Excel.
- Multimedia—Microsoft PowerPoint, PowerPoint, and PowerPoint.
- Desktop Publishing—Microsoft Publisher, PageMaker 6.5; Quark; CorelDraw.
- Dictation—DragonDictate.
- Web Page Design—Website Developer.
- Accounting—Peachtree Accounting; QuickBooks Pro.

EDUCATION

B.S. degree in Business Education, Smith University, Scarsdale, NY, 2000.
First National Bank's 400-hour Internship program, 1998-2000.
Bank of New York Cohen Brown Proactive Relationship Banking course, 2000.
Bank of New York Cohen Brown Extraordinary Sales & Leadership course, 2000.

EXPERIENCE

Was hired at Bank of New York as a temporary employee; quickly advanced to full-time and was promoted to a position of increased responsibility.
REGIONAL SALES ANALYST. Bank of New York, Huntington, NY (2000-present). Act as liaison to 30 branch offices of this large regional bank, compiling various data and preparing documents for dissemination throughout the company.
- Provide each of the 30 branches with campaign goals and weekly updates of campaign information to be distributed to the employees.
- Compile data from various sources and enter the pertinent information into a Microsoft Excel spreadsheet, generating monthly reports.
- Order analytic data, and issue the information in its final form to Branch Managers, Relationship Bankers, and City Executives.
- Instruct and assist Branch Managers in operation and information retrieval via Mobius, a proprietary computer report system.
- Produce and develop new spreadsheets in Excel.
- Developed electronic forms for lending and mortgage department to be used in E-mail.

MORTGAGE LOAN PROCESSOR. Bank of New York (through Kelly), White Plains, NY (2000). Performed a variety of loan processing and clerical functions in this busy office.
- Processed incoming mortgage loans, completing the initial preparation of the application before forwarding it to the appropriate processor.
- Responsible for office accounting, writing disbursement vouchers, keeping accounts, and paying bills.
- Photocopied mortgage files that were distributed to processors for second level review.
- Sorted & delivered all incoming mail to the appropriate person.

OFFICE ASSISTANT. Smith University, Scarsdale, NY (1997-99). Worked in a clerical/secretarial capacity while I was pursuing my college education.
- Answered phones for professors; photocopied documents and ran errands.

PERSONAL

Excellent personal and professional references are available upon request.

GOAL: Finding a Completely Different Type of Work to Do

Date

BY FAX TO: Mrs. Maryanne Snider
District Manager
Pfizer

Banking Services Background Seeking to Transfer into Pharmaceutical Sales

This sales professional is actually seeking to transfer her skills into a new industry. She is hoping to convince employers in the pharmaceutical industry that she could excel in pharmaceutical sales through applying the same highly motivated nature which has helped her achieve outstanding results recently in banking and earlier in the human services field.

Dear Mrs. Snider:

With the enclosed resume, I would like to make you aware of my interest in employment as a Pharmaceutical Healthcare Representative with Pfizer. I believe you are aware that Don Smith, one of your Healthcare Representatives, has recommended that I talk with you because he feels that I could excel in the position as Pharmaceutical Healthcare Representative.

As you will see from my enclosed resume, I offer proven marketing and sales skills along with a reputation as a highly motivated individual with exceptional problem-solving skills. Shortly after joining my current firm as a Mortgage Loan Specialist, I was named Outstanding Loan Officer of the month through my achievement in generating more than $20,000 in fees.

I believe much of my professional success so far has been due to my highly motivated nature and creative approach to my job. For example, when I began working for my current employer, I developed and implemented the concept of a postcard which communicated a message which the consumer found intriguing. The concept has been so successful that it has been one of the main sources of advertisements in our office and the concept has been imitated by other offices in the company.

In addition to my track record of excelling in the highly competitive financial services field, I have also applied my strong leadership and sales ability in the human services field, when I worked in adult probation services. I am very proud of the fact that many troubled individuals with whom I worked told me that my ability to inspire and motivate them was the key to their becoming productive citizens.

If you can use a creative and motivated self starter who could enhance your goals for market share and profitability, I hope you will contact me to suggest a time when we could meet in person to discuss your needs and goals and how I could meet them. I can provide strong personal and professional references at the appropriate time.

Yours sincerely,

Irene S. Lane

IRENE S. LANE

1110½ Hay Street, Fayetteville, NC 28305 • preppub@aol.com • (910) 483-6611

OBJECTIVE

To offer my experience in sales, marketing, and customer service to an organization that would benefit from my aggressive style of developing customer relationships and my desire to work for an organization that seeks to maximize market share and profitability.

EDUCATION

B.S. in Business Administration, University of San Diego, CA 1998.
- Completed this degree in my spare time while excelling in my full-time job.

EXPERIENCE

SENIOR MORTGAGE LOAN SPECIALIST. First Mortgage Services, San Diego, CA (1997-present). Have continuously excelled in this position which requires excellent sales, customer service, decision making, and problem solving skills.
- In Jan. 2000 was named Outstanding Loan Officer for generating $20,000 in fees.
- Process VA, FHA, conforming, and nonconforming first and second mortgages while handling debt consolidations, refinancing, and other financial arrangements.
- Consult with attorneys, VA and FHA officials, appraisers, and other construction and lending officials in matters related to loan conveyances and loan closings.
- Research property to assess value, ensure liens, and assess credit worthiness of clients.
- Am known for my gracious style of communicating with the public and for my ability to explain technical concepts in language that is understandable to lay people.
- Have gained valuable experience in marketing services which are not well understood by the average consumer.

MORTGAGE LOAN SPECIALIST. Ramsey Mortgage, San Diego, CA (1995-97). Gained expertise in all aspects of mortgage loan processing while becoming an expert in handling slow payments and credit repairs.

ADULT PROBATION SERVICES OFFICER. California Department of Corrections, San Diego, CA (1990-95). Because of my exceptional work performance, excellent attitude, and superior work performance, was promoted in the following track record:
1994-95: **Adult Intensive Probation Parole Officer.** Was promoted to a supervisory position which involved providing guidance and supervising a case load of 50 clients per week.
- Earned widespread respect for my ability to establish rapport and cordial relationships with a wide variety of individuals from troubled backgrounds and with turbulent case histories.
1990-94: Adult Probation/Parole Officer. Took pride in the fact that an extremely high percentage of my clients completed their probation and went on to become well adjusted and productive citizens; was frequently told that it was my leadership and motivation skills which made the difference in their lives.
- Provided supervision and guidance for up to 150 clients per month who were on court-ordered probation; completed paperwork and reports in a timely fashion.

DEPUTY CLERK. County Clerk of Superior Court, San Diego, CA (1988-90). Processed affidavits for court traffic tickets, misdemeanors, and felonies in the Criminal Division; was known for my professional style of interacting with others.

Other sales experience: Gained sales experience as an Account Representative for a company which sold sleep systems; also worked as a Sales Representative for a company marketing the Canon Facsimile line.

PERSONAL

Enjoy tackling, achieving, and exceeding ambitious goals through my ability to work effectively with others. Excel in prospecting for new business. Resourceful and high energy.

GOAL: Finding a Completely Different Type of Work to Do

Date

Exact Name of Person
Exact Title or Position
Name of Company
Address (number and street)
Address (city, state, and zip)

**Banking Sales,
Assistant Vice President**

This aggressive young professional is on the "fast track" in his company, but he is feeling restless and wants to "see what's out there." The resume and cover letter are designed to interest employers in numerous fields.

Dear Exact Name of Person: (or Dear Sir or Madam if answering a blind ad.)

With the enclosed resume, I would like to formally initiate the process of being considered for a position within your organization which can use my exceptionally strong marketing, communication, and consulting skills.

As you will see from my resume, since earning my B.S. degree in Business Administration with a Marketing major, I have enjoyed a track record of success in highly competitive banking and consumer product environments. Most recently I was named the top producer in my region based on my results in establishing the most new accounts, achieving the highest loan volume, and obtaining the most referrals. In an earlier position, I consistently led my office in sales and received the Sales Leadership Award as well as other honors recognizing my aggressive marketing orientation and highly refined customer service skills.

Even in summer and part-time jobs while earning my college degree, I was selected for highly responsible positions at companies including R.J. Reynolds/Nabisco, where I managed 30 employees. My summer jobs prior to college graduation helped me acquire excellent skills in merchandising, marketing, and sales.

If you can use an ambitious, results-oriented marketing professional, I hope you will contact me to suggest a time when we might meet to discuss your needs and goals and how I might help you achieve them.

Sincerely,

Jason Vetter

JASON VETTER

1110½ Hay Street, Fayetteville, NC 28305 • preppub@aol.com • (910) 483-6611

OBJECTIVE   To offer strong marketing and sales experience to an organization in need of a professional with the ability to motivate others to exceed expectations through excellent communication and consulting skills.

EXPERIENCE   **ASSISTANT VICE PRESIDENT, CONSUMER BANKING.** FirstBank, N.A., Seattle, WA (1996-present). In May, 2000, was ranked the **Top Consumer Banker** in the Central Washington Region based on my results in establishing the most new accounts, achieving the highest loan volume, and obtaining many referrals.
- Have achieved record productivity for two years in a row.
- Assisted customers while educating them on the merits of different products such as checking and savings accounts, Certificates of Deposit, and IRAs.
- As a loan officer, met with customers and explained differences between types of loans available and made decisions on their qualifications for loans.

PERSONAL BANKER and **RETAIL MANAGEMENT ASSOCIATE.** Nations Bank of Washington, N.A., Seattle, WA (1995-1996). Achieved record productivity while completing a comprehensive management training program with this major financial institution; maintained and managed a portfolio of approximately 1,000 customers.
- Increased the size of my customer base by 30%.
- Played a key role in achieving the highest number of loan and credit card sales and the highest dollar volume of any branch in the region (April and May).
- Learned all aspects of banking including teller operations, investment and loan procedures, and account management; continued to attend training classes to refine and add to my store of knowledge.
- Emphasized quality customer service and set an example for other bank employees while helping existing customers and selling the bank's services to new ones.
- Supervised teller staff and daily operations; conducted staff sales meetings.

ACCOUNT REPRESENTATIVE. Dictaphone Corporation/Pitney Bowes, Midlands, WA (1994-95). Managed more than 300 new and existing accounts while selling communications equipment including Dictaphone, voice mail, and time management equipment in a three-county area.
- Consistently led the office in sales: received the "Sales Leadership Award" for achieving 206% of my quota two months ahead of schedule and later received recognition in the "Achievement Club" for 210% of quota.
- Worked mainly with medical and legal accounts while selling systems valued from $400 to more than $100,000 in a generally long-term sales process.
- Opened more than 25 accounts.

EDUCATION   **B.S. in Business Administration,** Seattle State University, Seattle, WA, 1993.
- Majored in Marketing; was a member of the American Marketing Association.
- Held leadership roles in Delta Chi Fraternity including vice president and rush coordinator; was honored as "Brother of the Year" and currently serve as a trustee on the alumni board.

Completed professional development programs related to consumer finance and consumer loans sponsored by FirstBank, 1996-present.

PERSONAL   Have volunteered with the United Way, Hospitality House, and Watauga Hunger Coalition. Knowledgeable of Microsoft Word, Lotus 1-2-3, dBase III. Excellent references.

GOAL: Finding a Completely Different Type of Work to Do

Date

Exact Name of Person
Title or Position
Name of Company
Address (number and street)
Address (city, state, and zip)

Business Sales and Management

This successful entrepreneur started a lawn and garden business which grossed $250,000 in its fourth year. She could stay comfortably where she is, but she finds herself in a small town missing the "action" of a larger company and a larger town. She has decided to sell her business and job-hunt in a large metropolitan area, and she is seeking a position where she can utilize her sales abilities.

Dear Exact Name of Person: (or Sir or Madam if answering a blind ad.)

With the enclosed resume, I would like to acquaint you with my background and begin the process of exploring opportunities within your organization which could utilize my versatile strengths in management, marketing, and financial control.

As you will see from my resume, after graduating from Alabama University I obtained my Real Estate Broker's License and was consistently in the Top Ten in my county with sales and listings of over $5 million annually. After a sustained track record of outstanding performance, I became involved in large-scale industrial development; I initiated and directed the design of a high-tech digital global telecommunications system which required me to organize extensive collaboration and cooperation among engineers from various competing telecommunications giants. With a partner, I pioneered the concept of and then developed Alabama's first "business incubator" for start-up businesses; after we transformed the concept into a successful operating reality, I became a consultant to 25 foreign countries and a guest lecturer on entrepreneurism at Alabama University's School of Business.

Subsequently, I was recruited by a consulting firm to market and sell industrial buildings and sites for clients such as Burlington Industries, Cone Mills, Jefferson Pilot, and NationsBank. In addition to utilizing my strong negotiating and communication skills, I was involved in planning Alabama's largest commercial development, and I provided leadership in creating a state-of-the-art retirement community based on extensive input from both the public and private sectors.

Most recently I have utilized my proven visionary thinking skills and creative conceptual abilities in simultaneous jobs as a Business Manager/Property Manager and General Manager for two separate businesses. Although I am excelling in handling these responsibilities, I am eager to take on new challenges. I am single and will cheerfully relocate and travel as your needs require. With an outstanding personal and professional reputation, I offer a proven ability to take an idea and transform it into a viable operating entity.

I could make valuable contributions to your organization, and I hope you will contact me. I have a strong bottom-line orientation and outstanding references.

Sincerely,

Martha Woolcott

MARTHA WOOLCOTT

1110½ Hay Street, Fayetteville, NC 28305 • preppub@aol.com • (910) 483-6611

OBJECTIVE

To benefit an organization that can use a creative problem-solver and resourceful manager with excellent negotiating skills along with a proven ability to transform ideas into operating realities while maximizing profitability and satisfying customers.

EDUCATION

B.S. in Political Science, *magna cum laude*, Alabama University, Macon, AL, 1980. Numerous executive development courses in communication/supervision, 1980-1997.

AFFILIATIONS

Have been prominent as a leader in state, local, and business organizations:
- Appointed to Macon County Strategic Planning Commission; was active in site selection for a major shopping center; recruited new business to the county; and am developing feasibility plans for a small industrial and business park.
- Developed Alabama's first business incubator for start-up businesses; became a leading spokesperson in the state for entrepreneurial development and also became a consultant on the federal and state level to 25 foreign countries.
- Sold 2,000 acres of land for construction of an innovative and comprehensive new retirement community after working extensively with legislators, retirement groups, and numerous public officials to sell them on the concept.

EXPERIENCE

Am excelling in management roles in two separate organizations:

1993-present: **GENERAL MANAGER.** Quality Lawn & Garden, Macon, AL. Combined my strategic planning skills with my management ability in identifying a need and a niche for this successful business; started "from scratch" a business which grossed $250,000 in its fourth year.
- Manage a diversified company which provides landscaping services to 50 new homes annually while managing a retail garden center which sells top-quality trees, flowers, and gardening supplies; also operate a related side business which rakes, bales, and markets 50,000 bales of pine straw a year.
- Hired, trained, and managed a work force of between 6-10 employees.

1991-present: **BUSINESS MANAGER/PROPERTY MANAGER.** Bryson's, Inc., Macon, AL. Represent a diversified multiplex consisting of a furniture store, grocery store, and rental properties; negotiated the multimillion-dollar sale of 200 acres of prime commercial property; developed infrastructure plans and obtained permits/inspections in spite of complicated county procedures.
- Sold prime commercial sites for a service station and an auto parts business.

VICE PRESIDENT & BROKER. XYZ Industrial Relations, Lincoln, AL (1986-91). Marketed and sold industrial buildings and sites for such clients as Burlington Industries, Cone Mills, Jefferson Pilot, and NationsBank while providing the key leadership in two major projects:
- *Project 1:* Assembled a 28,000-acre parcel of land, devised plan for infrastructure and funding and then wrote and presented a proposal to the Governor for Alabama's largest planned commercial development.
- *Project 2:* Pioneered the development of new concepts now routinely used in many retirement communities; obtained several patents on designs for handicapped bathrooms and kitchens while also inventing new concepts in financing retirement living which banks and insurance companies now accept; sold 2,000 acres of land for a new "model" retirement village after engaging public and private sector leaders in "think-tank" activities which ultimately led to their support of the project.

REAL ESTATE BROKER. Trainor Realtors, Duluth, AL (1981-86). Was consistently in the Top Ten in the county in sales and listings with over $5 million annually.

PERSONAL

Can provide outstanding personal and professional references. Single and will relocate.

GOAL: Finding a Completely Different Type of Work to Do

Date

Exact Name of Person
Title or Position
Name of Company
Address (number and street)
Address (city, state, and ZIP)

Catering and Dining Services Manager

This is an excellent example of an all-purpose resume and cover letter. The cover letter is designed to make this individual appealing to employers in numerous industries, and the Objective on the resume highlights skills and abilities which are transferable to all types of work environments. Notice how the Personal Section of the resume emphasizes his ability to adapt easily to new environments—a subtle hint that he is in career change.

Dear Exact Name of Person: (or Dear Sir or Madam if answering a blind ad.)

Can you use an articulate, detail-oriented professional who offers outstanding abilities in the areas of sales program development and management, financial management, and the training and supervision of employees?

You will see by my enclosed resume that I have built a track record of accomplishments with Holiday Inn Management Services where I am currently the Account Director at Yale University in New Haven, CT. During my six years in this position I have reduced labor costs and increased auxiliary sales while overseeing a program with a $900,000 annual operating budget. I oversee two supervisors and a 30-person staff which provides resident dining, catering, conference, and retail dining services on a private college campus.

In addition to my business, inventory control, personnel, and human resources management responsibilities, I also am heavily involved in the development and management of promotional materials and programs. I have refined natural verbal and written communication skills while acting as liaison between corporate headquarters and the university, training and dealing with employees, and handling customer service activities.

I believe that you would find me to be an articulate professional with the ability to learn quickly and apply my organizational skills and common sense.

I hope you will welcome my call soon to arrange a brief meeting at your convenience to discuss your current and future needs and how I might serve them. Thank you in advance for your time.

Sincerely yours,

Callahan Warren

Alternate last paragraph:
I hope you will call or write me soon to suggest a time convenient for us to meet and discuss your current and future needs and how I might serve them. Thank you in advance for your time.

CALLAHAN WARREN

1110½ Hay Street, Fayetteville, NC 28305 • preppub@aol.com • (910) 483-6611

OBJECTIVE	To offer my expertise in reducing costs as well as increasing profits and customer satisfaction while displaying exceptional sales, leadership, and financial management abilities and refining organizational, training, and time management skills.
EXPERIENCE	*Built a track record of accomplishments with Holiday Inn Management Services at Yale University, New Haven, CT:*

SALES MANAGER & ACCOUNT DIRECTOR. (1996-present). During a six-year period in this role, have reduced total labor costs more than $96,000 while operating a $900,000 program providing this campus with resident dining, catering, conference, and retail dining services.

- Provided outstanding customer satisfaction in all areas of dining services with a staff of two supervisors and approximately 30 employees.
- Increased Operating Profit Contributions (OPC) from $25,000 to $90,000 and auxiliary sales to more than $228,000 over a six-year period by identifying opportunities, developing strategy, and implementing new plans.
- Polished managerial abilities while developing budgets and business plans along with making revisions in procedures which led to increases in sales and production.
- Managed a procurement program for more than 1,000 line items.
- Reconciled profit and loss statements and balance sheet management.
- Supervised accounts payable and receivable, payroll, and weekly financial reports sent to the corporate office while acting as liaison between the corporation and client.
- Assisted the regional sales director in the development of sales proposals by using sales and cost analysis modules.
- Used my communication skills to prepare brochures, calendars, and other promotional materials as well as in the development of a client communication manual.

FOOD SERVICE MANAGER. (1993-96). Gained exposure to a wide range of day-to-day operational activities related to campus dining, catering, and conference food services.

- Applied time management and organizational skills overseeing fiscal areas of operations which included purchasing as well as inventory, labor cost, and cash-handling controls.
- Handled additional activities ranging from vendor specifications, to menu development and implementation, to promotions and marketing, to catering, to sanitation and safety.
- Updated the automated procedures which reduced unit labor costs.
- Implemented a computerized system used to handle associate payroll, accounts payable, accounts receivable, and billing.

MANAGEMENT TRAINEE. (1993). As a food service management trainee, became familiar with customer service, scheduling, and employee training.

STUDENT MANAGER. Holiday Inn Management Services, Davidson University, Augusta, SC (1992). Hired by the corporation while attending the university, was in charge of food-handling controls and supervised 10 part-time employees.

EDUCATION & TRAINING	**B.A., Business Administration** (minors: Marketing, Finance), Davidson University, SC, 1992. Completed extensive corporate training programs in major areas of emphasis including:

public relations	safety training	human resource management
sales & cost analysis	internal accounting systems	labor productivity I and II
Total Quality Management 1 and II		diversity/sensitivity training
Hazard Analysis Critical Control Points (HACCP)		food handling & food-borne illness

CERTIFICATION	Am a licensed food handler with certification in food-borne illness.
PERSONAL	Fast learner capable of easily adjusting to new environments. Excellent references.

GOAL: Finding a Completely Different Type of Work to Do

Date

Exact Name of Person
Title or Position
Name of Company
Address (number and street)
Address (city, state, and zip)

Dear Exact Name of Person: (or Sir or Madam if answering a blind ad.)

With the enclosed resume, I would like to formally make you aware of my interest in your organization. As you will see, I have excelled in jobs which required originality and creativity in prospecting for new clients, business savvy and financial prudence in establishing new ventures, as well as relentless follow-through and attention to detail in implementing ambitious goals.

I was recruited for my current job when the company decided that it wanted to set up a new commercial division and needed someone with proven entrepreneurial skills and a make-it-happen style. Under my leadership we have set up a new commercial division which has targeted the healthcare and pharmaceutical industry as a primary customer base in addition to major financial institutions and large corporations. Although I now manage several individuals, I personally prospected for the initial accounts and I discovered that my extensive training and background related to chemistry and microbiology was of great value in interacting with healthcare industry decision makers.

Although I can provide outstanding personal and professional references and am being groomed for further promotion within my company, I have decided that I wish to transfer my skills and knowledge to the healthcare industry. You will notice from my resume that I have been a successful entrepreneur and previously started a company which I sold to a larger industry firm. I succeeded as an entrepreneur largely because of my ability to communicate ideas to others, my strong problem-solving skills, and my naturally outgoing and self-confident nature. I am certain I could excel in the healthcare industry in any role which requires extraordinary sales, marketing, and relationship-building abilities.

If my background interests you, and if you feel there is a suitable position in your organization in which you could make use of my sales and marketing strengths, I hope you will contact me to suggest a time when we might meet to discuss your goals and how I might help you achieve them. Thank you in advance for your consideration and professional courtesies.

Yours sincerely,

Parsival Flanagan

PARSIVAL FLANAGAN

1110½ Hay Street, Fayetteville, NC 28305 • preppub@aol.com • (910) 483-6611

OBJECTIVE

To contribute to an organization that can use a dynamic professional who wishes to transfer my exceptionally strong sales and marketing abilities to the pharmaceutical industry.

EXPERIENCE

MANAGER, COMMERCIAL DIVISION. Drayton Enterprises, Augusta, ME (1995-present). Was aggressively recruited by this company which wanted to establish a new commercial division targeting the healthcare and pharmaceutical industry as a primary client base; provided the leadership in developing the strategic plan for the new division which has annual revenues of more than half a million dollars; now manage several technicians and sales reps.

- Personally prospected for all the initial accounts.
- Utilized my background and extensive training in chemistry and microbiology to facilitate my sales effectiveness in the healthcare and pharmaceutical industry.
- Excelled in building relationships through creative lead generation, astute needs assessment and fulfillment, and strong skills in closing the sale.

FOUNDER/PRESIDENT. Termites Undone, Inc., Richmond, VA (1988-94). Started "from scratch" a company which was bought out by one of the largest pest elimination service companies in the country.

- Succeeded as an entrepreneur and business manager in a highly competitive industry because of my ability to communicate ideas to others, my problem-solving skills, my ability to formulate new ideas based on information obtained from multiple sources, and my outgoing and self-confident nature.
- Handled all financial matters including budgets, profit-and-loss quotas, tax planning, insurance, and purchasing.
- Acquired considerable experience in dealing with government regulatory agencies and in preparing the paperwork necessary to document programs in critical situations.

VICE PRESIDENT OF SALES AND TRAINING. Dana Exterminating Company, Inc., Augusta, GA (1980-88). Was a major force in the company's growth for over eight years; helped establish formal training and hiring policies.

- Began in sales and in my fourth year was promoted to supervisor responsible for 15 individuals, project management, as well as equipment maintenance and troubleshooting.
- In my fifth year was promoted to **Vice President of Sales & Training** responsible for setting/achieving branch goals, defining/implementing training programs, as well as overseeing safety and vehicle/equipment maintenance.

EDUCATION

More than two years of college coursework at **Maine University;** courses included biology and social sciences, accounting and economics.

- Corporate sales and technical training sponsored by leading firms.

PERSONAL

Business skills include marketing and sales, starting up new business operations, selecting and training employees, controlling inventory, purchasing materials, preparing strategic plans, dealing with regulators, accounting and financial control. Excellent references.

Date

Exact Name of Person
Title or Position
Name of Company
Address (number and street)
Address (city, state, and zip)

Consumer Products Sales, Transitioning from Buying to Sales

This young professional actually offers more experience in purchasing than in sales, but sales is what he wants to do. He is hoping to convince an employer to see his sales potential. Many employers feel that employees succeed because of their highly motivated nature, and many employers will see the relevance of his buying background as an advantage in sales.

Dear Exact Name of Person: (or Sir or Madam if answering a blind ad.)

With the enclosed resume, I would like to initiate the process of being considered for employment within your organization. Because of family ties, I am in the process of relocating to the San Diego area. Since I do not yet have a permanent address, I would prefer your contacting me at the e-mail address shown on my resume or at my current telephone number if you wish to talk with me.

Since graduating from the University of Iowa, I have established a track record of rapid promotion with a corporation headquartered in Bladen, IA. I began as an Assistant Branch Manager and Head Buyer, was cross-trained as a Sales Representative, and have been promoted to my current position in which I manage the selling process related to 3,500 different products. In that capacity, I am entrusted with the responsibility for nearly $15 million in annual expenditures, and I maintain excellent working relationships with more than 150 vendors of name-brand consumer products sold through chain and convenience stores.

In my job, rapid change is a daily reality, and I have become accustomed to working in an environment in which I must make rapid decisions while weighing factors including forecasted consumer demand, distribution patterns, inventory turnover patterns, and vendor capacity and character. I have earned a reputation as a persuasive communicator and savvy negotiator with an aggressive bottom-line orientation.

If you can use my versatile experience in sales, purchasing, distribution, and operations management, I hope you will contact me to suggest a time when we might meet to discuss your needs and how I might serve them. I can provide excellent personal and professional references, and I assure you in advance that I am a hard worker who is accustomed to being measured according to ambitious goals for profitability in a highly competitive marketplace.

Yours sincerely,

Charles Granquist

CHARLES GRANQUIST

1110½ Hay Street, Fayetteville, NC 28305 • preppub@aol.com • (910) 483-6611

OBJECTIVE

To contribute to an organization that can use a resourceful manager with proven skills in managing the selling process while prudently overseeing inventory carrying costs, maintaining excellent working relationships with vendors, and preparing strategic plans.

EDUCATION

B.S. in Business Administration, University of Iowa, Bladen, IA, 1995.
• Dr. Philip and Betsey Davis Scholarship award recipient.

EXPERIENCE

MIDLAND DOMINION DISTRIBUTORS (1995-present): **Since graduating from the University of Iowa, have a track record of success and rapid promotion with Midland Dominion Distributors, a company with seven locations throughout the Midwest, headquartered in Bladen, IA:**

HEAD BUYER. Bladen, IA. (1999-present). Personally handle more than half of the buying for a company which purchases up to $25 million annually in consumer products which are then distributed to the consumer through chain and convenience stores.
• Develop and sustain effective working relationships with more than 150 vendors including Hershey, Nabisco Foods, Quaker, and other vendors of name-brand juices, candy, health and beauty aids, and groceries.
• Maintain extensive liaison with sales representatives; coordinate contests and promotions for sales representatives and customers.
• Attend national trade shows and buying conventions.
• Was commended for playing a key role in my branch's being named "Branch of the Year" in 2000.
• Am responsible for prudently managing the selling process and making astute buying decisions related to 3,500 products in a highly competitive market in which rapid turnover is critical.

HEAD BUYER. Walton, IA (1997-99). Reported directly to the Vice President while handling the buying of more than $10 million worth of merchandise annually; purchased products supplied to five locations in Iowa from the Walton location.
• Established and maintained excellent working relationships with 50 vendors while purchasing juices, candy, health and beauty aids, and other consumer products.
• Was commended for my excellent decision-making ability in forecasting inventory needs and purchasing products on a timely basis at lowest cost; made weekly buying decisions.
• Maintained a close working relationship with warehouse managers to ensure inventory accuracy.
• Organized deliveries of products to locations served by the Walton branch.
• Conducted semiannual inventory of the Walton location.
• Maintained strict accountability; entered receiving documents into computer to update inventory status daily and reconciled all invoices monthly. Monitored inventory turnover.
• Learned to resourcefully troubleshoot a wide variety of inventory problems.

BUYER & ASSISTANT BRANCH MANAGER. Bladen, IA (1995-97). Became skilled in buying groceries and tobacco products while also functioning in the role of **Sales Representative**; was cross-trained as a Route Sales Representative.

AFFILIATIONS

Member, Leadership Development Division, a national group of young executives.
Member, Delta Sigma Pi, a professional business fraternity.

COMPUTERS

Lotus, Microsoft Excel, Microsoft Word, Harvard Graphics, and WordPerfect for Windows.

Date

Mrs. Veronica Lane
Owner
Braselton Gallery
185 Hazelwood Drive
Hilton Head, SC 99877

Environmental Professional Changing to Art Gallery Management

This professional has decided that the city where she is relocating does not have the high-powered environmental work in which she has been involved. So she is choosing her upcoming relocation as the ideal time to switch careers to the art gallery field. She has long had an interest in art gallery work, public relations, and public affairs and feels that her skills and personality would be well expressed in this new environment. In terms of career change, this is true: You don't know if it's possible until you try!

Dear Mrs. Lane:

With the enclosed resume, I would like to make you aware of my interest in exploring employment opportunities with your organization. I have recently relocated to South Carolina with my husband because of his new position, and I have much to offer an organization that can use a versatile hard worker with strong communication, management, computer operations, and budget skills. I am interested in the management position we recently discussed on the telephone.

In my most recent work experience, I have worked in the environmental compliance field and recently functioned as the only Environmental Compliance Inspector for my employer in Dallas, TX. In that role I acted as spokesperson for environmental issues and was involved in training employees at all levels. Continuously involved in quality assurance activities, I conducted announced and unannounced inspections to determine compliance with regulations.

Although I have excelled in my recent job, I have decided to explore opportunities outside the environmental field at this next phase in my career. You will notice from my resume that I offer strong computer knowledge. I am skilled in database management using Microsoft Access, and I am proficient with all Microsoft programs. I have worked effectively in situations where I was a bookkeeper, budget assistant, computer program analyst, and administrative assistant.

I believe one of my main strengths is my ability to adapt easily to new environments as I have a natural problem-solving orientation. Known for my attention to detail in all matters, I excel in situations in which excellent analytical and problem-solving skills are required. I also offer the ability to act as a spokesperson for an organization utilizing the public speaking and problem-solving skills which have been refined through experience.

If you can use a versatile and adaptable professional with knowledge in numerous areas to become a part of your team, I hope you will contact me to suggest a time when we might meet in person to discuss your needs. I can provide outstanding references at the appropriate time.

Sincerely,

Amy Vanderbilt

AMY VANDERBILT

1110 1/2 Hay Street, Fayetteville, NC 28305   •   preppub@aol.com   •   (910) 483-6611

OBJECTIVE

To benefit an organization that can use an articulate, experienced professional with exceptional planning and organizational skills who offers a versatile background related to customer service, public relations, bookkeeping, and project management.

**EDUCATION &
CERTIFICATION**

Completed two years towards B.S. in Business Management, University of Virginia. Attended numerous courses related to Environmental Laws and Regulations, Hazardous Material Waste Handling, and CPR/First Aid.

COMPUTERS

Completed formal coursework for Microsoft applications and the Windows operating system. Knowledgeable of Windows and Microsoft Access, Excel, Word, and Works.
- Skilled in database management using Microsoft Access.
- Have created presentations with PowerPoint.

EXPERIENCE

1994-2000: ENVIRONMENTAL COMPLIANCE INSPECTOR. Advanced from Environmental Assistant (1994-98) to Environmental Compliance Inspector with Bristol Corporation (1998-2000), Dallas, TX. Recently resigned this position in order to relocate with my husband.
- As the only inspector in Dallas for this major corporation, conducted announced and unannounced inspections of facilities to determine compliance with environmental regulations; provided guidance and made recommendations for corrective action, then prepared formal reports of the inspection.
- On my own initiative, updated the environmental compliance checklist/inspection form which was four years out of date.
- Was extensively involved in training personnel at all levels, from executives to entry-level personnel; conducted classes and briefed executives and personnel.
- Acquired expertise in quality assurance and environmental compliance inspection.
- Have acquired vast expertise related to environmental issues while serving in a highly visible capacity as the spokesperson for environmental compliance.
- Received the highest possible evaluations on all performance appraisals; was praised for "consistently exercising sound judgment," for my "hard work in improving compliance."

COMPUTER ANALYST. Department of Defense, Ft. Hood, TX (1993). Handled data entry and computer systems support for a project that computerized inventory data for eight schools.

ADMINISTRATIVE ASSISTANT. Department of Defense, Ft. Dix, NJ (1992-93). Maintained a student database using Lotus 1-2-3 while also handling purchase requisitions and assisting in contract modifications; worked closely with the Public Affairs office, and was Acting Public Affairs Officer in the absence of the Director.

BUDGET ASSISTANT. Womack Army Community Hospital, Ft. Bragg, NC (1991). Managed expenditures of the Supplemental Care Program utilizing automated accounting system, and performed audits of medical facility treatment activities and pharmacy inventory.

BUDGET ASSISTANT. U.S. Army, Belgium (1988-90). Maintained ledgers of fund distribution for major units while gathering data for budget analysts, confirming accuracy of reports, as well as reconciling and balancing ledgers.

PERSONAL

Have earned three Sustained Superior Performance Awards. Known as a service-oriented professional with strong analytical and problem solving skills. Excellent references available.

GOAL: Finding a Completely Different Type of Work to Do

Date

Exact Name of Person
Exact Title
Exact Name of Company
Address
City, State, Zip

Dear Exact Name of Person (or Dear Sir or Madam if answering a blind ad):

With the enclosed resume, I would like to make you aware of my exceptionally strong office skills and management abilities. I am interested in exploring employment opportunities within your organization.

As you will see from my enclosed resume, since graduating from high school I have earned two Associate's degrees in my spare time while earning rapid promotions in my full-time job. One of my Associate's degrees is in Business Administration and the other Associate's degree is in General Education. I have also excelled in extensive professional training sponsored by my employers related to customer service, operations management, and other areas. My computer skills are outstanding, and I own a home computer which I utilize frequently with software including Microsoft Word, Excel, PowerPoint, and other programs.

In my current management position with the McDonald's company, I have advanced rapidly from Cashier, to Crew Leader, to Shift Supervisor, and I am being groomed for further rapid promotion to Store Manager. I have decided, however, that I wish to make my career in the office technology and computer operations field, and I am confident that I could become an outstanding office manager and operations supervisor. In my current position, I manage up to 10 individuals, and I am responsible for bottom-line wage costs as well as for scheduling and supervising employees. With a reputation as a tactful and articulate young manager, I have become respected for my ability to adeptly manage human resources in an environment in which quality service must be provided under tight deadlines.

If you can use a smart and hard-working professional who offers excellent problem-solving and customer relations skills, I hope you will contact me to suggest a time when we might meet to discuss your needs. I can provide outstanding personal and professional references at the appropriate time, but I would ask that you not contact my current employer until after we have a chance to meet.

Yours sincerely,

Natalie Driscoll

NATALIE DRISCOLL

1110½ Hay Street, Fayetteville, NC 28305 • preppub@aol.com • (910) 483-6611

OBJECTIVE   To benefit an organization that can use a hard-working manager who offers strong computer operations know-how, excellent mathematical skills and accounting knowledge, as well as hands-on experience in the most efficient workflow methods and productivity techniques.

EDUCATION   Have earned two Associate's degrees from Kennesaw Technical Community College:
· **Associate of Applied Science in Business Administration,** May 2001.
· **Associate in General Education,** May 2001.
Extensive training related to business finance, marketing, management, supervision, accounting, business law, business applications, and typing.
Numerous professional and technical training programs sponsored by employers.

COMPUTERS   Proficient with MS Word, Excel, PowerPoint, and numerous other software programs.

EXPERIENCE   **SHIFT SUPERVISOR.** McDonald's, Kennesaw, MI (1999-present). Assist restaurant management in the training of all new customer service employees on all shifts and weekends; play a key role in the cross training and retraining of existing customer service employees, and attend routine meetings designated for training management purposes.
- When I was only 16 years old, began my employment as a Cashier and then was promoted to Crew Leader in charge of six people after only six months; then was rapidly promoted to Shift Supervisor and now supervise up to 10 people.
- Am being groomed for promotion to Store Manager and have been told that I possess all the qualifications and will be selected for this key management role; I have decided, however, that I wish to transfer my management skills into a new environment.
- Have become very skilled at customer service and public relations, and personally resolve all difficult customer problems on my shift.
- After extensive training in operational policies and procedures, have become skilled at scheduling and managing employees for maximum efficiency and productivity.
- Schedule employees in such a way that I meet budgetary expectations.
- Maintain a harmonious working relationship with all employees, and am respected for my effective management style.
- Played a key role in helping the store transition to a new status of becoming a "Star Store," which required me to retrain employees and implement new procedures.

ASSISTANT MANAGER. Blockbuster, Kennesaw, MI (1998-1999). Assisted the store manager in managing all daily operations, and became his trusted "right arm."
- Supervised up to six employees while also preparing bank deposits; became skilled in processing credits and refunds: and performed till audits to prevent customer and employee theft.
- Was responsible for product management; rectified shipment problems, merchandised inventory in order to maximize customer satisfaction, and protected inventory from external and internal theft.
- Gained extensive experience with credit and collections as well as auditing.
- Was frequently commended by management for my outstanding ability to initiate action, make decisions, and solve problems; earned a reputation as a young person who was highly motivated in accepting responsibility who could be entrusted to work independently.

PERSONAL   Outstanding personal and professional references upon request. Strong work ethic.

GOAL: Finding a Completely Different Type of Work to Do

Date

Exact Name of Person
Exact Title
Exact Name of Company
Address
City, State, Zip

Dear Exact Name of Person (or Dear Sir or Madam if answering a blind ad):

With the enclosed resume, I would like to make you aware of my background as an experienced manager with a track record of success in building sales and profitability while maintaining focus on customer service and satisfaction.

As you will see, I have advanced with the retail supermarket chain Food World while becoming recognized as a professional who could be counted on to provide sound control over wages, inventory, supplies, and shrinkage. In my current position as a Store Manager, I have increased sales and profitability in a store with $14 million in average annual sales. I am leading this location to excellent results which include year-to-date rates of 21% increase in sales and a shrinkage rate of +0.14%.

I began my career with Food World as a Stocker and soon advanced to Grocery Manager, to Assistant Manager, and then to Store Manager, and I have held this top management role in three area locations. In each store I have provided leadership which has led to my recognition with numerous "Outstanding Performance Awards" for sales increases and expertise in inventory control as well as for high ratings in customer satisfaction surveys.

If you can use an experienced manager who is known for the ability to identify and solve problems and to lead employees to outstanding results in all measurable areas of operations, please contact me to suggest a time when we might meet to discuss your needs. I can assure you in advance that I could rapidly become an asset to your organization.

Sincerely,

William McGowan

WILLIAM McGOWAN

1110½ Hay Street, Fayetteville, NC 28305 • preppub@aol.com • (910) 483-6611

OBJECTIVE	To benefit an organization that can use a strong manager with expert knowledge of inventory, wage, and shrinkage control as well as a well-developed sense of the value of customer service and satisfaction.
TRAINING	Continually add to my knowledge by reading and taking tests which have earned me approximately 1,000 continuing education units awarded by the Food World corporation.
EXPERIENCE	***Have built a track record of advancement with a large retail supermarket chain, Food World, which is headquartered in Macon, GA:***

STORE MANAGER. Duluth, GA (1997-present). Increased sales and profitability in a store with $14 million in annual sales while managing six department heads and overseeing the day-to-day performance of 70 employees.

- Am providing the leadership which has allowed this location to see a year-to-date shrinkage rate of +0.14% and a 21% sales increase.
- Increased this store's bottom-line profitability by 4%.
- Oversee all phases of store operations ranging from wage control and processing, to inventory control and supply, to utilities, to maintenance, to security and safety, to cleaning and sanitation, to merchandising.
- Hire, train, and schedule employees.

STORE MANAGER. Smithfield, GA (1994-97). Increased sales 8% a year in a store which had an average annual sales volume of $10 million while supervising five department heads and 50 employees.

- Demonstrated my dedication to the success of store operations by working an average of 60 to 70 hours a week.
- Maintained outstanding results in all measurable areas of wages, shrinkage reduction, and bottom-line profitability.
- Oversaw all operational areas to include wage control and payroll actions, inventory control and supply, utilities management, building maintenance, security and safety, cleaning and sanitation, and merchandising as well as hiring, training, and scheduling.

STORE MANAGER. Crayfish, GA (1992-94). Supervised five department heads and 50 employees in a store which posted sales of $9 million annually.

- Increased sales; learned to share responsibilities with my department heads while still working an average of 60-70 hours a week; maintained high levels in all measured areas of operation (wages, shrinkage, and profitability).

ASSISTANT MANAGER. Malvern, GA (1991-92). Supervised one department head and seven employees in the grocery department while working as acting manager in his absence for a store with a $10 million annual sales volume.

- Was recognized for my excellent inventory control abilities as well as for my skills in scheduling, ordering, and building displays.

SKILLS	Through my years of retail experience, have become familiar with equipment and procedures which include using computerized cash registers and automated systems for recordkeeping and inventory control.
PERSONAL	Earned numerous "Outstanding Performance Awards" based on sales increases, inventory control, and customer satisfaction surveys. Have not missed one day of work due to illness in ten years with Food World. Excellent references available on request.

GOAL: Finding a Completely Different Type of Work to Do

Date

Mr. William Monroe
Gruber Properties
222 McPherson Church Rd.
Charlotte, NC 27803

Real Estate Sales

Dear Mr. Monroe:

This young professional has recently relocated back to his hometown to help his mom settle the estate of his deceased dad, and he is seeking a career change from store management to real estate sales. Notice that he is using the "direct approach" in his job hunt: he is approaching a select number of employers for whom he would like to work.

I would appreciate an opportunity to talk with you soon about how I could contribute to your organization through my sales and management experience along with my formal education and technical training related to real estate.

As you will see from the enclosed resume, I am licensed by the North Carolina Real Estate Commission as a sales person and am currently completing Brokers Certification courses. I completed the "North Carolina Fundamentals of Real Estate Course" at The Charlotte School of Real Estate.

My resume also will show you my "track record" of achievement in sales and management. Although I was born and raised in the Charlotte area and am living here permanently, most recently I worked in Ft. Lauderdale and Jacksonville, FL, as a Store Manager for Camelot Music. I managed other employees, decreased inventory shrinkage, opened new stores, converted acquisition stores to Camelot systems and procedures, and was specially selected to manage a new "superstore" of more than 10,000 square feet.

I am sending you this resume because, after conducting extensive research of real estate companies, your company is the one I would most like to be associated with. I hope you will find some time in your schedule for us to meet at your convenience to discuss your needs and goals and how I might serve them. I shall look forward to hearing from you, and thank you in advance for your time.

Yours sincerely,

Michael Jenkins

MICHAEL JENKINS

1110½ Hay Street, Fayetteville, NC 28305 • preppub@aol.com • (910) 483-6611

OBJECTIVE   To contribute to an organization that can use a resourceful and congenial sales professional with excellent customer relations skills who offers a proven "track record" of accomplishment in both sales and operations management.

REAL ESTATE
- Licensed by North Carolina Real Estate Commission.
- Currently completing Brokers Certification courses.
- Completed "North Carolina Fundamentals of Real Estate Course" at the Charlotte School of Real Estate.

EXPERIENCE SUMMARY
- Eight years of restaurant and retail management experience.
- Skilled in hiring, training, scheduling, and maintaining sales staff dedicated to superior customer relations.
- Proven commitment to meeting deadlines and serving customers.
- Exceptionally strong analytical and problem-solving skills.
- Known for my positive attitude and cheerful disposition.

EXPERIENCE   **STORE MANAGER**. Camelot Music, Jacksonville, FL, and Ft. Lauderdale, FL (1993-2000). Earned a reputation as a skilled store manager who was equally effective in starting up new retail operations, "turning around" existing stores experiencing sales and profitability problems, and managing "superstores."
- After managing three Camelot Music retail stores in Jacksonville and Ft. Lauderdale, was selected to manage a new 10,000 square foot freestanding "superstore."
- Was responsible for opening new stores and converting acquisition stores to Camelot's procedures, methods, and systems.
- Devised and implemented effective merchandising techniques.
- Specialized in maintaining superior inventory conditions.
- Achieved consistent sales increases and ranked among the chain's highest volume stores.
- Diminished shrinkage and substantially increased profits.
- Implemented effective off-site sales locations utilizing radio and television as well as popular musicians and bands at successful local events.

Other experience:
After earning my Associate of Arts degree, excelled in restaurant management and was selected for management training programs.
- Worked in Hardee's and was selected for their corporate training program; was hand-picked as co-manager of a Hardee's at Myrtle Beach.
- Worked in Quincy's Restaurant as an assistant manager after completing their corporate training program.

EDUCATION   **Associate of Arts** (A.A.) degree in Restaurant and Hotel Management, Baltimore's International Culinary College, 1990.
- Completed renowned management training programs with established restaurants, Hardee's and Quincy's.
Completed high school at Hargrave Military Academy and Flora McDonald Academy.

PERSONAL   Am an accomplished guitarist and musical collector. Excellent health. Single.

GOAL: Finding a Completely Different Type of Work to Do

Date

Exact Name of Person
Exact Title
Exact Name of Company
Address
City, State, Zip

Retail Buying Transitioning into Marketing

This successful professional found herself in a job hunt one day when her employer announced that it was relocating the buyers to the head office, 100 miles away. She didn't want to move, and she decided that she'd had enough of retail buying, anyway. So she used this resume and cover letter to open numerous doors, and she finally chose a job as a Marketing Manager of a nonprofit organization.

Dear Exact Name of Person (or Dear Sir or Madam in answering a blind ad):

With the enclosed resume, I would like to make you aware of my extensive sales, merchandising, and management skills as well as my interest in exploring the possibility of utilizing my experience to benefit your organization.

After earning a B.S. degree (cum laude) from the University of Idaho at Boise, I was recruited by Lord & Taylor as an Associate Buyer in 1997. I achieved unusually rapid advancement to Buyer after only one year and four months, and since 1999 I have excelled in handling a $10 million volume while buying for 22 stores. The buying function had been handled in New York City for the previous five years, and I instituted a major reorganization which led to increased sales.

My sales and gross margin results have been consistently superior, and I have never received anything less than "above average" on annual performance evaluations of my business, sales, marketing, merchandise planning, and inventory control skills. I am well known for my ability to establish and maintain effective working relationships with people at all levels, from top-level buying and merchandising experts in New York City to store managers and vendors. I pride myself on my ability to react quickly to emerging trends and to respond decisively in averting problems before they happen.

If you can use a dynamic and results-oriented individual with excellent communication skills, I hope you will contact me to suggest a time when we can meet to discuss your goals and needs and how I might help you. I can provide excellent references.

Thank you in advance for your time and professional courtesies.

Yours sincerely,

Lurene Rhoades

LURENE RHOADES

1110½ Hay Street, Fayetteville, NC 28305 • preppub@aol.com • (910) 483-6611

OBJECTIVE I want to contribute to an organization that can use a dynamic and results-oriented young professional who has enjoyed promotion to increasing responsibilities because of an ability to produce outstanding bottom-line results.

EDUCATION **Bachelor of Science in Criminal Justice,** *cum laude,* University of Idaho at Boise, 1996.
- Named to Social Science Honor Society (Pi Gamma Mu), the freshman Honor Society (Phi Eta Sigma), and Who's Who Among College Students.
- Worked as a Writing Lab Tutor; elected Vice President of Criminal Justice Club; was honored by selection as a University Ambassador.
- Excelled in numerous professional development courses related to purchasing, sales, merchandising, and finance sponsored by Lord & Taylor Department Stores.

COMPUTERS Highly proficient with computers including Lotus 1-2-3 and AmiPro; utilize LAN to provide timely information; also proficient with all merchandise systems including POM, Markdown, IMS, Store SKU Database, MPO/MPT, and SAR.

EXPERIENCE *Have excelled in the following track record of advancement with Lord & Taylor Department Stores, Boise, ID (1997-present).*
1999-present. BUYER. Was promoted to Buyer because of my exceptional performance as an Associate Buyer. Am now responsible for a $10 million sales volume while buying for the Juniors departments for 22 stores.
- **Superior sales results**: Increased sales 1.1% in 1999 compared to the previous year; am currently showing an 8.9% sales increase in 2000 compared to 1999; reorganized the Juniors area and increased sales after taking over buying which had been handled in New York City for the previous five years.
- **Gross margin increase:** Increased GM from 36.2 in 1999 to 37.1 in 2000.
- **Sales and marketing management:** Consistently maintain "above average" on annual performance evaluations, and have been verbally commended for my insightful sales and marketing management.
- **Communication:** Maintain outstanding relationships with store management.
- **Business and professional management:** React prudently to changing market trends to maximize sales; work with vendors to build profitable relationships.
- **Merchandise planning and inventory management:** Am skilled in planning and achieving balanced assortments that meet customer demand.

1997-99: ASSOCIATE BUYER. In unusually rapid advancement, was promoted to buyer after only 1 year and four months in this job and was given responsibility for a $10 million sales volume; learned the duties of a buyer while working with Ladies Ready to Wear, Ladies Sportswear, Accessories, Cosmetics, Fragrances, Lingerie, Jewelry, and Hosiery.
- Played a key role in increasing sales in the Misses Suit Department.

Other experience*:* **Partially financed college education working 30 hours a week.**
1994-97: Sales Representative & Sales Support Specialist. Chic Boutique, Boise, ID. In addition to sales, handled additional responsibilities which included maintaining security and adhering to a strict theft reduction system; verified status of incoming and outgoing merchandise and processed price reductions.

PERSONAL Outstanding decision maker and problem solver who thrives on multiple responsibilities.

GOAL: Finding a Completely Different Type of Work to Do

Date

San Diego Public Utility
Human Resources
RE: Inventory Technician
P.O. Box 9547
San Diego, CA 34235

Sales Background Trying to Find "Anything But Sales!"

This young professional found himself in two outside sales jobs in his most recent positions, and they convinced him that sales is not for him! In writing his resume, his job titles were changed from Outside Sales Representative to the jobs titles you see on his resume. Nothing is misrepresented in terms of what he did, but his background is being presented to show the personality he most wants to express in his next job. He has decided that he would feel most comfortable in an industrial environment where he could provide some customer service or utilize management skills.

Dear Sir or Madam:

With the enclosed resume, I am responding to your recent ad for a Power Plant Inventory Technician for San Diego Public Utility. I believe you will see that my background seems tailor-made to your requirements, and I would appreciate an opportunity to talk with you in person about the position.

A permanent native of San Diego, I graduated from San Diego State University with a Bachelor of Business Administration (B.B.A.). Prior to college I served my country in the U.S. Army, and I worked as a Power Generation Equipment Repairer and Materials Handler. While completing my college degree, I also worked in an internship at a local hospital related to engineering maintenance. I have operated forklifts, and I am proficient in identifying parts from specifications and technical manuals. In addition to my work related to power plant maintenance in the U.S. Army, I have taken courses related to industrial maintenance, inventory control, and accounting principles.

In two separate positions with companies which specialized in heavy equipment rentals, I worked with construction industry companies to set up long-term leases and payment schedules. I am skilled at performing mathematical computations and have knowledge of accounting principles related to purchasing and warehouse operations. I have utilized computers with numerous software programs to verify shipments, control inventory, and track supplies and shipments. I have become skilled in working with vendors and in providing excellent customer service.

I am confident I would excel in handling inspection, quality control, and scheduling responsibilities for you as I have done for my previous employers, and I hope you will contact me to suggest a time when we might meet in person to discuss the position you are trying to fill. I can provide excellent references.

Sincerely,

Jackson Draughton

JACKSON DRAUGHTON

1110½ Hay Street, Fayetteville, NC 28305 • preppub@aol.com • (910) 483-6611

OBJECTIVE   To benefit an organization that can use a professional with technical knowledge and management ability along with strong decision-making, problem-solving, and communication skills.

EDUCATION   **Bachelor of Business Administration (B.B.A.),** San Diego State University, San Diego, CA, 1996.
- Coursework related to Management, Human Resources, Environmental Science, Public Speaking, Business Communication, and Economics.
- Received **Big South Conference Athlete Award;** named **Team Most Valuable Player.** Graduated from San Diego Senior High School where I was voted **Conference Most Valuable Player** in Wrestling.

Technical: Excelled in professional training related to reading blueprints and electrical schematics; completed extensive training related to power generation equipment and systems repair and maintenance management, U.S. Army and National Guard.
- Am skilled at identifying parts from specifications and technical manuals.

Customer Service and Sales: Completed training sponsored by my employers.

COMPUTERS   Use computers to verify shipments, control inventory, track supplies ordered, maintain records.

EXPERIENCE   **CUSTOMER SERVICE REPRESENTATIVE.** Prime Rentals and Prime Equipment, San Diego, CA (1998-2000). Served an existing customer base while developing new accounts in the construction industry; worked with construction companies and electrical contractors in setting up long-term leases for construction equipment such as backhoes and bulldozers.
- Determined payment schedules; performed mathematical computations daily.

EQUIPMENT COORDINATOR. Hertz Equipment Rental, San Diego, CA (1996-98). Frequently functioned as Acting General Manager in the absence of the General Manager while handling a variety of duties; served a customer base of construction industry companies to whom we rented equipment and sold supplies.
- Provided quotations while also providing pre-order and post-order technical and administrative support for the field sales staff; assessed market conditions and analyzed data; formulated sales plans for specific geographic areas and for periods of known cyclical fluctuation.
- Prepared and maintained rental/lease agreements; handled collections when needed.
- Utilized a computer daily to maintain customer and account information.
- Negotiated prices, payment schedules, financial terms, and other matters.

ENGINEERING MAINTENANCE INTERN. San Diego State University, San Diego, CA (1993-95). While completing my college degree, completed an **internship related to engineering maintenance** at a local hospital; repaired and maintained ceiling tiles, sinks, and drains; planned preventive maintenance.

POWER GENERATION EQUIPMENT REPAIRER & MATERIALS HANDLER. U.S. Army, Ft. Dix, NJ (1988-92). Maintained and repaired 40 diesel generator systems throughout the organization while assigning work duties to junior employees; operated forklifts.
- Inspected paperwork; utilized a computer daily for entering customer data.
- Served with distinction in the Persian Gulf War; received Army Commendation Medal.
- Selected for advanced management training and Primary Leadership Course.

PERSONAL   Resourceful individual with strong combination of technical knowledge and management skills. Can provide excellent personal and professional references on request.

GOAL: Seeking a Change But (Probably) Staying in the Same Industry

Date

Exact Name of Person
Exact Title
Exact Name of Company
Address
City, State, Zip

Cosmetics Sales, Cosmetologist Seeking Outside Sales

This cosmetologist is seeking a sales position in the beauty and makeup products line. Her ideal situation would be a position in outside sales selling premier-line cosmetology products to salons and other establishments.

Dear Exact Name of Person (or Dear Sir or Madam if answering a blind ad):

With the enclosed resume, I would like to make you aware of my extensive cosmetics and cosmetology knowledge as well as my desire to put that knowledge to work for your organization in some role in which I could contribute to your bottom line.

As you will see from my resume, I have completed extensive training related to numerous premier-line cosmetics courses and seminars from cosmetics industry firms such as Lancôme, Mary Kay, Aveda, Sebastian/Trucco, and Goldwell. I am a CO State Board licensed Cosmetologist, and I am the graduate of a 1500-hour Cosmetology certification course. I also hold an Associate of Arts degree in Fashion Merchandising.

Currently working as a freelance Beauty Consultant/Makeup Artist, I worked previously for Lancôme Cosmetics in California and Nevada, where I created innovative displays and merchandising concepts while coordinating fashion shows and special events to market Lancôme products. I also worked for Lancôme Cosmetics in Colorado, where I played a key role on a sales team which generated the highest sales of all military exchanges in the U.S. while working at Ft. Carson.

In earlier experience in the cosmetology industry, I excelled as a Cosmetologist with Galliard's Hair Design in Colorado and I also worked in Nebraska as a Salon Manager and Cosmetologist. While at the Marriot Grand Hotel & Salon in Lincoln, NE, I interviewed and hired employees while managing all aspects of a salon catering to high-end customers.

If you can use my considerable sales and customer service experience, I hope you will contact me to suggest a time when we might meet to discuss your needs. I can assure you in advance that I can provide excellent references.

Sincerely,

Samantha T. Yurko

SAMANTHA T. YURKO

1110½ Hay Street, Fayetteville, NC 28305 • preppub@aol.com • (910) 483-6611

OBJECTIVE   To benefit an organization that can use an enthusiastic sales professional with exceptional communication and organizational skills who offers a track record of accomplishment as a premier-lines cosmetics advisor, consultant, aesthetician, and salon manager.

EDUCATION   **Associate of Arts in Fashion Merchandising,** Long Beach City College, Long Beach, CA, 1990. Graduated from a 1500-hour Cosmetology certification course, Boulder Technical Community College, Boulder, CO 1992.
Completed numerous premiere-lines cosmetics courses and seminars, including:
- Mary Kay Beauty Seminar, 40-hour course in product line, sales, and productivity.
- Lancôme Cosmetics Beauty Seminars, 120 hours; trained in proper application, developed knowledge of product lines, learned sales and merchandising techniques.
- Redken Color Class, 80 hours; learned proper application, product lines, sales techniques.
- Sebastian/Trucco Hair Academy, 160 hours; trained in product lines, sales techniques, and proper application of Sebastian Hair and Trucco Cosmetics products.
- Goldwell Color Class & Color Analysis, 80 hours; learned hair coloring, highlighting, and color-matching techniques.

LICENSES   Colorado State Board licensed Cosmetologist, 1992-present.

AFFILIATIONS   Member, Colorado Medical Society Alliance, 1998-present.
Member, Boulder Area Chamber of Commerce, 1999-present.
Patron, Colorado Museum of Arts, 1995-1999.
Member, National Association of Business Women's League.

EXPERIENCE   **BEAUTY CONSULTANT & MAKEUP ARTIST.** Boulder, CO (1998-present). Freelance.

BEAUTY ADVISOR and **FREELANCE MAKEUP ARTIST.** Lancôme Cosmetics, California and Nevada (1998). Performed cosmetic makeovers and facials, presenting Lancôme's premier line of cosmetics to customers and training them in techniques for applying makeup.
- Created innovative and effective displays and merchandising concepts; coordinated fashion shows and other special events to present Lancôme products to potential customers.
- Developed strong relationships with clients, generating repeat customers and sales of Lancôme products; met or exceeded all store, district, and regional sales quotas.
- Monitored sales and inventory to ensure a strong in-stock position on fast-moving items.
- Provided service to Lancôme clients, averaging eight makeovers per four hour shift.

MARKETING REPRESENTATIVE. Lancôme Cosmetics, Ft. Carson, CO (1997-1998). Performed inventory control, merchandising, customer service, bookkeeping, and events promotion while professionally representing Lancôme's premiere line of cosmetics.
- Provided makeovers, manicures, facials, and Personal Image Consulting to new and existing Lancôme customers, generating sales of premiere line cosmetics.

COSMETOLOGIST. Galliard's Hair Design, Boulder, CO (1992-1997). Provided a full range of cosmetology, hair care, manicure/pedicure, and therapeutic massage services while assisting the management of this busy salon with bookkeeping, inventory control, and sales.

PERSONAL   Excellent personal and professional references are available upon request.

GOAL: Seeking a Change But (Probably) Staying in the Same Industry

Date

Exact Name of Person
Exact Title
Exact Name of Company
Address
City, State, Zip

Financial Services Sales, Applying for Internal Public Relations Position

Sometimes the best way to change careers is within your own organization! This young professional enjoys her company but seeks a change from a sales role to a public relations activity. She feels that her strengths lie in her strong written communication skills. She is applying for a newly created public relations position which will allow her to use her writing skills and company knowledge to sell the bank's products.

Dear Exact Name of Person: (or Dear Sir or Madam if answering a blind ad):

With the enclosed resume, I would like to make you aware of my education related to Mass Communications and Marketing as well as my in-depth knowledge of the bank's financial services. I am interested in applying for the Public Relations Coordinator position recently created, and I feel I am the ideal candidate for the position.

As you will see from my resume, I am presently employed by Citizen's Bank where I am respected for my exceptional sales and customer service skills as well as for my resourcefulness and attention to detail. In August 2000 I was a Pinnacle Club Recipient, an honor given in recognition of sales achievements. I was singled out for this award specifically for my second quarter sales of bank products ranging from credit cards, to home equity lines of credit, to new savings and checking accounts. Previously I excelled in jobs in retail management and sales.

With my extensive knowledge of the bank's operations as well as strong communication skills, I feel I would be the ideal candidate to serve as the bank's Public Relations Coordinator. I would enjoy the opportunity to talk with you in person to discuss your goals and how my background might serve your needs.

Sincerely,

Nancy Childs

NANCY CHILDS

1110½ Hay Street, Fayetteville, NC 28305   •   preppub@aol.com   •   (910) 483-6611

OBJECTIVE   To contribute analytical, communication, and problem-solving skills as well as expertise in managing fiscal and human resources to an organization that can use a mature detail-oriented professional with high levels of initiative and self-motivation.

EDUCATION & TRAINING   **B.S. degree, Mass Communications and Marketing,** Indiana State University, IN, 1991.
•   Completed a course in banking procedures sponsored by Citizen's Bank (1999), a Real Estate course leading to licensing by the State of Michigan (1991) and extensive training by K-Mart in management and financial operations.

COMMUNITY INVOLVEMENT   Am serving on a second task force with the Ridge County Partnership for Children and Families, Troy, MI: the current group is developing goals and guidelines for a mobile preschool unit while an earlier task force focused on the development of the organization's goals, objectives, and operational guidelines for a program called Child Care Connections.

EXPERIENCE   **FINANCIAL SERVICES SALES ASSOCIATE.** Citizen's Bank, Troy, MI (1998-present). Was recently honored by the bank's Pinnacle Club for **second quarter sales achievements** while excelling in a job which requires the adaptability to adjust to traveling between four different locations to provide financial services and sales support.
•   Utilize computer systems with proprietary software programs unique to banking.
•   Am known for my accuracy while balancing large amounts of funds to include weekly balancing of cash drawers and Automated Teller Machines (ATM).
•   Have been cited for my attention to detail while preparing a variety of daily reports and providing exceptional customer service.
•   Handle sales of a variety of bank products including credit cards, loans, credit lines, and home equity lines of credit as well as new checking and savings accounts.

RETAIL STORE ASSISTANT MANAGER. K-Mart Stores, Inc., Troy, MI (1993-97). Gained knowledge and built strong skills in all aspects of daily operations while overseeing the activities of up to 60 employees in 15 different departments.
•   Became skilled in reading and understanding a variety of financial statements from profit-and-loss, to inventory, to budget statements.
•   Was entrusted with the control of a successful and effective project which established and set up third-shift receiving procedures and operations.
•   Utilized computers daily basis for inventory control, accounting, budgeting, scheduling.

HUMAN RESOURCES AND CONTRACTING MANAGER. Megaforce Temporary Services, Birmingham, MI (1992-93). Developed business contracts and met with existing corporate customer representatives in order to understand their requirements and manage an office which provided skilled and qualified temporary personnel to order.
•   Developed and refined human resource management skills while interviewing and screening prospective employees and making decisions on their placement.
•   Learned how to market the organization and its services to prospective clients.
•   Refined time management skills in a simultaneous job as a supervisor/training specialist with Food Mart Stores: handled activities ranging from balancing registers, to making deposits, to opening or closing the store, to processing shipments, to managing funds.

PERSONAL   Have enrolled in a college Spanish class and am the only person on the bank staff who speaks enough Spanish to help the approximately 300 non-English speaking customers.

GOAL: Seeking a Change But (Probably) Staying in the Same Industry

Date

Exact Name of Person
Title or Position
Name of Company
Address (number and street)
Address (city, state, and zip)

Firearms Sales, Pawnshop Owner and Firearms Dealer Background

This entrepreneur found himself in a job hunt because his wife graduated from college and her job took them to a new city. He decided to try to represent one of the product lines which he used to purchase when he owned his own business.

Dear Sir or Madam:

With the enclosed resume, I would like to introduce the proven sales skills and extensive firearms industry knowledge which I could put at the disposal of your company.

As you will see, I recently sold a gun store which I transformed from an unprofitable company saddled with debt into a very profitable business with an excellent reputation.

As a former dealer, I am very familiar with your company's products, and I have dealt personally with salesmen and sales representatives from all manufacturers and distributors. I strongly believe that my sales skills and congenial personality were the keys to my success as a dealer, and I am certain I could be a highly effective representative of your products.

I have grown up around guns since I was a child. Before my father became a Baptist minister, he owned the largest firearms business in eastern KY, and I helped him with everything in the store. I have used the products of every manufacturer.

I attend gun shows frequently and have developed an extensive network of contacts and friends within the industry who know me and my fine personal reputation. I feel certain that I could make significant contributions to your bottom line through my expert product knowledge, outstanding personal reputation, and exceptional sales abilities. I am writing to you because I am familiar with your company's fine reputation, and I feel it would be a pleasure to become associated with your product line.

If you can use a dynamic and hard-working individual to complement your sales team, please contact me to suggest a time when we might meet to discuss your needs and how I could help you. I am married with no children, and I can travel as extensively as your needs require. Thank you for your consideration, and I look forward to hearing from you.

Sincerely,

Robbie J. Goins

ROBBIE J. GOINS

1110½ Hay Street, Fayetteville, NC 28305 • preppub@aol.com • (910) 483-6611

OBJECTIVE	To contribute to an organization that can use an experienced sales professional with expert knowledge of firearms products along with a network of outstanding relationships which I have developed with firearms dealers, manufacturers, and distributors who know of my fine reputation and trust me personally.

EXPERIENCE

Since 1989-present, have been associated with Carolina Firearms Sports, Inc.:

GENERAL MANAGER & SALESMAN. Carolina Firearms Sports, Inc., Matthews, SD (1989-present). In 1991, bought this company after working for the company as a Salesman for two years; continued as General Manager after selling the business in 2000.

- When I purchased the company, it was unprofitable and in debt; I relocated the company to a better market and utilized effective sales and management techniques to transform an ailing organization into a highly profitable and respected company which I sold in 2000.
- Combined my expert knowledge of manufacturers and distributors with my marketing sense in determining the correct inventory for the store; carried more than 1,000 individual guns and accessories needed by shooters.
- As a dealer, have become very familiar with the products, product lines, and sales policies of all manufacturers including Smith and Wesson, Ruger, Weatherby, Colt, Browning, and Winchester.
- Worked with distributors including Outdoor Sports Headquarters, Inc., Nationwide, Bill Hicks, Go Sportsman, Bangers, and Acusport.
- On a daily basis, used my common sense in solving uncommon problems.
- Strongly believe that my sales skills and congenial personality were the keys to my success in this business.

Other experience:

- **MANAGER.** Traders Antiques, Vass, SD (1984-89). Managed all aspects of a small furniture refinishing business; personally handled sales and customer service.
- **SALESMAN.** Furniture Traders, Rowland, SD (1982-84). Upon graduation from high school, became employed by a furniture refinishing business and rapidly discovered that I have exceptional sales and customer relations skills.
- **GUN STORE ASSISTANT.** Quaker Neck Gun Exchange, Greenville, KY. As a young boy, grew up around guns since my father, who later became a Baptist minister, owned the largest firearms business in eastern KY.
- **LAW ENFORCEMENT OFFICER—Reserve.** (1988-97). As an unpaid volunteer, served as a reserve Law Enforcement Officer helping to enforce the law and keep the peace.

MEMBERSHIPS	Member, National Rifle Association; Member, Capel Baptist Church.
HOBBIES	Hunting, shooting, reloading, and collecting.
EDUCATION	Completed numerous courses in Law Enforcement, Matthews Technical Community College, Matthews, SD.
PERSONAL	Can provide outstanding references inside and outside the firearms industry. Am married with no children; will travel extensively if needed. Excel in establishing strong relationships.

GOAL: Seeking a Change But (Probably) Staying in the Same Industry

Date

Exact Name of Person
Title or Position
Name of Company
Address (number and street)
Address (city, state, and zip)

Food Industry Sales and Purchasing

In the first paragraph, this junior professional makes it clear that he is relocating to Seattle. Although his background will be of interest to food companies, his experience in sales and purchasing is transferable to other fields.

Notice that, although he has a license to sell Life and Health insurance, he doesn't plan on approaching the insurance industry, so his license is shown in a low-key fashion in the Personal section of his resume rather than in a separate License section.

Dear Exact Name of Person: (or Sir or Madam if answering a blind ad.)

With the enclosed resume, I would like to make you aware of the considerable sales and purchasing experience which I could put to work for your company. I am in the process of relocating to Seattle, and I believe my background is well suited to your company's needs.

As you will see from my resume, I have been excelling as the purchasing agent for a large wholesale food distributor with a customer base of schools, restaurants, and nursing homes throughout the western states. While negotiating contracts with vendors and handling the school lunch bid process, I have resourcefully managed inventory turnover in order to optimize inventory levels while maximizing return on investment. I have earned a reputation as a prudent strategic planner and skillful negotiator.

In a prior position as a Sales Trainer and Sales Representative with a food industry company, I increased sales from $250,000 to $1.3 million and won the Captain Max award given to the company's highest-producing sales representative.

With a B.S. degree, I have excelled in continuous and extensive executive training in the areas of financial management, purchasing, contract negotiation, and quality assurance.

I can provide outstanding personal and professional references at the appropriate time, and I hope you will contact me if you can use a resourceful hard worker with a strong bottom-line orientation. I am in the Seattle area frequently and could make myself available to meet with you at your convenience. Thank you in advance for your time.

Sincerely,

Benjamin Brainerd

BENJAMIN BRAINERD

Until 12/15/00: 1110½ Hay Street, Fayetteville, NC 28305   (910) 483-6611

After 12/16/00: 538 Pittsfield Avenue, Seattle, WA 89023   (805) 483-6611

OBJECTIVE

To benefit an organization that can use my exceptionally strong sales and marketing skills as well as my background in purchasing, inventory management, and contract negotiation.

EDUCATION

Bachelor of Science Degree, Denver University, Denver, CO, 1980.
- Majored in Health and Physical Education
- Minor in Business Administration

Graduated from W.G. DuBois High School, Denver, CO.
- Was named one of the "Ten Most Outstanding Seniors."
- Was selected to receive the Cayman Sportsmanship Award during my senior year. This award is presented annually to only one athlete in the Denver area.
- Earned varsity letters in football, basketball, and baseball.

EXPERIENCE

PURCHASING MANAGER. Culloughby Co., Denver, CO (1993-present). For this wholesale food distributor with a customer base of schools, nursing homes, and restaurants throughout the western states, purchase $750,000 of canned, dry, and staple goods.
- Am responsible for turning the inventory and maximizing return on investment (ROI); have resourcefully developed methods of purchasing products in a timely manner in order to optimize inventory turnover and ROI.
- Have earned a reputation as a skilled negotiator in the process of negotiating contract pricing as well as other terms and conditions with vendors.
- Have acquired eight years of experience with school lunch bid process; conduct product availability research, secure guarantee bid pricing, handle bid quoting.
- Utilize a computer with Target software for purchasing activities.

SALES REPRESENTATIVE. Mason Brothers, Denver, CO (1986-1993). Sold portion control meat and seafood to established and newly developed accounts.

SALES REPRESENTATIVE & SALES TRAINER. Bryan Foods, Bodega Bay, CA (1979-1986). Excelled in numerous positions of responsibility related to sales and sales management during my eight years with this company.
- As a Sales Representative, boosted annual sales from $250,000 to $1.3 million.
- As "Equipment and Supplies Specialist," initiated sales efforts in the western California region and helped produce sales in excess of $200,000 during the first quarter of the 1985 fiscal year.
- As "Sales Representative," produced growth of over $900,000 in annual sales revenue between 1979 and 1984, which resulted in my winning the "Captain Max" Award, presented to the company's most outstanding salesperson.
- Managed and coordinated divisional sales meeting; trained sales personnel.

Other experience:
- As **Co-Manager** of a seafood restaurant in Denver, was in charge of hiring, training, scheduling, and supervising all employees.
- Worked as a **Sales Representative and Staff Manager** for Pilot Life Insurance Company in Los Angeles; sold life and health products and served as Staff Manager.

PERSONAL

Can provide outstanding references. Have been licensed to sell **Life and Health** insurance.

GOAL: Seeking a Change But (Probably) Staying in the Same Industry

Date

Exact Name of Person
Exact Title
Exact Name of Company
Address
City, State, Zip

**Furniture Sales,
Transitioning to Outside
Sales Position as a
Manufacturer's
Representative**

After a career in a family furniture business, this gentleman found himself in a job hunt when the business closed. When he decided that he most enjoyed sales as a functional area, he then determined that he would be happy in a job as a manufacturer's representative of the kinds of furniture lines his store used to sell. He used this resume and cover letter to approach furniture manufacturers.
P.S. He can omit paragraph four when approaching a company outside the furniture industry.

Dear Exact Name of Person: (or Dear Sir or Madam if answering a blind ad):

With the enclosed resume, I would like to make you aware of my extensive sales background and my interest in putting my expertise to work for your company.

As you will see from my resume, I have established a reputation as an articulate, personable, and persuasive communicator while functioning as Sales Manager and President of a small family-owned business which was recently sold. I have decided that I wish to embark on a full-time career in sales, and I am a proven sales performer. With an instinctive sales personality fortified by years of on-the-job training, I played a valuable role in building and maintaining the company's reputation for value and an emphasis on quality customer service. I have trained and developed numerous effective sales professionals.

Although I am single and would relocate according to your needs, I believe I could be of enormous use to a company which desired to employ my sales skills in the Shreveport and surrounding area. I offer an outstanding business reputation and would have a ready-made ability to network with key decision makers in the region.

You will notice from my resume that I offer an extensive background of knowledge and contacts related to the furniture and textile industry. I am knowledgeable of the product line and reputation of most furniture and appliance makers, and I am certain I would be highly effective in a manufacturer's representative role.

I hope you will welcome my call soon to try to arrange a brief meeting to discuss your goals and how my background might serve your needs. I can provide outstanding references at the appropriate time.

Sincerely,

Kenneth Soifer

Alternate Last Paragraph:
I hope you will write or call me soon to suggest a time when we might meet to discuss your needs and goals and how my background might serve them. I can provide outstanding references at the appropriate time.

KENNETH SOIFER ("KEN")

1110½ Hay Street, Fayetteville, NC 28305   •   preppub@aol.com   •   (910) 483-6611

OBJECTIVE

To contribute to an organization in need of an articulate, personable sales professional with expert knowledge of the effective methods of buying, merchandising, displaying, and selling furniture and of the value of providing quality service for a positive bottom-line impact.

EDUCATION

Earned a **B.A. in Business Administration,** Shreveport College, Shreveport, LA.

EXPERIENCE

SALES MANAGER & PRESIDENT. Smithson & Associates, Shreveport, LA (1988-present). In my first job after college, joined my family's business—a well-respected downtown furniture, hardware, and appliance retailer—and became thoroughly knowledgeable of all aspects of customer service and sales. Became highly respected by clientele interested in buying quality products at reasonable prices; sell furniture which ranged from promotional to medium high-end products.

- **Sales management:** Train and manage numerous sales representatives; personally lead the store in sales and personally handle the large-volume sales of up to $15,000 and more since those purchases usually involve financing arrangements.
- **Diverse product line:** Am thoroughly familiar with products from manufacturers which include:
    Furniture: Huntington House, Pioneer, Colony House, Standard, Bemco, Carolina, Florida, and Webb living rooms, dining rooms, and bedroom furniture
    Appliances: Magic Chef, White-Westinghouse, and Gibson
    Floor covering: Sentry Rug Co. and Armstrong linoleum
    Other: Holiday Lamp lamps and Lyon-Shaw outdoor furniture
- **Affiliations:** Hold membership in the Shreveport Chamber of Commerce, Servistar Corp., and other trade associations for retailers and furniture industry firms.
- **Excellent credit and accounting policies:** Play a highly visible role in helping the business maintain an excellent reputation for providing customers with value while selling good products at fair prices. Skillfully manage accounts payable.
- **Collections:** Handle the delicate issue of making collection calls and dealing with customers who are behind in their payments which are being financed internally.
- **Vendor relations:** Make decisions on which manufacturers can provide the best quality products for the cost and carry out purchasing activities; negotiate terms.
- **Customer service:** Recognized for my ability to establish trust with potential customers, ensure they receive one-on-one attention to their needs and financial circumstances and that they receive the highest quality of service.
- **Business management:** Became president in 1998 after several years as vice president; became skilled in the hiring, termination, and training of new employees.
- **Extensive trade contacts:** Attend numerous trade shows and am highly skilled in finding small manufacturers who can produce the type of goods which will appeal to the clientele we service.
- **Negotiating skills:** Played the key role in negotiating the sale of the business and the physical building in September 2000.

AFFILIATIONS

Hold memberships in organizations which include the Shreveport Chamber of Commerce and furniture and hardware trade associations as well as the Knights of Columbus.

- Am a member of the Administrative Council of my church (United Shreveport Church).

PERSONAL

A native of Shreveport, graduated from Lawrence High School. Am single and available for travel and/or relocation. Enjoy a reputation for dedication, integrity, and high standards.

Date

Exact Name
Exact Title
Exact Name of Company
Exact Address
City, State, Zip

Industrial Products Sales and Sales Management

A short cover letter such as this one can be highly effective. This accomplished sales manager could transfer his skills and knowledge to numerous industries. "Short and sweet" could describe this cover letter which makes powerful points about how he has developed new territories, improved margins, and boosted profit.

Dear Exact Name:

With the enclosed resume, I would like to introduce myself and the substantial sales and marketing background I could put to work for you.

As you will see, I offer a proven track record of outstanding results in producing a profit, improving the profit margin, developing new accounts, increasing market share, satisfying customers, and expanding territories. In my current position, I have developed a new territory while training and managing an eight-person sales staff. I am contributing significantly to the company's bottom line through my results in delivering a 40% profit margin. Prior to being recruited for my current position, I was part of a four-person team which boosted sales 15% at a plant in Toronto.

I am known for my ability to creatively and resourcefully apply my considerable knowledge, and I am always on the lookout for new ways to refine my own selling techniques. I am confident of my ability to produce a highly motivated team of sales professionals.

If you can use my talents and knowledge, please contact me and I will make myself available for a meeting with you to discuss your needs and how I might help you. I can provide outstanding personal and professional references.

Sincerely,

Rodney Lewis

RODNEY LEWIS

1110½ Hay Street, Fayetteville, NC 28305 • preppub@aol.com • (910) 483-6611

OBJECTIVE To become a valuable member of an organization that can use an outgoing and highly motivated sales professional who offers a proven ability to produce a profit, improve the profit margin, develop new accounts, satisfy customers, as well as motivate employees.

EDUCATION Received Bachelor of Arts degree in **Psychology**, University of Miami, Miami, FL, 1986. Have excelled in numerous sales and sales management training programs sponsored by major industrial suppliers.
- Pride myself on my ability to creatively and aggressively apply any and all sales training.
- Have especially benefited from advanced training related to product marketing, cold calling and other sales skills, and techniques for increasing sales, profits, and motivation.

EXPERIENCE **SALES MANAGER.** TrueTest Supply Network, Macon, GA (1995-present). Was recruited by key marketing officials in the parent company for this job which has involved developing a new territory as well as hiring and supervising an eight-person sales staff.
- In addition to my management responsibilities, am actively involved in sales; call on colleges, major retailers, hospitals, military accounts, and large industrial facilities.
- Sell virtually any product needed for the daily operations; provide products ranging from cleaning supplies to televisions, VCRs, refrigerators, nuts and bolts, and light bulbs.
- Have trained and organized the eight-person sales team so that it is now a sales machine known for outstanding product knowledge, customer service, and resourcefulness.
- Taught my sales peers how to improve profit in each sale by at least 5%.
- Have learned how to "work smart" in order to increase sales and sales calls by 32%.
- Trained sales personnel to establish aggressive goals and then helped them learn the practical tools which would help them achieve those goals.
- Am contributing significantly to the company's bottom line through my ability to deliver a 40% profit margin.

SALES MANAGER. Braxton & Co., Chicago, IL and Toronto, Canada (1993-95). Was recruited to join a four-person sales team responsible for increasing by 5% the sales of a plant in Toronto which was affiliated with a company with total annual sales of $368 million.
- Greatly exceeded management expectations and our targeted goals; increased sales by 15% instead of the projected 5%.
- Retrained sales personnel in Canada in all aspects of their jobs; significantly improved their ability to prospect for new commercial and retail accounts and refined their ability to close the sale.
- Personally established numerous new commercial accounts and dramatically expanded the territory which the company had been servicing.

SALES CONSULTANT & SALES REPRESENTATIVE. Dallas, TX (1986-93). Worked for one of the country's leading sales/marketing consulting firms; acted as a management consultant under contract with numerous companies that wanted expert help in expanding their territories, boosting sales, and improving profitability. Called on and established new retail and commercial accounts.

PERSONAL Am skilled at dealing with people and earning their confidence. Hard working, dependable, honest. Am always seeking new opportunities to improve my sales presentation skills. Known for my ability to creatively apply the knowledge I already have. Will relocate.

GOAL: "I'm changing fields but I have no idea what I want to do next..."

Date

Background in Sales and Consulting, Semi-Functional Resume

One interesting feature of this resume is that it is in a semi-functional format, which may interest those of you who are curious about functional resumes. Even his cover letter is set up in a functional format, so that he can identify key areas of competency to prospective employers.

Dear Sir or Madam:

With the enclosed resume, I would like to inquire about employment opportunities in your organization and make you aware of my extensive background related to sales and marketing, customer service, and management.

Sales, Customer Service, and marketing background

As you will see from my resume, I have most recently excelled in handling sales and customer service responsibilities in both the financial services and automobile sales field. In my earliest positions as an Auto Sales Representative, I refined my communication and negotiating skills and then advanced in a track record of accomplishment as a Sales Manager and then General Sales Manager. In my current job in the financial services field, I am excelling as a Mortgage Consultant in a highly competitive marketplace, and I am known for my excellent communication and negotiating skills.

Experience in contracting and purchasing

In a previous job, I refined my decision-making and problem-solving skills as an Assistant Contract Officer. I was authorized to approve contracts under $500,000 for the procurement of goods and services, and I was commended for my ability to maintain excellent working relationships while overseeing strict quality assurance related to the expenditure of public money.

Military and security background

As a young airman in the Air Force, I proudly served my country and was entrusted with one of the nation's highest security clearances: Top Secret. After military service, I worked in the law enforcement and corrections field and continued to serve my country in the National Guard in administrative capacities.

I can provide outstanding references at the appropriate time, and I would enjoy an opportunity to talk with you in person about your needs. If you can use a versatile young professional who is accustomed to excelling in multifaceted complex assignments, I hope you will contact me. Thank you in advance for your time.

Yours sincerely,

Mark R. Graham

MARK R. GRAHAM

1110½ Hay Street, Fayetteville, NC 28305   •   preppub@aol.com   •   (910) 483-6611

OBJECTIVE
I want to contribute to an organization that can use an accomplished sales professional who offers a proven ability to establish strong working relationships, generate profitable bottom-line results, and provide outstanding customer service.

EDUCATION
College: Completed three years of college at these institutions: studied **General Studies** and **Sociology**, Boston College, MA; studied **Business Administration**, Northeastern University, MA; and studied **Business Administration**, Boston Business College, MA.
Military Training: Completed technical training and professional development courses sponsored by the U.S. Air Force; areas studied included administration and operations management.
Sales: Completed numerous courses related to sales and customer service sponsored by my employers.

EXPERIENCE
Sales and Financial Field:
MORTGAGE CONSULTANT. New England Mortgage, Brookline, MA (1997-present). As a mortgage consultant for a regional mortgage brokerage company, provide services related to debt consolidation while refinancing VA, FHA, conforming, and nonconforming loans.

GENERAL SALES MANAGER. Peter David Used Cars, Lexington, MA (1995-97). Was recruited by the founder of the company to serve as his General Sales Manager; supervised up to 10 sales professionals including assistant sales managers.
- Trained sales professionals in winning techniques related to sales and customer service.
- Helped my sales staff become skilled at "closing the sale" and negotiating final details.

SALES MANAGER. Revere Chrysler-Suzuki, Lexington, MA (1994-95). Was credited with being a major force in helping the company achieve gross sales of $32 million a year along with an extremely healthy after-tax income.
- Resigned from this job when I was recruited by my former employer, Peter David, to become his General Sales Manager.

Corrections and Law Enforcement Field:
CORRECTIONAL OFFICER. (1977-84). Worked in a 1,000-man corrections facility in Maryland State Penitentiary, Potomac, MD and in the Bethesda City Jail, Bethesda, MD.

Contracting and Finance Field:
ASSISTANT CONTRACT OFFICER. Defense Control Administrative Services, Bethesda, MD (1974-77). Was authorized to approve contracts under $500,000 for the procurement of goods and services for the U.S. government; refined my communication and negotiating skills while fine-tuning the details of complex contracts.

Military Service:
ADMINISTRATIVE SPECIALIST. Strategic Air Command, Andrews AFB, MD (1970-74). Held a Top Secret security clearance and was entrusted with receiving Top Secret documents and other classified documents. Was promoted rapidly from Airman to Sergeant.

PERSONAL
Enjoy helping others and being in business situations in which my product knowledge can help consumers make a wise decision about products and services. Have proven my ability to provide the finest customer service in a highly competitive marketplace.

Date

Exact Name of Person
Title or Position
Name of Company
Address (number and street)
Address (city, state, and zip)

Background in Property Management

Although the Objective on the resume is versatile and all-purpose, just in case she wishes to job-hunt outside the property management field.

Dear Exact Name of Person: (or Dear Sir or Madam if answering a blind ad.)

With the enclosed resume, I would like to indicate my interest in your organization and my desire to utilize my management skills for your benefit.

As you will see from my resume, I offer extensive experience in property management and am known for my strong bottom-line orientation. You will notice that I have handled all aspects of property management including administration, maintenance management, public relations, inspection and inventory control, as well as collections and delinquency management.

I hope you will welcome my call soon to arrange a brief meeting at your convenience to discuss your current and future needs and how I might serve them. Thank you in advance for your time.

Sincerely yours.

Dianne Jones Weaver

Alternate last paragraph:
I hope you will call or write me soon to suggest a time convenient for us to meet and discuss your current and future needs and how I might serve them. Thank you in advance for your time.

DIANNE JONES WEAVER

1110½ Hay Street, Fayetteville, NC 28305 • preppub@aol.com • (910) 483-6611

OBJECTIVE
I want to contribute to an organization that can use a highly motivated self-starter who offers strong public relations and communication skills along with experience in managing people, property, finances, and daily business operations.

EXPERIENCE
PROPERTY MANAGER. Bladenboro Apartment Community, Canby, OR (1997-present). While managing this large apartment complex, raised and maintained occupancy by 17% in a 6-month interval.
- Collect rent, make deposits, and balance books at end of each month.
- Prepare activity, occupancy, and market reports for Broker-in-Charge and property owner.
- Maintain a monthly operating budget and explain any variances; manage a budget of $82,000.
- Coordinate with contractors and oversee all maintenance on units; lease apartment, process applications, and expedite lease agreements.

Began with The Affiliated Real Estate Consortium in 1992, and excelled in handling both sales/marketing and property management responsibilities on a large scale:
PROPERTY MANAGER. The Affiliated Real Estate Consortium, Property Management Department, Canby, OR (1992-1997). Excelled as a property manager for one of the area's most well-known real estate/property management firms; was responsible for an inventory of between 180 to 200 residences.
- *Maintenance Management*: Supervised maintenance activities; coordinated and scheduled staff and independent contractors; obtained estimates for work to be performed and monitored major repairs as work proceeded.
- *Public Relations*: Screened potential residents and conducted rental showings.
- *Inspections and Inventory*: Conducted biannual inspections of every property and conducted house inventories; ordered goods and materials as needed.
- *Administration*: Prepared reports for top management while also preparing lease renewals, inspection reports, and other paperwork.
- *Court Liaison*: Handled evictions and represented the company in small claims court.
- *Negotiation*: Mediated between owners and tenants as needed in situations where disputes arose over damages, security deposits, or rent owed.
- *Accomplishments*: Made significant contributions to office operations through my talent for organizing office policies and procedures; brought more than 125 new properties into management.

REALTOR. The Johnson Agency Realtors, Canby, OR (1990-92). Became a $1.2 million dollar producer within 12 months!
- Gained valuable skills in sales, marketing, and contract negotiating while acquiring expert knowledge of most aspects of the real estate business.

OFFICE ADMINISTRATOR. Killeen Real Estate Corp., Killeen, TX (1989-90). Handled a wide range of activities for this real estate company.
- Processed sales contracts and revisions; verified sales prices, financing, option pricing, and lot premiums with approved documents; deposited and accounted for all earnest money received; prepared sales, closings, and construction reports; maintained land files including settlement statements and title insurance commitments.
- Compiled information on approved houses for start of construction; handled building permits, color selections, and related matters; ordered trusses, brick, and cable; issued job assignments and construction schedules; assembled and evaluated plans and specifications for use by real estate appraisers.

PERSONAL
Can provide outstanding personal and professional references on request.

GOAL: "I'm changing fields but I have no idea what I want to do next..."

Date

Exact Name of Person
Exact Title
Exact Name of Company
Address
City, State, Zip

Dear Exact Name of Person (or Dear Sir or Madam if answering a blind ad):

With the enclosed resume, I would like to make you aware of my interest in becoming associated with your fine product line in a sales role. Although I have excelled in retail management for the past 13 years with Macy's, I have decided that I wish to change careers and embark on a career in sales. I am particularly interested in your product line and would like to explore suitable opportunities with you.

Until a few weeks ago, I excelled in a track record of advancement with the Macy's organization, where I started as a management trainee and advanced into a senior management position in charge of 25 individuals. After earning my undergraduate degree in Business Administration with a minor in Economics, I was attracted to the Macy's organization because of its tradition of regarding its managers as profit centers and treating them essentially as entrepreneurs.

Although I was excelling in my job and held in high regard, I made the decision to resign from Macy's recently for two reasons: first, I wanted to spend a few weeks caring full-time for my widowed mother, who had undergone a serious operation, and second, I had decided that I wished to pursue a career in sales. I left on excellent terms and can provide outstanding personal and professional references within the Macy's organization including from my immediate supervisor, Bob Kleinstein, who would gladly welcome me back at any time.

While performing my buying function at Macy's, I became aware of your fine products and I would enjoy discussing with you the possibility of my representing your products to retailers such as Macy's.

I am single and would cheerfully travel as your needs require. If you feel that my skills and background might be of interest to you, I hope you will contact me to suggest a time when we might meet in person to discuss your needs.

Sincerely yours,

Nells Acampora

NELLS ACAMPORA

1110½ Hay Street, Fayetteville, NC 28305 • preppub@aol.com • (910) 483-6611

OBJECTIVE

To benefit an organization that can use an experienced manager who offers a background in managing budgets and performing financial analysis, buying and controlling inventory, supervising personnel, and handling public relations.

EDUCATION

Bachelor of Arts, Business Administration major with a minor in Economics, Newark College, Newark, NJ, 1987.
Pursuing MBA in my spare time from Davidson University, Davidson, NJ.
Completed extensive management training sponsored by Macy's.

EXPERIENCE

Excelled in a track record of promotion at Macy's Department Store in Newark, NJ; recently resigned from Macy's in order to devote my full time to caring for my widowed mother in the aftermath of a serious operation, and to seek a career outside retailing.

- **Resigned under excellent conditions; can provide an outstanding reference from Bob Kleinstein, my immediate supervisor, and from numerous other Macy's executives.**

1995-2000: SENIOR MERCHANDISE MANAGER. Was promoted to manage 25 sales associates while controlling a $5 million inventory; this position placed me in charge of this large-volume Children's Department; also managed the Home and Infant Departments.

- Interviewed and hired new sales associates.
- Consistently increased department sales by a minimum of 5% annually.
- In the Macy's environment, the Senior Merchandise Manager is in an essentially entrepreneurial role and, unlike in most department stores, the Senior Manager undertakes the buying function; performed extensive liaison with suppliers and manufacturers who acted as vendors to Macy's.
- Prepared business plans four times a year; reviewed goals monthly.
- While performing in the role of Senior Manager/General Manager, have been extensively involved in leadership and public relations roles in the community; worked with the YMCA to coordinate a "Kid of the Year" event.

1994: PROJECT MANAGER. Because of my reputation as an excellent communicator and public speaker, was selected to take on a special project related to implementing a new Designer Implementation Program; as coordinator of this program, traveled extensively to talk with store managers.

- Was commended for my ability to articulate the concepts of this new program in ways managers could understand.

1993: MANAGER. Men's Clothing and Men's Accessories.
1992: MANAGER. Infant Department.
1991: MANAGER. Housewares Department.
1989-91: MANAGEMENT TRAINEE. Was attracted by Macy's outstanding management training program and by the opportunity as a manager to function in an essentially entrepreneurial role with broad decision-making abilities after advancing into management.

MERCHANDISE MANAGER. Penney's, Newark, NJ (1985-89). Worked part-time at Penney's for two years while completing my college degree which I earned in 1987.

- Received the Manager's Award for achievement in hourly productivity.

PERSONAL

Am seeking a career outside retailing primarily so I can attend classes two nights a week in pursuit of my MBA. Work well under pressure and am known for attention to detail. Proficient with Word. Single; will travel extensively. Excellent references.

Date

Exact Name of Person
Title or Position
Name of Company
Address (number and street)
Address (city, state, and zip)

Retail Store Management, Transitioning into Another Industry

A desire to finish her degree is what has prompted this experienced retail manager to look for employment outside retailing.

Dear Exact Name of Person: (or Dear Sir or Madam if answering a blind ad.)

With the enclosed resume, I would like to indicate my interest in your organization and my desire to explore employment opportunities.

As you will see from my enclosed resume, I am an experienced manager of people, assets, and financial resources. In my current position I am managing the store which is the Top Volume Store in sales in the region. Although I am excelling in my current position and am held in high regard by upper management, I am interested in transferring my considerable management skills to another industry.

I hope you will welcome my call soon to arrange a brief meeting at your convenience to discuss your current and future needs and how I might serve them. Thank you in advance for your time.

Sincerely yours.

Gerry Reeves

Alternate last paragraph:
I hope you will call or write me soon to suggest a time convenient for us to meet and discuss your current and future needs and how I might serve them. Thank you in advance for your time.

GERRY REEVES

1110½ Hay Street, Fayetteville, NC 28305 • preppub@aol.com • (910) 483-6611

OBJECTIVE   To benefit an organization that can use a persuasive and dynamic professional who combines outstanding sales and marketing abilities, management experience, and a proven ability to make sound decisions and achieve ambitious bottom-line goals.

EDUCATION   Completing Bachelor's degree in my spare time at night; completed three years (98 credit hours) of course work from Baptist College, Austin, TX with a concentration in Marketing. Have excelled in numerous management and executive development training programs.

EXPERIENCE   **STORE MANAGER.** Toys "R" Us, Denton, TX (1996-present). Manage up to 50 employees while controlling a $625,000 inventory level and maintaining tight operational control of a $2 million store.
- Am managing the store which is considered the Top Volume Store in sales in the entire region.
- Have hired, trained, and developed several managers who have gone on to become key management professionals for the Toys "R" Us chain.
- Increased profit margin from 37% to 39.2% in a one-year period while also increasing profit by $15,000 year-to-date through effective cost-cutting measures on store-controlled expenses without jeopardizing overall store productivity.
- Although I am highly regarded in my current position and enjoy the fast pace of this bustling retail environment, I am seeking an equally challenging position which will fully energize my leadership and energy while permitting me to complete, in my spare time, the year of studies remaining for my college degree.

MANAGER. Fashion Coordinators, San Antonio, TX (1996). Was recruited by this company to take over its multiunit operations; raised sales at the Dellwood Park Mall location 80% over the previous year's figures in my first month supervising that location, and then played a key role in closing the Centerfield Mall location.
- At the Centerfield Mall location, inventoried equipment, supplies, and client records and selected team members to be transferred.
- Was successful in raising sales average from $120-130 per client to $190-200 per client consistently per pay period.
- Sought new acquisitions in client base to increase business, and serviced existing clients with a standard of excellence in customer service; was effective in statistical management, including sales average, client survey scores, and payroll management.

SENIOR STORE MANAGER. The Paladium, San Antonio, TX (1992-96). Worked alone with no direct supervision on implementing company guidelines and goals among three stores generating $2.3 million in sales.
- Promoted to Senior Store Manager after consistently exceeding expectations in all aspects of managing overall operations
- Set sales goal and payroll allocations with given budget among the three stores.
- Kept shortage levels consistently under goal, and brought a high-shortage store down from a 3.8% shortage to .96% in a six-month period.
- Was the Liaison between corporate and six stores in Texas through 4th Quarter.

CO-MANAGER. New York Fashions & Accessories, Houston, TX (1990-92). Supervised the daily operations of a store with annual sales exceeding $1.5 million after being promoted from Assistant Manager to Co-Manager in a 10-month period; responsible for productivity of a 13-member sales team, and led by example with personal sales always exceeding given goals.
- Organized and presented merchandise to create a unique fashion image tailored by watching customer trends.
- Utilized available fixtures and equipment for optional usage.

PERSONAL   Excellent references on request.

GOAL: "I'm changing fields but I have no idea what I want to do next..."

Date

Exact Name of Person
Exact Title
Exact Name of Company
Address
City, State, Zip

Teacher

Dear Exact Name of Person: (or Dear Sir or Madam if answering a blind ad):

Employers are *very* inquisitive about why you want to make a change. The way you present yourself on a resume will influence how the potential employer "sees" you. For that reason, this teacher says very little about teaching and emphasizes previous experience.

With the enclosed resume, I would like to make you aware of my background as a dynamic and articulate professional whose exceptional skills in developing, coordinating, and marketing programs and services have been proven in a variety of challenging environments.

Although I have recently excelled as an English teacher in the Salt Lake City School system, you will see from my resume that I have previously marketed my skills in a number of different venues, achieving success through my natural leadership and exceptional sales ability. While simultaneously running a prosperous business as a private instructor in music, language arts, and gymnastics, I planned, developed, coordinated, and marketed the "Jump the Gun" athletic readiness program. In addition to producing the fliers and other marketing materials, I made "cold calls" to local child care center directors and civic officials, as a result of which I "sold" the program to a number of child development centers and to the Salt Lake City Parks & Recreation Department.

Although I am highly regarded as an educator and can provide exceptional personal and professional references at the appropriate time, I am very interested in exploring career opportunities in the areas of sales and marketing. When we have the opportunity to meet in person, I think you will agree that my outgoing personality, strong bottom-line orientation, and energetic, "take-charge" attitude would be well suited to a selling environment.

If you can use a motivated professional with exceptional problem solving skills and the proven ability to sell ideas and services, I hope you will welcome my call soon to arrange a brief meeting to discuss your goals and how my background would serve your needs.

Sincerely,

Chris M. Vogt

Alternate Last Paragraph:
If you can use a motivated professional with exceptional problem solving skills and the proven ability to sell ideas and services, I hope you will write or call me soon to suggest a time when we might meet to discuss your needs and goals and how my background might serve them.

CHRIS M. VOGT

1110½ Hay Street, Fayetteville, NC 28305 • preppub@aol.com • (910) 483-6611

OBJECTIVE To benefit an organization that can use an articulate, experienced professional with exceptional planning and organizational skills who offers skills related to .sales and marketing, public relations, and project management.

EDUCATION **Bachelor of Science** in **Education**, with a major in Language Arts, Dixie College, St. George, UT, 1991.

EXPERIENCE **ENGLISH TEACHER** and **VOLLEYBALL COACH.** Childs High School, Salt Lake City, UT (1998-present). Provided classroom instruction in English and American Literature as well as in grammar and composition to eleventh and twelfth grade students and served as coach for the volleyball team.

MUSIC and **PHYSICAL FITNESS & COORDINATION INSTRUCTOR.** Self-employed (1986-1998). In addition to marketing my skills as a private piano and language arts instructor, also developed, successfully marketed, and was contracted to implement an athletic skills development program at child development centers as well as through the Salt Lake City Parks & Recreation Department.
- Designed, planned, and implemented the "Jump the Gun" program, an athletic readiness skills program for classes of up to 15 students ages three to seven.
- Developed and produced informational flyers and other marketing and promotional materials for the program.
- Succeeded in "selling" the program to child development centers and to the Salt Lake City Parks & Recreation Department, which implemented it at several Recreation Centers; made "cold calls" to local child care directors and civic officials to present the program.
- Trained and directed the work of two teaching assistants in addition to coordinating the advertising, curriculum development, and class schedules for the program.
- Devised a program using piano and gymnastics to assist children with visual perception problems or dyslexia in overcoming obstacles and understanding "how" to learn.
- Instructed high school students privately in English grammar and composition, with a special emphasis on the elements of effective essay writing.
- Expanded my business to the point that prospective students had to be placed on a waiting list, through advertising in newsletters of home schooling resources.
- While serving as a Gymnastics Instructor for a summer nonprofit program, taught classes of up to 25 underprivileged students the rudiments of gymnastics; devised curriculum for the course and trained teaching assistants.

EDUCATIONAL SERVICES COORDINATOR. Cubby Hole, Salt Lake City, UT (1996). In this challenging temporary position, was recruited to serve as facilitator and coordinator for tours of up to 500 students attending this traveling exhibit of robotic dinosaurs.
- Tasked with resolving logistical problems and performing liaison between the exhibit's management and local tour organizers, successfully handled scheduling conflicts.

Highlights of earlier experience: Excelled in earlier positions as a **FREELANCE TECHNICAL WRITER** preparing proposals for an engineer, **VETERINARY ASSISTANT** at a local animal clinic, and **SOCCER COACH** for the Youth Soccer League.

PERSONAL Former member of the Dixie College gymnastics team and Instructor for Dixie College Recreation Department. Known for leadership ability and exceptional problem-solving skills.

GOAL: "I'm changing fields but I have no idea what I want to do next..."

Date

Exact Name of Person
Title or Position
Name of Company
Address (no., street)
Address (city, state, zip)

Teaching Background

Dear Exact Name of Person: (or Dear Sir or Madam if answering a blind ad.)

Teachers generally do well in career change situations because they usually offer strong communication skills. Here you see an all-purpose resume and cover letter that will help this professional explore opportunities in numerous fields.

I would appreciate an opportunity to talk with you soon about how I could contribute to your organization through my maturity, friendly and caring personality, and reputation as a resourceful professional with outstanding communication and organizational skills.

While most of my experience is in education and I am a successful classroom teacher, I have been singled out on numerous occasions to develop and manage special projects, contribute to management teams, and find solutions to problems. I have been chosen ahead of more experienced professionals to take over where others have been unsuccessful and correct problems where services are not up to standards.

In earlier jobs I displayed a different set of skills while involved in activities such as providing clerical, dispatching, and accounting support for businesses in the transportation field. I worked with people who were shipping their household goods and saw that all documentation was in compliance with government regulations. At a trucking company I processed requests, checked forms for accuracy, calculated and typed bills, and posted accounts receivable and payable.

I feel that I have proven myself capable of dealing with the public tactfully and graciously, communicating clearly and concisely both verbally and in writing, and making sound decisions quickly—abilities which would be valuable to organizations of any size or type. I feel that I am capable of bringing out the best in others as a team leader or contributor to a group's efforts.

I hope you will welcome my call soon to arrange a brief meeting at your convenience to discuss your current and future needs and how I might serve them. Thank you in advance for your time.

Sincerely yours,

Margaret Frances Stieg

MARGARET FRANCES STIEG

1110½ Hay Street, Fayetteville, NC 28305 • preppub@aol.com • (910) 483-6611

OBJECTIVE	To contribute to an organization that can use a mature professional known for possessing a friendly and enthusiastic personality and being truly interested in other people as well as for resourcefulness, creativity, and the ability to handle pressure, stress, and emergencies.
EDUCATION	**B.S., Elementary Education,** Butler University, Indianapolis, IN, 1995. • Completed additional course work in accounting, business law, and economics. • Maintained a GPA of at least 3.65 in all elementary education courses.
EXPERIENCE	**PROGRAM DEVELOPMENT SPECIALIST** and **EDUCATOR**. Toole County Board of Education, Indianapolis, IN (2000-01). Was handpicked by the school's principal to participate in leadership roles and develop special programs designed to build morale and self confidence in students on the basis of my success as a first-grade teacher.

- Displayed flexibility and managerial talents while participating on a site-based management team to fill a vacancy previously held by the assistant principal.
- Transformed the "Terrific Kids" program from complete disorganization and chaos to a respected, well-organized method of singling out children for their accomplishments.
- Coordinated the efforts of a committee which planned programs and assemblies honoring successful academic efforts, attendance records, and other achievements.
- Honed my organizational skills planning three assemblies each nine-weeks period to include decorating, ordering and stocking supplies, and assigning responsibilities to teachers and staff members in order to achieve success.
- Designed a form for maintaining statistics which in turn made preparing regular reports easier and less time consuming and helped in prioritizing for better time management.
- Selected to receive special training in developmental education, applied my communication skills while presenting county-wide staff development courses.
- Wrote a grant which was approved and resulted in funds for purchasing microscopes for first grade classes.
- Contributed the "voice" for a video produced by the county which is currently available at school libraries and is recommended for people moving into Toole County.
- Coordinated an international dinner which represented ten countries.
- Contributed my time as a teacher for an after-school reading program for fourth graders.

TEACHER. Toole County Board of Education, Indianapolis, IN (1995-2000). Was specially selected to step in after the school year had begun and provide continuity for reading and math classes for fourth-grade students.

- Provided guidance and supervision for two student teachers completing their internships by preparing lesson plans and gaining exposure in actual classroom settings.

Highlights of earlier experience: Gained practical work skills in summer jobs including marketing, inventory, accounting, and clerical support for a trucking company, clerk/typist for a transportation company, and as a lifeguard.

PERSONAL	In excellent health, am interested in physical fitness and hold certification in aerobics, creative floor work and conditioning, and choreography. Have demonstrated skills as a public speaker. Have been trained in first aid and have the ability to react quickly in emergencies. Enjoy working with IBM-compatible and Macintosh computers and plan to expand my knowledge of computer science.

GOAL: "I'm changing fields but I have no idea what I want to do next..."

Date

Teaching Background

Once you realize that the occupation or profession or career field isn't your "fit," you must take some action, even if it is simply exploring options. There is no reason to stay with a career field that you don't enjoy. This teaching professional is stressing management and problem-solving skills which should be transferable to most industries.

Dear Sir or Madam:

With the enclosed resume, I would like to express my interest in exploring employment opportunities with your organization and make you aware of my strong skills and abilities.

As you will see from my resume, I have earned a Bachelor of Science degree as well as a Master's degree, and I have applied my knowledge as a teacher. While I have thoroughly enjoyed the challenge of educating young minds and stimulating young children to excel academically, I have made the decision to change careers and transfer my skills into another arena. I have acquired a reputation as an outstanding communicator, problem solver, and organizer, and I can provide outstanding personal and professional references at the appropriate time.

During my leisure time, I have gravitated toward volunteer work in which I could contribute to the well being of others. With strong organizational skills as well as a high degree of intelligence, I have become skilled at managing projects which required me to make prudent decisions about the best use of scarce resources. I have been told numerous times during my life that I have a "natural" sales personality. Indeed, I believe much of what I did as a teacher was to "sell" concepts and ideas to both students and their families. While working on numerous school committees and task forces, I became known as a resourceful problem solver who could always be counted on to come up with fresh ideas about how to implement new programs.

If my considerable talents and skills interest you, I hope you will contact me to suggest a time when we might meet. I am sure that it would be an honor to learn more about your fine organization, and I hope I will have the pleasure of meeting you. Thank you in advance for your time and professional courtesies.

Yours sincerely,

Nancy Goguen

NANCY GOGUEN

1110 1/2 Hay Street, Fayetteville, NC 28305   •   preppub@aol.com   •   (910) 483-6611

OBJECTIVE

To benefit an organization that can use an articulate and outgoing professional with outstanding written and oral communication skills along with strong natural abilities in the areas of public relations, customer service, management, and sales.

EDUCATION

Master's degree in Education, Ohio State University, Columbus, OH, 1989.
Bachelor of Science in Social Service, Ohio State University, Columbus, OH, 1984. Completed two years of course work toward Master's degree in Counseling, Ohio University, Athens, OH.
Extensive training in arbitration, mediation, and conflict resolution techniques.

EXPERIENCE

EDUCATOR. Lockton Public Schools and Miller County Schools, Ohio (1997-00). Excelled in all aspects of this job teaching math, social studies, art, science, reading, and other subjects to second graders.
- Refined my management skills in training and supervising a Teacher's Assistant.
- Played a key role in developing programs to motivate students to excel while working as a member of the Motivational/Academic Committee.
- Served on the committee to develop intervention strategies for "at risk" students.
- Was well known for my nurturing and caring personality as well as for my ability to inspire and motivate students.

GRADUATE STUDENT. Ohio University, Athens, OH (1993-97). Worked part-time in customer service positions while also completing course work towards a Master's degree in Counseling.
- Learned how to counsel individuals experiencing marital, child rearing, spouse abuse, and employment problems.
- Gained knowledge related to administering the Strong-Campbell Interest Inventory and other tools designed to help job hunters figure out their best fit in the job market through determining their strongest interests.
- Completed a practicum in Career Counseling that included freshman orientation, Wittenburg University, fall 1995.

EDUCATOR. Ft. Goddard, OH (1987-93). At a military base, taught second and third grade.
- Became known as a highly creative problem solver and vibrant communicator while working with a population which was culturally diverse in nature.
- Because of my enthusiastic and outgoing nature, was appointed to numerous committees which developed new programs aimed at strengthening internal and external communication, motivating students to aim for excellence, and integrating new technology in the classroom.

Other experience: In my leisure time, have provided leadership to community organizations; was a popular counselor at the Women's Center in Athens.

COMPUTERS

Knowledgeable of computers and possess the ability to rapidly master new software and applications; familiar with Microsoft Word and conversant with Internet.

PERSONAL

Although I have loved teaching and excelled in educating young minds, I have decided that I wish to transfer my skills into a new arena in which I can contribute to an organization that can use a dynamic self-starter with unlimited personal initiative.

GOAL: "I'm changing fields but I have no idea what I want to do next..."

Date

Exact Name of Person
Title or Position
Name of Company
Address (number and street)
Address (city, state, and ZIP)

Dear Exact Name of Person: (or Dear Sir or Madam if answering a blind as.)

Can you use an energetic, and intelligent young professional who offers a reputation as a talented and persuasive communicator who can sell ideas and concepts to others? I am known as a detail-oriented individual who is determined to excel and provide a business with sound ideas and the organizational skills to carry those ideas to their successful completion.

As you will see from my enclosed resume, I have been effective in positions and volunteer roles which called for the ability to relate to others and often to persuade them to listen to my suggestions. With a keen eye for detail and strong time management abilities, I feel that my experience as an educator has given me a chance to hone skills which would effectively transfer to other industries.

While attending Atlanta Metropolitan College in Atlanta where I was a Dean's List student, I refined my time management skills while strengthening my public relations, communications, and project management abilities as a junior high school math tutor, coordinator for freshmen orientation activities, and volunteer in the pediatric section of the Emory University Hospitals.

From my resume you will gather the facts about my success as an educator, what may not be as obvious is the fact that I possess a strong interest in sales and marketing. I feel that the very qualities that have made me effective are readily transferable to other fields: a persuasive and informative style of communication, the ability to feel at ease and make others at ease in a variety of situations, and the dedication to quality apparent in everything I attempt.

I hope you will welcome my call soon to arrange a brief meeting at your convenience to discuss your current and future needs and how I might serve them. Thank you in advance for your time.

Sincerely yours.

Deirdre R. Hackett

DEIRDRE R. HACKETT

1110 ½ Hay Street, Fayetteville, NC 28305　•　preppub@aol.com　•　(910) 483-6611

OBJECTIVE

To offer a reputation as a detail-oriented, well-organized professional with excellent written and verbal communication and sales skills to a business in need of a quick thinker who is known as a talented manager of human, material, and fiscal resources.

EXPERIENCE

ADMINISTRATIVE AND PLANNING SPECIALIST and **CLASSROOM TEACHER.** Kappel Primary School, Atlanta, GA (1994-present).
As a fifth grade teacher, handle a wide variety of administrative, budgeting, public relations, and management activities in addition to preparing lessons and working with approximately 26 students on a daily basis.
- Helped prepare an annual operating budget: conducted research and prioritized needs resulting in $134,570 being allocated for personnel and $7,630 for maintenance.
- Wrote material which was used on local radio stations and excelled in selling my ideas on numerous subjects to others.
- Applied my organizational skills planning and carrying out events for 72 faculty and staff members as well as an awards banquet for 200 people including 75 students.

PROJECT COORDINATOR. Jaycees, Atlanta, GA (1995-present). Enjoy giving my time to help in planning and carrying out various service projects ranging from organizing a Halloween haunted trail, to visiting an area boys home, to participating in sharing ideas with other chapters, to planning a Christmas party for 200 people.

Strengthened public relations, communications, and organizational abilities while learning to manage my time effectively in part-time and volunteer positions while attending college:
TUTOR. Liza Middle School, Atlanta, GA (1993). As a volunteer for seventh grade math classes, prepared lessons and worked with at-risk students to help them improve their skills and learn how to develop good study habits.

ORIENTATION COUNSELOR. Atlanta Metropolitan College, Atlanta, GA (1993). Was selected to help in a program which provided incoming freshmen with guidance while they were becoming adjusted to college life: gave tours, provided information about campus facilities and activities, and addressed their questions and concerns.
- On my own initiative, approached representatives of major area companies to solicit contributions; gathered materials and assembled welcome packets.

PATIENT RELATIONS VOLUNTEER. Emory University, Atlanta, GA (1992). Was cited as a caring and compassionate individual while interacting with the parents of children who were hospital in-patients; organized games and spent time with children while also helping the parents by providing comfort and reassurance to parents.

CUSTOMER SERVICE SPECIALIST. The Riverside Cafe, Atlanta, GA (1992). Learned how to be patient, diplomatic, and courteous while dealing with the public.

EDUCATION

B.A., Psychology and Education, Atlanta Metropolitan College, Atlanta, GA, 1994.
- Placed on the Dean's List with a GPA above 3.5 for three semesters.

SKILLS

Excellent computer skills; highly proficient in Internet research.

PERSONAL

Working knowledge of the French language. Easily adapt to changing situations.

GOAL: "I'm changing fields but I have no idea what I want to do next..."

Date

Exact Name of Person
Exact Title
Exact Name of Company
Address
City, State, Zip

Textile Industry Changing to a New Industry

If you notice the first job on his resume, you will see that he doesn't go into much detail. He used this resume and cover letter to transition out of textile sales, so he didn't want to "talk the talk" of the textile industry. He wanted his resume and cover letter to work in a "generic" way, so that he could approach employers in any industry.

Dear Exact Name of Person (or Dear Sir or Madam if answering a blind ad):

With the enclosed resume, I would like to make you aware of my background in sales and management and express my interest in discussing the possibility of employment with your company. Although I am held in high regard in my current job and can provide an excellent reference at the appropriate time, I am writing confidentially and would appreciate your not contacting my current employer until after we talk.

I am currently excelling as an Area Sales Manager, and I have developed innovative marketing ideas for new products while establishing and maintaining effective working relationships with my accounts. In my previous experience, I worked as a supervisor for both Hanes and Clothes-Knit Industries. While with Clothes-Knit, I was promoted from a supervisory position to Technical Service Representative, a job which required me to resolve problems and issues among customers, sales, manufacturing, quality control, process development, and management. I have earned a reputation as an exceptionally strong problem solver with an ability to think strategically and operationally when tackling a complex issue.

While earning my Bachelor of Business Administration degree, I financed my college education by working at a prominent bakery, and upon college graduation I took over the management of this 12-employee operation with wholesale and retail accounts in several cities. I was instrumental in developing accounts with industry and convenience stores, and I developed and implemented innovative marketing strategies.

If you can use a versatile professional who has excelled in both sales and management positions in the textile industry as well as in other environments, I hope you will contact me to suggest a time when we might meet to discuss your needs and how I might serve them. Thank you in advance for your time.

Sincerely,

George Louik

GEORGE LOUIK

1110½ Hay Street, Fayetteville, NC 28305　　•　　preppub@aol.com　　•　　(910) 483-6611

OBJECTIVE　　To benefit an organization that can use an enthusiastic, highly motivated sales professional and experienced general manager with a proven ability to establish and maintain strong working relationships while utilizing my problem-solving and communication skills.

EDUCATION　　**Bachelor of Business Administration (BBA),** Texas State University, Austin, TX, 1989.
& TRAINING　　•　Minor in Economics and Management.
　　　　　　　　Excelled in sales and management training and professional development courses.

EXPERIENCE　　**AREA SALES MANAGER.** Lowe & Associates, Birmingham, AL (1999-present). Sell textile replacement and OEM parts to textile mills.

　　　　　　　　ACCOUNT REPRESENTATIVE. Mader, Inc., Dothan, AL (1998). Developed marketing ideas for new products while developing and maintaining effective working relationships with new and existing accounts; left the company when it went into Chapter 11.
　　　　　　　　•　Refined my ability to deliver the highest possible customer service by learning the function of our products in customers' operations, both fiberfill and nonwoven.
　　　　　　　　•　Became respected for my ability to communicate effectively both orally and in writing.

　　　　　　　　Was promoted in the following track record because of my exceptional bottom-line results and sales ability, Clothes-Knit Industries:
　　　　　　　　1995-97: TECHNICAL SERVICE REPRESENTATIVE. Plano, TX. Was promoted to serve as a Technical Service Representative resolving problems and issues among Clothes-Knit customers, sales, manufacturing, quality control, process development, and management personnel.
　　　　　　　　•　Assured customer satisfaction related to quality complaints and technical assistance.
　　　　　　　　•　Developed excellent problem-solving and conflict resolution skills while negotiating claims and disposition of "off-quality goods."
　　　　　　　　•　Gained experience in open-end yarn manufacturing, knitting, and weaving, as well as dyeing and finishing through my involvement with 10-yarn manufacturing facilities with combined shipments of 4.5 million pounds per week.
　　　　　　　　•　Conducted numerous courtesy visits in order to market and promote Clothes-Knit.

　　　　　　　　1995: SUPERVISOR. Connell Textiles, Corpus Christi, TX. Excelled as a Supervisor in open end yarn production with capacity of more than 1 million pounds per week; motivated and managed 40 employees and led them to achieve and exceed ambitious production goals.
　　　　　　　　•　Continuously ran high efficiencies while emphasizing the highest quality standards, implementing cost reduction goals, and promoting intense safety consciousness.
　　　　　　　　•　Was responsible for the carding and spinning departments; equipment consisted of Trutzschler opening and carding, Rieter 851 drawframes, and Schlafhorst SE 9s.

　　　　　　　　GENERAL MANAGER. Sweet & Tasty Bakery, Inc., Corpus Christi, TX (1987-94). For this wholesale and retail bakery serving Corpus Christi, Deer Park, Bellaire, and Arlington, developed marketing strategies for a wide range of quality baked goods, and developed large accounts with local industry and convenience stores; supervised 12 employees daily.

PERSONAL　　Can provide outstanding personal and professional references.

GOAL: "I'm changing fields and I have a pretty good idea what I'd like to do..."

Date

Dear Sir or Madam:

With the enclosed resume, I would like to express my interest in exploring employment opportunities with your organization and make you aware of my versatile skills and talents. I am in the process of permanently relocating to Idaho for family reasons, and I would appreciate the opportunity to discuss job openings which might utilize my versatile skills.

As you will see from my enclosed resume, I have excelled in several functional areas. While serving my country in the U.S. Army, I was promoted ahead of my peers to mid-management. I served with distinction as a Computer Operator, and I became known for my exceptionally strong mathematical and computational skills. I became accustomed to operating in an environment in which there was "no room for error" as I was involved in performing precise mathematical calculations used to calculate targets in live firing projects.

While serving my country, I was also cross-trained as a Vehicle Operator and Communications Operator. I became skilled in operating a 12-ton tracked vehicle and safely transporting people and equipment in all types of terrain and weather. I also worked as a Communications Operator and became skilled in using field telephones, digital message systems, and radio transmitters/receivers.

After military service, I went to work as a Maintenance Worker I and I have been promoted to Maintenance Worker II. Although I am excelling in this job which involves carpentry, plumbing, masonry, and maintenance knowledge, I am seeking to transfer into a job which could make more extensive use of my communication, sales, and customer service skills.

I can provide excellent references at the appropriate time, and I hope you will contact me to suggest a time when we might meet in person to discuss your needs. Please feel free to contact me at the Idaho address and phone on my resume or at my current location.

Yours sincerely,

Belton Jones

BELTON JONES

1110½ Hay Street, Fayetteville, NC 28305 • preppub@aol.com • (910) 483-6611

OBJECTIVE

I want to contribute to an organization that can use a versatile employee who offers skills related to training and supervising employees, maintaining and operating vehicles, handling sales and customer service, as well as operating computers.

EDUCATION

Completed numerous training programs sponsored by the U.S. Army including programs pertaining to computer operations, radio and telecommunications, management and supervision, and vehicle maintenance.
- Received a Certificate, Primary Leadership Course, 1995. Also received a Certificate from the Computer Operator Course, 1992.

Completed training sponsored by Vernon County, Georgia, pertaining to the management of maintenance operations, 1998-present.

Graduated from Plummer County High School, Butler, ID, 1990.

LICENSE

Hold a current Pesticide License issued by the County of Vernon in GA.

EXPERIENCE

EQUIPMENT OPERATOR & MAINTENANCE WORKER II. Vernon County, GA (1998-present). For the county, perform general carpentry and renovation work related to the construction, repair, or alteration of floors, roofs, stairways, partitions, doors, windows, and screens; build, erect, and repair a wide range of items such as partitions, cabinets, and bookcases; play a key role in the demolition of structures.
- Maintain plumbing systems and change faucet washers, stems, and seals; repair toilets by changing tank bulbs, overflow tubes, and guide wires.
- Perform preventive maintenance and minor repairs on tractors, mowers, string trimmers, power and hand tools, compactors, and other items.
- Perform liaison with the public and communicate the policies of the county; exercise tact and courtesy with the general public.
- Have refined my knowledge of the procedures, materials, and equipment related to the plumbing, carpentry, and grounds maintenance trades.
- Have become skilled in the use and care of a variety of hand and power tools necessary to perform plumbing, masonry, carpentry, and maintenance tasks.
- Read and interpret blueprints and specifications.
- Have received the highest possible evaluation of my performance in the following areas:

Quality of Work	Quantity of Work
Dependability	Attendance and Punctuality
Initiative and Enthusiasm	Judgment
Cooperation	Relationships with Others
Coordination/Scheduling	Safety and Quality Assurance

- Began as a Maintenance Worker I and was promoted to Maintenance Worker II.

COMPUTER OPERATOR. U.S. Army, Ft. Benning, GA (1994-97). Became known for my exceptionally strong mathematical and computational skills while performing precise calculations in a state-of-the-art computerized center which provided precise data used to determine targets for live-fire training projects.
- Advanced to the rank of E-4 (middle management) ahead of my peers; was responsible for training/supervising four people operating a sophisticated computer system.
- Operated a computer while also using graphs, tables, charts, and maps for manual computation.

PERSONAL

Possess an outgoing personality which is well suited to customer service and sales.

GOAL: "I'm changing fields and I have a pretty good idea what I'd like to do..."

Date

From Bookselling to Office Management

This experienced bookseller is tired of bookselling! She is making major changes in her life which include moving to another state to live closer to family and finding dramatically different work. She has her eye on office jobs, and she is hoping that her experience in serving customers and selling products will transfer into a new environment.

To whom it may concern:

With the enclosed resume, I would like to make you aware of the considerable management, problem-solving, and customer service experience I could put to work for you. I am currently in the process of relocating permanently to Arizona, where most of my family lives.

As you will see from my resume, I am currently involved in sales, customer service, and inventory control for a major book and magazine center in South Carolina. In my prior position in one of the southeast's largest malls, I managed all aspects of store operations for a prominent retailer of fine jewelry. Prior to that, I excelled in a track record of promotion to increasing responsibilities with the county clerk's office in Riverton, SC, where I completed four years of college studies in Communication Arts at the College of Charleston. You will notice from my resume that I was active in drama and theater while in college and received a Best Actress Award for my role as Annie Sullivan in *Miracle Worker*.

In addition to my strong customer service and operations management skills, I am skilled with Windows, including Word, Excel, and Access. I am also experienced in setting up and utilizing spreadsheets and in handling accounting including accounts receivable, accounts payable, and inventory control. In my job at the county clerk's office in South Carolina, I was praised for the leadership and initiative I displayed in transforming a troubled billing function with a pattern of chronic late payments into a punctual and accurate accounts payable operation.

An enthusiastic individual, I have always found resourceful ways to contribute to increased efficiency in all of my jobs. For example, I have expressed my creativity in developing exciting point-of-sale displays that have multiplied inventory turnover. Known as a cheerful and enthusiastic team player with unlimited personal initiative and resourcefulness, I can provide outstanding personal and professional references.

If you can use a versatile young professional known for an excellent attitude as well as superior work habits including reliability, dependability, and honesty, I hope you will contact me to suggest a time when we might meet to discuss your needs. I can assure you in advance that I could rapidly become an valuable permanent asset to your organization. I will be in Arizona on June 2nd and will contact you at that time if we have not already spoken.

Sincerely,

Tofali Chou

TOFALI CHOU

1110½ Hay Street, Fayetteville, NC 28305 • preppub@aol.com • (910) 483-6611

OBJECTIVE

To contribute to an organization that can use a skilled professional with extensive customer service and operations management experience along with an ability to expertly operate all office machines and equipment.

EDUCATION

Completed four years of course studies in **Communication Arts,** the College of Charleston, 1990-94.
- Worked in numerous part-time jobs in order to finance my college education.
- Received the **Communications Arts Award** for contributions to the drama department through my acting, directing, and managerial services.

Received Certificates of Completion from courses in Windows and MS Office.

On my own initiative, completed numerous courses related to computer operations, personal development, communication skills, and other areas in order to improve my poise.
- Completed Peter Lowe's Success Seminar which focused on motivational techniques.

SPECIAL SKILLS

- Skilled with Word and Windows including Word, Excel, Access, PowerPoint.
- Experienced in setting up/utilizing spreadsheets with software including QuattroPro.
- Experienced in accounts receivable and payable as well as inventory control.

HONORS

Received numerous awards and honors including the following:
- Received a Best Actress Award for my role as Annie Sullivan in *Miracle Worker*
- Numerous Certificates of Achievement for contributions to employers
- Received Honorable Mention for a poem published in *The Poetry Collection.*

EXPERIENCE

SALES CLERK. Tyler's Magazine and Book Center, Riverton, SC (1999-present). Have been credited with making significant contributions to store profitability through my ability to create and implement exciting point-of-sale displays as well as my skills in sales and customer service.
- Am involved in purchasing and controlling inventory; maintain a wide range of records.

MANAGER TRAINEE. Bopie's Pearls and Beads, Riverton, SC (1998-99). Managed all aspects of operation in a fine jewelry store.

OFFICE ASSISTANT II. Riverton County Clerk and Recorder, Riverton, SC (1995-98). Began working for this organization as a temporary worker and was offered a full-time job; continuously promoted to increasing responsibilities.
- Received, set up, and tracked the status of multiple jobs.
- Set up and maintained spreadsheets; prepared monthly billing and time sheets.
- Inventoried office supplies and micrographic supplies on a monthly basis and placed orders for products and equipment needed.
- Assisted my boss in producing the statewide Clerk and Recorder's Newsletter.
- Was cross-trained as a Microtechnician, and learned to prep and film documents.
- Was praised for the leadership and initiative I displayed in taking over a troubled billing function in which the organization was sending out its quarterly bills late; after a short time, the bills were being produced on time and our accounts balanced to the penny.

PERSONAL

Can provide outstanding references. Am known as a very outgoing and enthusiastic professional who prides myself on attention to detail and organizational skills.

GOAL: "I'm changing fields and I have a pretty good idea what I'd like to do..."

Date

Exact Name of Person
Title or Position
Name of Company
Address (number and street)
Address (city, state, and zip)

From Business Executive to Sports Team Management

Dear Exact Name of Person: (or Sir or Madam if answering a blind ad.)

After playing basketball in college, this professional excelled in a Fortune 500 company environment. In the back of his mind, he has always wanted to try his hand at managing in a sports environment. With this cover letter and resume, he is going to take a shot at finding a management position with a professional sports team. He figures his sales and management skills are transferable to the environment he enjoys most—basketball.

With the enclosed resume, I would like to make you aware of my interest in exploring management positions within your organization in which you could utilize my strong strategic thinking and problem-solving abilities as well as my proven strengths in sales, sales management, and general management.

Although I have excelled in sales, sales management, and general management in a Fortune 500 company environment, I am seeking to transfer my skills into the sports industry. I graduated from college after playing college baseball for four years. I then spent two years traveling the U.S., trying to sign a free agent contract as a professional player. Although professional baseball did not become my first full-time career, I feel that I "learned the ropes" about the ground floor of professional sports through that experience. I was recruited by my current employer, an international firm with $1.5 billion in annual sales, and I have an excellent track record based on superior results and performance.

After excelling as a Sales Representative, I was promoted rapidly to Sales Manager. I was then selected from among the corporation's 85 sales managers to act as National Sales Trainer, and in that job I developed and instituted programs that reduced turnover while increasing sales and boosting profits. I advanced to manage a $4 million district in Washington and then a $15 million district in Oregon. Most recently I have turned around a troubled major operation in Washington.

I feel certain that my strong management, communication, and organizational skills would be of great value to your team.. I would like to talk with you personally about the possibility of my playing a role in your continued bottom-line success.

If you can use my considerable skills and talents, I hope you will contact me to suggest a time when we might talk in person about your needs. I can assure you in advance that I have a reputation as a hard worker and highly effective communicator with a gift for thinking strategically, managing resourcefully, and operating with a strong bottom-line orientation. It would certainly be a pleasure to meet with you in person to discuss your needs and goals.

Sincerely,

Juan Osario

JUAN OSARIO

1110½ Hay Street, Fayetteville, NC 28305 • preppub@aol.com • (910) 483-6611

OBJECTIVE   I want to contribute to an organization that can use a skilled executive who offers a track record of outstanding results in profit center management, sales, and sales management along with a reputation as an insightful strategic thinker and resourceful problem solver.

EXPERIENCE   *Have excelled with Granger Worldwide, Inc., a $1.5 billion company which has evolved from a U.S. company selling business equipment into a global corporation selling network solutions; am being groomed for further promotion into senior management.*
DISTRICT MANAGER. Seattle, WA (1999-present). Because of my reputation as an exceptional problem solver with an ability to turn around troubled operations, was asked to take over the troubled Seattle district.
- Have taken over an unprofitable district with a damaged sales force and have reshaped attitudes, restored productivity, and instilled a winning attitude in a short time.

DISTRICT MANAGER. Portland, OR (1996-99). Was promoted to manage one of Granger's top five largest districts which has four branches in Seattle, Portland, Houston, and Detroit.
- Trained, motivated, and managed 65 sales, service, and administrative personnel.
- Exceeded every goal and objective and boosted revenue from $10 million to $15 million in less than three years.
- Held accountable for ambitious objectives related to asset management, revenue/profit growth, customer satisfaction in multiple locations, P&L, as well as human resources recruiting, training, and management.

DISTRICT MANAGER. Seattle, WA (1990-96). Operated as General Manager of a $4 million business, and succeeded in increasing revenues and profits every year; managed 30 people including sales, service, and support personnel.
- In 1992 and in 1995, was named **District Manager of the Year** among the company's 85 district managers; no one else in company history has ever won this award **twice.**
- Managed the district ranked as #1 in market penetration in the company for six years.
- Achieved a 267% growth in revenue over six years.
- Accomplished 100% quota for sales, revenue, and profits for a six-year period.

NATIONAL SALES TRAINER. Seattle, WA (1989-90). Was handpicked from a field of 85 sales managers for this assignment training and motivating the national sales force.
- Developed and instituted training programs that reduced turnover in the sales force.
- Became recognized for my ability to identify talented individuals, for my skill in recruiting them, and for my effective training style.
- Revised the corporate sales training program with the result that sales increased 12%, profits increased 14%, and turnover was reduced by 20%.

BASEBALL PLAYER. After playing four years of college baseball, I traveled the U.S. for two years with the goal of becoming a professional baseball player; was recruited by Granger in 1992.

EDUCATION   B.S. degree in Business Administration, University of South Carolina, 1991.
- Attended college on a four-year athletic scholarship; four-year letterman in baseball.

PERSONAL   Offer highly refined problem-solving and opportunity-finding skills. Have a proven ability to motivate individuals to achieve high goals and to work together as a team.

GOAL: "I'm changing fields and I have a pretty good idea what I'd like to do..."

Date

Exact Name of Person
Exact Title
Exact Name of Company
Exact Address
City, State, Zip

Dear Exact Name of Person (or Dear Sir or Madam if answering a blind ad):

I am writing to express my strong interest in a position as a Pharmaceutical Sales Representative with your organization. As you will see from the enclosed resume, I have excelled throughout my career in sales and teaching positions which required strong communication and negotiation skills.

As a native of Germany, I earned a Bachelor of Arts in Japanese Language and Literature and have developed and presented Japanese Language instructional materials as a Department of Defense employee. I worked with the Defense Language Institute and with prominent university officials on a multimedia series of Japanese language lessons that were later published on CD-ROM. While providing translation services for visiting Japanese delegates, I demonstrated my ability to communicate effectively with individuals at every organizational level.

Although I have been highly successful in my entrepreneurial endeavors and could continue in my present career, I have decided to pursue my long-term interest in the field of pharmaceutical sales. Through the local physicians who patronize our business, as well as our sponsorship of numerous charity events, I have developed a solid network of contacts within the medical community in my local area, which I feel would make me a great asset to any pharmaceutical company.

If you can use a dynamic communicator with a talent for establishing effective relationships and managing profitable business activities, I hope you will call or write me to suggest a time when we might meet in person to discuss your needs. I can provide outstanding references at the appropriate time.

Yours sincerely,

Mesaki Shang

MESAKI SHANG

1110½ Hay Street, Fayetteville, NC 28305 • preppub@aol.com • (910) 483-6611

OBJECTIVE   To contribute to an organization that can use a motivated professional with exceptional communication and organizational abilities who offers a strong bottom-line orientation and a "track record" of accomplishment in sales and management, education, and accounting.

EDUCATION   Earned a **Bachelor of Arts** in Asian Literature, Heidelberg University, Germany.
Completed studies in **Bookkeeping** at the Boseman School of Accounting and **Computer Programming** at Central Texas College, Fort Bliss, TX.
Excelled in specialized training courses from the U.S. Department of Defense, which included: Microsoft Excel, Harvard Graphics, and WinCalis 2.0, as well as the Instructor Training Course (ITC) and Instructor Certification Course (ICC).

COMPUTERS   Familiar with many of the most popular computer operating systems and software including Windows, Microsoft Word, Excel, and Access; and the PrintMaster desktop publisher.

EXPERIENCE   **OWNER** and **GENERAL MANAGER.** The Bountiful Boutique, Fort Bliss, TX (1997-present). Managed all phases of the opening and operation of this exclusive women's boutique; interviewed, hired, trained, and now supervise the sales staff, ensuring that each customer receives the highest possible levels of customer service.
- Monitor daily, weekly, and monthly sales of all merchandise, overseeing all purchasing and inventory control to guarantee a strong in-stock position on popular items.
- Oversee advertising and promotions for the store; negotiate with sales representatives from print, radio, and television media to obtain the best possible advertising rates.
- Direct all visual merchandising efforts, designing and implementing creative and effective displays throughout the store.

LANGUAGE INSTRUCTOR and **COURSE DEVELOPER.** Department of Defense, Fort Bliss, TX (1991-1996). Served as subject matter expert for the Japanese language; developed course materials and conducted formal classroom training and platform instruction for military and civilian instructors and students.
- Coordinated with the Defense Language Institute (DLI) while developing and reviewing the Basic Military Language Course (BMLC) in German.
- Completed the WinCalis 2.0 course, then trained ten other instructors in the proper use of this program used to develop computerized, multimedia lessons.
- Using audiovisual and graphic effects in WinCalis 2.0, authored and developed a series of Japanese language lessons presented at Michigan State University, considered for use by the National Security Agency (NSA), and later published in a CD-ROM format.
- Presented workshops on "Instructional Techniques and Methodology" to other instructors.
- Recognized for my exceptional performance; was selected as **Instructor of the Year** and received the Commander's Award and two Achievement Medals.

LANGUAGE INSTRUCTOR. Central Texas College, Fort Bliss, TX (1990-1991). Instructed military and civilian students and teachers in proper pronunciation, comprehension, and grammar of the Japanese language.

Highlights of earlier experience: **SENIOR ACCOUNTANT.** Bryson's Large Ladies Store, Dallas, TX. Provided accounting services to an upscale ladies' clothing store.

PERSONAL   Excellent personal and professional references are available upon request.

Date

From Day Care Worker to Franchise Owner

This hard-working professional has long envisioned the goal of owning her own business, and she believes she has found the perfect niche. She is attempting to transfer her experience and knowledge of day care into a business opportunity by applying to own a franchise in that industry.

Dear Exact Name:

With the enclosed resume, I would like to express my interest in franchising opportunities with your organization and make you aware of the many skills and abilities I could bring to the management of a Gymboree Play Programs business.

As you will see from my resume, I am a highly motivated self-starter who offers a proven ability to excel in any job I take on. After graduating from high school in Williamsburg, VA, I worked briefly for a temporary agency and then became employed as a Nanny for a professional couple with two adopted children. I thoroughly enjoyed the experience of helping young children find creative ways to develop their motor skills, intellectual abilities, and express themselves in play. After marrying and having two children of my own, I established a day care facility in my own home, and I provided full day care to children ranging from toddlers to older preschool children. I have thoroughly enjoyed working with children, and Gymboree offers the opportunity to own and manage a business catering to children.

I offer medical skills which would be useful in the role of Gymboree franchisee. Always seeking to improve myself and refine my knowledge, I have excelled in training programs including Certified Nursing Assistant, Emergency Medical Technician, as well as firefighting and rescue training. As a professional C.N.A. and Home Health Nurse, I have provided therapy and rehabilitation to victims of strokes and heart disease, and I have been told by many patients that my cheerful and enthusiastic personality was instrumental in their recovery. I was voted C.N.A. of the Month.

You will notice from my resume that I offer business management experience. For a popular hair styling and tanning salon in North Carolina, I became the trusted "right arm" to the owner. On my own initiative I implemented numerous new scheduling changes and procedures which improved customer satisfaction and profitability. I have a strong bottom-line orientation.

A hard worker by nature, I have extensively examined the Gymboree franchise opportunity and I feel that the franchise opportunity is an excellent fit with my love for children, technical medical knowledge, and management abilities. I am confident that I could become a distinguished franchisee within the Gymboree organization. Please review the materials I am sending and advise me about the next step I should take in the process of becoming a Gymboree franchisee. I can provide outstanding references such as the references which I am enclosing at this time.

Sincerely yours,

Grace Everett

GRACE EVERETT

1110½ Hay Street, Fayetteville, NC 28305 • preppub@aol.com • (910) 483-6611

OBJECTIVE

I wish to join the Gymboree organization as a franchisee; I seek to apply my strong business management skills along with my proven abilities related to serving customers, marketing programs and products, as well as maintaining bottom-line controls to ensure profitability.

EDUCATION

College and Professional education and training:
Certified Nurses Assistant (C.N.A.), College of William and Mary, Williamsburg, VA, 1996.
Completed 168 hours of training as an **Emergency Medical Technician**, College of William and Mary, Williamsburg, VA, 1998.
Completed more than 200 hours of training related to **firefighting and rescue operations,** College of William and Mary, Williamsburg, VA, 1997.
CPR Certified; **HAZMAT** Certified.
High School: Graduated from Williamsburg High School, Williamsburg, VA.

HONOR

Named "C.N.A. of the Month" in August 2001 because of my outstanding skills in establishing relationships with patients and their families.

EXPERIENCE

HOME HEALTH NURSE. TriCare Alternatives, Radford, VA and self-employed, Radford, VA (1999-present). Provide therapy and rehabilitation to victims of stroke and heart disease.
- Provide wound care therapy, order supplies, administer catheters, and help patients gain a new zest for life and an appreciation of their capabilities and limitations.
- Have been told by many patients that my outgoing and enthusiastic personality has been a motivating influence in their recovery.

CERTIFIED NURSES ASSISTANT. Highmount Hospital, Radford, VA (1997-98). Provided skilled nursing care in this major hospital environment; expertly handled charting, and became known for my gracious style of dealing with patients.

PATIENT CARE ASSISTANT & CERTIFIED NURSES ASSISTANT. Rest Haven Nursing, Radford, VA (1996-97). In this long-term care environment, provided skilled nursing care to the elderly; fed and bathed patients; took vital signs; performed charting.
- Assisted senior nursing professionals and physicians as needed.

ASSISTANT MANAGER. Shear Dimensions, Williamsburg, VA (1995-96). Became the trusted "right arm" of the owner of this popular hair and tanning salon with multiple stylists.
- On my own initiative, extended the salon's hours in order to increase profitability.
- Prepared payroll; handled bank deposits; purchased supplies; opened/closed salon daily.
- Became skilled at resolving customer problems in a tactful manner.

OWNER & MANAGER, DAY CARE FACILITY. Self-employed, Williamsburg, VA (1992-95). Established a day care center in my own home, and became knowledgeable of the local, state, and federal guidelines regarding such businesses.
- Provided care 10 hours a day for five children from toddlers to older preschool children.
- Designed play activities suitable for different age groups, and created an environment in which children were stimulated to explore, learn, and discover their creative abilities.

PERSONAL

Enjoy helping others, especially children and the elderly. Have excellent people skills.

Date

Mr. Bill Martin
Spaulding Products Division
P.O. Box 2560
Marietta, GA 30062

From Golf Pro to Manufacturer's Representative

Dear Mr. Martin:

Who would be a more knowledgeable sales representative for golf products than a golf pro? Although this golf pro has enjoyed his experience teaching and managing in golfing and country club communities, he would like to try his hand at sales.

I would appreciate an opportunity to talk with you soon about how I could contribute to your organization through my strong desire to represent your product line throughout eastern North Carolina and southeast Virginia.

As you will see from my resume, since earning my B.A. degree in 1996, I have been promoted to increasing responsibilities at Pinehurst Country Club. I began as an Assistant Golf Professional, was promoted to Head Golf Professional, and am currently Director of Golf Operations. Although many clubs and organizations have approached me over the years with other employment opportunities, I was determined to remain at Pinehurst Country Club until I developed its golf program to the highest possible standard. By every measure, I have achieved that goal and, in the process, have gained a reputation as an exceptionally strong communicator and motivator. I have frequently been called a "born salesman" and have become skilled in retail management while owning and managing the golf shop which grosses $165,000 annually.

As a lifetime resident of eastern North Carolina, I am well acquainted with the region and have an extensive network of contacts who know of my fine personal and professional reputation. I believe my name would make an excellent "calling card" for Spaulding, and I am certain I could contribute to your goals and continued success. I am an enthusiastic advocate of Spaulding already, and I would enjoy the opportunity to talk with you about the position of sales representative which is available. Of course I can provide outstanding personal and professional references.

I hope you will call or write me soon to suggest a time convenient for us to meet and discuss your current and future needs and how I might serve them. Thank you in advance for your time.

Sincerely yours,

Tom Wilson

TOM WILSON

1110½ Hay Street, Fayetteville, NC 28305 • preppub@aol.com • (910) 483-6611

OBJECTIVE

To contribute to an organization through my expertise as a golf professional, outstanding personal and professional reputation, exceptionally strong communication and sales skills, as well as my proven ability to manage operations, budgets, people, events, and assets.

EDUCATION

Bachelor of Arts (B.A.) degree in History, Grinnell College, Grinnell, Iowa, 1996.
- Areas of concentration were Business Administration, Psychology, and Sociology.

EXPERIENCE

Pinehurst Country Club, Pinehurst, NC (1996-present). On numerous occasions, have been approached by other clubs and organizations, but have steadfastly remained at Pinehurst Country Club in order to achieve the goal of elevating this golf program to the highest standard; have been promoted in the following progression:
DIRECTOR OF GOLF OPERATIONS. (1999-present). At this 625-member private club, own and operate a retail shop grossing $165,000 annually and supervise its four employees while also managing all aspects of golf operations, including supervising a staff of eight performing course maintenance.
- Combined my creativity and writing skills to improve communication with members through the monthly newsletter.
- Directed installation of a state-of-the-art irrigation system tee-to-green.
- Added senior tees, which were greatly appreciated by the members.

HEAD GOLF PROFESSIONAL. (1997-99). Planned and administered a $130,000 operational budget for golf shop operations while promoting, supervising, directing, and coordinating the overall golf program.
- Trained and supervised four employees retailing products in the golf shop.
- Created and directed a Junior Golf League which began as a four-club league in 1997 and grew to 15 member clubs in three divisions by 1998.
- Established and created a Junior Golf Association.
- Was golf coach for Pinehurst High School, 1997-98.
- Was featured in *Golf World Magazine* for walking and playing a 100-hole golf marathon for Junior Golf, July 1998.
- Coordinated numerous tournaments and golf promotions.

ASSISTANT GOLF PROFESSIONAL. (1996-97). After graduating from college, served as apprentice under Maynard Griffin, PGA Professional, while planning and conducting golf clinics and club tournaments, coordinating the junior golf program, and serving as Secretary of the Men's Golf Association.
- On my own initiative, organized a junior golf team to compete with area clubs.

PROFESSIONAL HIGHLIGHTS
- PGA National Education Committee, 2000.
- Extensive Carolinas PGA Section involvement.
- *Winner of eight Pro-Ams and qualified for PGA Club Pro Championship, 1996-present.*
- CPGA Winter Seminar Pro-Am Champion, 1999.
- Birchwood Pro-Lady, 1998.
- Duck Woods Pro-Am Champion, 1998.
- Pepsi-Brook Valley Country Club Pro-Am Champion, 1997.
- Pizza Inn-Willow Springs Pro-Am Champion, 1996.

PERSONAL

Can provide outstanding personal and professional references. Will relocate.

GOAL: "I'm changing fields and I have a pretty good idea what I'd like to do..."

Date

Exact Name of Person
Title or Position
Name of Company
Address (number and street)
Address (city, state, and zip)

From Management to Sales

Different jobs provide you with opportunities to gain insights into which skills you enjoy using and which skills you don't enjoy as much. This talented professional has tried management and has succeeded in that arena, but she has learned that she enjoys sales and consulting the most. Even in a career change, it's usually best not to abandon everything you know. In Elizabeth's case, she will approach manufacturers of eye products about representing their product line.

Dear Exact Name of Person: (or Sir or Madam if answering a blind ad.)

With the enclosed resume, I would like to make you aware of my interest in exploring employment opportunities with your organization. I offer a track record of outstanding bottom-line results based on my strong personal initiative, sales ability, and management skills, and I can provide outstanding references at the appropriate time.

As you will see from my resume, after completing two years of college I became a Sales Representative in the optical industry and rapidly distinguished myself because of my strong customer service skills.

In 1993 I was recruited to become a Sales Representative for a company which was pursuing an ambitious strategic growth strategy. After distinguishing myself in sales, I was promoted to a newly created position as Field Operations Coordinator and Trainer. Although I was considered quite young to handle the senior management responsibilities involved in that job, I quickly excelled and was instrumental in establishing "from scratch" seven new optometric practices which are still ongoing and which have contributed significantly to the company's bottom line. For those seven practices I played the major role in establishing them from the construction phase through the staff training and recruiting phase, and I spent up to three months at each practice to get it firmly established and operating in a sound manner.

After excelling as a Field Operations Coordinator, I was promoted to Manager in 1996, and I have succeeded in all aspects of sales, customer service, and personnel management. While managing seven employees, I motivated them to achieve bonus-level results for 33 out of 36 months. I have become skilled at working with doctors' offices, and I am experienced in negotiating the details of business agreements.

If you can use a proven performer with unlimited personal initiative and an ability to deliver exceptional bottom-line results, I hope you will contact me to suggest a time when we might meet to discuss your needs. Thank you in advance for your time and professional courtesies.

Sincerely,

Elizabeth Smitherson

ELIZABETH SMITHERSON

1110½ Hay Street, Fayetteville, NC 28305 • preppub@aol.com • (910) 483-6611

OBJECTIVE

I want to contribute to an organization that can use a dedicated young professional who offers a proven ability to achieve excellent bottom-line line results while also applying my strong customer service, sales, and management skills.

EDUCATION

Completed two years of college course work, College of Saint Elizabeth, Morristown, NJ. Completed numerous sales and customer service seminars sponsored by my employer. Graduated from Morristown High School, Morristown, NJ, 1993.

EXPERIENCE

Have worked for the same employer since 1993, and made significant contributions to the bottom line while excelling in the following track record of advancement with Optometric Eye Care Center, various locations in NJ:

1996-2000: MANAGER. Morristown, NJ. Was promoted to a key position which involved recruiting, training, and supervising seven individuals.

- In an essentially entrepreneurial role, took the initiative to establish "from scratch" vision programs with local companies and employers which contributed greatly to the growth and revenue of the company.
- Received the **Dedicated Service Award** in 2000 for two years of dedicated service.
- Worked closely with doctors in following up on patient referrals.
- Was responsible for payroll, insurance filing and billing, optical store sales, supervising staff and patient scheduling, coordinating with vendors for purchasing and inventory purposes, reconciling expense registers, and conducting inventory audits every six months.
- Met routinely with the President and Operations Manager of the company.
- Worked daily on a computer, and became proficient in utilizing RLI Optical software.
- Motivated the seven people I managed to achieve the office bonus level for 33 out of 36 months; the bonus was calculated on revenue figures and customer goals.
- Became known for my exceptional emphasis on customer service, and trained the people I managed to provide the finest level of customer service in the industry.

1994-96: TRAINER & FIELD OPERATIONS COORDINATOR. NJ Region. Worked in the corporate office of the company and traveled extensively in this job.

- Played a major role in the success of seven optometric practices in NJ; all practices are now extremely successful and profitable; was instrumental in opening the new facilities, hiring and training staff, and then worked in each office for 2-3 months to assure proper implementation of all policies and procedures.
- Trained employees in sales, customer service, office procedures, computer operations.
- Performed extensive liaison with doctors, and was called in to troubleshoot the most difficult customer service and operational problems.

1993-94: SALES REPRESENTATIVE. Morristown, NJ. Became skilled in all aspects of sales as I assisted patients in frame selection; fitted and dispensed new glasses; educated patients on lens options; wrote up sales orders; and relayed sales orders to the lab.

- Became skilled in working with doctors and gaining their confidence.
- Because of superior performance, was promoted by the company to manage its field operation during an ambitious time in the company's history.

PERSONAL

Can provide outstanding references. Skilled in working with Windows.

GOAL: "I'm changing fields and I have a pretty good idea what I'd like to do..."

Date

Exact Name of Person
Exact Title
Exact Name of Company
Address
City, State, Zip

Dear Exact Name of Person (or Dear Sir or Madam if answering a blind ad):

I would appreciate an opportunity to talk with you soon about how I could contribute to your organization through my marketing and communication skills as well as my experience in solving problems and supervising personnel in highly technical environments. My wife and I are permanently resettling in the Ohio area, and I am seeking to aggressively contribute to the bottom line of a company that can use a versatile professional with extensive technical knowledge and proven management abilities.

As you will see from my resume, I recently completed my B.S. degree with dual majors of Business Management and Marketing from DePauw University, Greencastle, IN, in December 1999. I am highly proficient with many software programs including Microsoft, and I can program in C++.

Prior to college, I served my country in the U.S. Navy, which gave me an opportunity to become involved in numerous projects which required an astute problem solver known for attention to detail. As a Navy diver, I was promoted to supervise complex diving operations which included salvage operations such as recovering the remains of the Shuttle Challenger. In my final position in the Navy as a Division Officer, I coordinated diving operations at an elite Research and Development facility in Texas where I supervised 15 specialists including electricians, mechanics, and other technical specialists. As a Quality Assurance Inspector in my previous job, I managed complex repair and overhaul projects and was recognized for my exemplary leadership ability and technical skills. I have managed budgets of up to $1 million and have coordinated all aspects of complex maintenance management projects.

After leaving the Navy, I devoted myself full time to completing my college degree and, in that process, I have refined my natural sales and marketing skills. If you can use an experienced professional with strong management, technical, and sales skills, I hope you will contact me to suggest a time when we might meet to discuss your needs. I can assure you in advance that I could rapidly become an asset to you.

Sincerely,

Crawford McKeithan

CRAWFORD MCKEITHAN

1110½ Hay Street, Fayetteville, NC 28305 • preppub@aol.com • (910) 483-6611

OBJECTIVE

To benefit an organization that can use a professional with excellent communication and problem-solving skills who offers experience in industrial environments where I have applied my excellent communication skills as well as my ability to train and motivate others.

EDUCATION

B.S., dual major in Business Management and Marketing, DePauw University, Greencastle, IN, December 1999.
A.A., Technical Studies, University of Indiana, IN, October 1995.

COMPUTERS

Am familiar with Microsoft Word, Excel, and Access.
Program in C++ and various other DOS and Windows environments.

EXPERIENCE

COLLEGE STUDENT. DePauw University, Greencastle, IN (1995-99). Completed degree requirements and was awarded a B.S. in Business Management and Marketing.

Became a member of the U.S. Navy's elite deep-water diving professionals and excelled in technical and supervisory roles:
DIVISION OFFICER. Corpus Christi, TX (1992-95). Coordinated diving operations at an elite Research and Development facility while conducting diving operations and overseeing a staff of 15 specialists including electricians, mechanics, and technicians.
- Acted as 3-M Coordinator scheduling all maintenance for multimillion-dollar equipment.
- Implemented a program to automate diving logs which streamlined tracking activities.
- Saved $20,000 in Navy funds and received a Letter of Commendation for directing clean-up efforts following the devastation of a military base by Hurricane Andrew.

QUALITY ASSURANCE INSPECTOR. Homeport: Corpus Christi, TX (1990-92). Contributed as a member of the repair department team with primary responsibilities for inspecting, maintaining, and repairing submarine engine systems.
- Completed a money-saving project during which a diving boat's main engine was over-hauled and was recognized with an Achievement Medal for my accomplishments.
- Was praised for my willingness to contribute many off-duty hours to complete repairs or overhaul projects which allowed equipment to be available sooner than expected.
- Achieved excellent results as a **Work Center Supervisor** managing logistics and maintenance for more than $1 million worth of equipment.

TECHNICAL INSPECTOR and **DIVING SUPERVISOR.** Homeport: Corpus Christi, TX (1987-90). Managed a $1 million operating budget while supervising highly complex programs which provided quality assurance support for a submarine rescue ship

Highlights of earlier U.S. Navy experience: Advanced in supervisory and technical jobs.
- Participated in salvage operations which recovered valuable orbiter and payload components and the remains of the Shuttle Challenger crew.
- In one position, played a key role in developing statements defining job knowledge, skills, and abilities needed in technical jobs which were adopted as standards by the Navy.
- In another job in Puerto Rico, functioned as a Purchasing Manager while working with local vendors to identify sources of supply for hard-to-obtain supplies and equipment.

PERSONAL

Thrive on challenges, deadlines, and pressure. Have basic knowledge of Spanish.

GOAL: "I'm changing fields and I have a pretty good idea what I'd like to do..."

Date

Exact Name of Person
Exact Title
Exact Name of Company
Address
City, State, Zip

From Military Officer to Civilian Public Relations

This accomplished military executive discovered his knack for public relations and was trained in media relations while serving his country as an officer. His first choice of a new career is in a corporation that can use his background related to creating communications products and coordinating media relations.

Dear Exact Name of Person: (or Dear Sir or Madam if answering a blind ad):

With the enclosed resume, I would like to make you aware of my interest in exploring employment opportunities with your organization. After several years of distinguished service as a military officer with the Army's highly trained Special Forces, I have resigned my commission as an officer and am relocating to the west to live and work near my family. I joined the Army after excelling for two years as a Hockey and Soccer Coach with a high school in Olympia, where I molded young athletes into winning teams which won league titles two years in a row.

While rising to the rank of Captain, I was selected for tough and complex assignments which required a strong leader with excellent problem-solving and decision-making skills. For example, I was handpicked to lead the attack which put down the coup attempt in Panama. I was also chosen over other highly qualified officers to lead sensitive military operations in stressful environments where meticulous planning and execution were critical to survival and mission success. As I was promoted to increased responsibilities I became responsible for planning and developing training activities and schedules. For example, I developed a two-year comprehensive training plan for 18 Special Forces team totaling 200 employees.

In 1999, I was selected to attend an intensive training program in marketing and public relations, and I have had an opportunity to refine my abilities related to public relations and marketing as the Public Affairs Officer for the famed Special Forces. I routinely perform liaison with media including CNN, ABC, CBS, FOX, the Discovery channel, and the History channel as well as numerous magazines and newspapers. I have coordinated eight film projects and two book projects, and I have developed highly successful community relations programs that sparked civic involvement and community-wide problem-solving. With outstanding written and public speaking skills, I am proficient with numerous software applications including PowerPoint and other presentation software. Although I was strongly encouraged to remain in military service and assured of continued promotion, I decided that my marketing, public relations, and communication skills would be best expressed in a civilian environment.

If you can use an astute communicator and experienced manager who could contribute strong problem-solving and strategic thinking skills to your staff, I hope you will contact me to suggest a time when we might meet to discuss your needs. I can provide excellent personal and professional references at the appropriate time.

Yours sincerely,

David Castleman, Jr.

DAVID CASTLEMAN, JR.

1110½ Hay Street, Fayetteville, NC 28305 • preppub@aol.com • (910) 483-6611

OBJECTIVE

To offer strong planning, organizational, and communication skills along with exceptional abilities in developing and implementing projects, mediating disputes, and solving problems through an innovative style of management, marketing, and public relations.

EDUCATION & TRAINING

Received **B.A. in History,** University of Puget Sound, Tacoma, WA., 1990.

Completed intensive executive education program in marketing and public relations, **The Defense Information School Program for Public Relations,** 1999.

Attended advanced leadership/management programs including a risk management course and Ranger School, the military's 72-day "stress test" of mental and physical capabilities.

EXPERIENCE

Advanced to the rank of Captain while building a reputation as an articulate, intelligent, and creative manager with the U.S. Army's elite Special Forces:

PUBLIC AFFAIRS OFFICER. United States Army Special Forces, Ft. Campbell, KY (Oct 1998-present). Coordinate with newspapers, magazines, and media including CNN, ABC, CBS, FOX, the History channel, Discovery channel, and numerous other broadcasting media while acting as the "voice" of the Special Forces to the outside world.

- Work with film crews to create awareness of what Special Forces does; have coordinated eight film projects and two book projects.
- Teach media relations and public relations, and have trained more than 200 people.
- Developed community relations programs that helped resolve community problems and ignited civic pride and citizen involvement.
- Coordinated internal and external information releases; conducted media analyses.
- Developed and published public affairs guidance for units deploying overseas.
- Write articles for unit magazine; utilize PowerPoint, Word, Excel, PageMaker.

TRAINING AND OPERATIONS MANAGER. Ft. Campbell, KY (1998). Handpicked from among 19 well-qualified managers, excelled in planning and scheduling long-range training for an organization with 1,000 employees; developed a two-year comprehensive training plan for 18 Special Forces teams while managing projects worldwide.

- Integrated intelligence, psychological operations, and administrative support.
- Managed an operations control center and integrated its functions into international activities directed at the highest levels of national security management.
- Earned widespread praise for my communication skills while delivering briefings.
- Reorganized a staff to achieve outstanding results in an environment of constant change.

GENERAL MANAGER. Ft. Campbell, KY (1996-99). Officially evaluated as one of the top six of 18 managers in the parent organization and as **"a superb performer with unlimited drive and initiative,"** supervised two junior managers and ten employees in five fields.

- Directed the efforts of weapons, engineering, medical, intelligence, and communications specialists carrying our politically sensitive missions vital to national security.
- Applied computer expertise to develop and implement a staff-level tracking system for monitoring training status which helped officials make resource management decisions.

Highlights of other experience: Refined my motivational skills while teaching and mentoring student athletes on teams which won league titles two consecutive years as a **Hockey and Soccer Coach,** Billings High School, Tacoma, WA.

PERSONAL

Earned numerous honors and medals. Excellent references. Offer strong computer skills.

Date

From Paralegal to Airline Stewardess

For a long time, this talented woman has entertained the thought of becoming an airline stewardess. She never acted on her desire until now, however. After excelling as a paralegal and then establishing a business which built on her knowledge in that area, she finally used her strong analytical skills to investigate which airlines were hiring. She made a telephone connection with an airline and then she responded to their initial expression of interest with this cover letter and resume.

Dear Sir or Madam:

I am writing to express my strong interest in pursuing a career as an Airline Flight Attendant with American Airlines. With the enclosed resume, I would like to make you aware of my strong background in leading, training, and motivating others and to acquaint you with my reputation as an outgoing, detail-oriented professional whose exceptional communication and interpersonal skills could benefit your company.

While earning my Associate's degree in Paralegal Technology, I completed coursework in Spanish. I also have a working knowledge of German language and culture, gained during the six years that I lived in that country. I have traveled extensively throughout the United States and to Panama as well as in Europe, where I visited Germany, Austria, Switzerland, and Spain.

As you will see from my resume, I have recently excelled as the General Manager of Tangle Title Agency, a company that I founded shortly after entering the legal field as a paralegal for a local law firm. At Tangle, I oversaw all human resources for the company, to include interviewing, hiring, and training all employees. I supervised as many as 15 paralegals and office assistants involved in conducting title searches for local law firms and attorneys. The exceptional communication skills and natural leadership that allowed me to succeed in establishing and marketing this venture will also make me a valuable addition to American's team of customer service professionals.

If you can use a self-motivated, enthusiastic individual whose decision-making skills and ability to deal effectively with others have been proven in challenging environments, I hope you will write or call me soon to suggest a time when we might meet to discuss your needs and goals and how my background might serve them. I can provide outstanding references at the appropriate time.

Sincerely,

Kathryn Barefoot

KATHRYN BAREFOOT

1110½ Hay Street, Fayetteville, NC 28305 · preppub@aol.com · (910) 483-6611

OBJECTIVE

To benefit an organization that can use an articulate professional with an outgoing personality, exceptional organizational skills, and strong attention to detail gained through a background in customer service, training, and management.

EDUCATION

Associate of Applied Science degree in Paralegal Technology, University of Miami, Coral Gables, FL, 1992; graduated with a **3.9 cumulative GPA.**
Completed additional coursework in Spanish.

TRAVEL EXPERIENCE

Traveled extensively throughout the U.S. as well as Europe; countries visited included Italy, Germany, Austria, Denmark, Luxembourg, Netherlands, France, Belgium, Switzerland, Spain, and Panama; lived in Germany for six years.

LANGUAGES

Have a working knowledge of both written and spoken **German** gained during my time living in that country.
Completed several courses in **Spanish** and have some knowledge and a great interest in that language; have a personal goal to become fluent.

EXPERIENCE

GENERAL MANAGER. Tangle Title Agency, Inc., Coral Gables, FL (1992-2000). After working briefly as a Paralegal with Smith & Whitman Attorneys at Law, launched my own company providing title insurance to attorneys in the area.

- Interviewed, hired, and supervised as many as 15 paralegals and office professionals while establishing and managing multiple offices.
- An acknowledged expert in searching titles, instructed paralegal staff in the proper methods for conducting accurate title searches.
- Known for my outgoing personality, personally oversaw all marketing efforts, presenting the company's services to local attorneys and law firms.
- Learned to adapt and interact effectively with a wide range of personalities, from builders, to real estate agents, to attorneys.
- Honed my ability to make sound judgments, negotiate contracts, and commit to decisions under tight deadlines and in stressful situations.
- Personally performed a large number of title searches, in addition to monitoring the performance of my staff in an industry in which no mistakes could be tolerated.
- Was recognized by the County Legal Association with a luncheon in my honor for my efforts in training paralegals in the community.

AFFILIATIONS

Past member, Chamber of Commerce
Member, National Association of Women in Law

PERSONAL

Am in excellent physical condition and health and work out daily in order to remain slim, trim, and strong. Known as a highly outgoing individual.

GOAL: "I'm changing fields and I have a pretty good idea what I'd like to do..."

Date

Exact Name of Person
Title or Position
Name of Company
Address (no., street)
Address (city, state, zip)

From Probation Services to Private Industry

There are a variety of situations and emotions that can spark the desire for a career change. In the case of Cynthia Willis, she found herself increasingly uncomfortable working in an environment in which she dealt with adult offenders in the criminal justice system. She also often worked late at night. She used this cover letter and resume to attract potential employers in a variety of industries, and she finally accepted a job in the insurance industry as a claims adjuster.

Dear Exact Name of Person: (or Dear Sir or Madam if answering a blind ad.)

With the enclosed resume and this letter of introduction, I would like to begin the process of formally applying for the job you recently advertised as a program manager.

As I believe you will see from my resume, I offer the skills, experience, and personal qualities which you are seeking. Since graduating with my B.A. degree, I have excelled in what is generally considered one of the most high-stress jobs in the world: administering parole services. While handling a large caseload of 150 clients, I supervise a wide variety of parole conditions and assist people in finding employment, obtaining help for substance abuse problems, managing their personal affairs and finances, and generally reorganizing their lives in creative and productive ways. I believe my positive and cheerful attitude has been the key to my excelling in a profession known for its high "burnout" and turnover rate.

I have become skilled in finding creative solutions for difficult problems, and I can provide strong personal and professional references describing my character and professional abilities. Computer literate, I offer a reputation as a tactful and diplomatic communicator with excellent writing skills. I have become adept at working with people at all levels, from judges to police officers, while also performing liaison with attorneys, prison administrators, business managers, and private sector employers.

You would find me to be a warm and enthusiastic professional who offers an exceptionally creative approach to problem solving and public relations.

I hope you will write or call me soon to arrange a brief meeting at your convenience to discuss your current and future needs and how I might serve them. I feel certain I could become a valuable asset to your organization, and I would enjoy an opportunity to show you in person that I am the qualified individual you are seeking.

Yours sincerely,

Cynthia Willis

CYNTHIA WILLIS

1110½ Hay Street, Fayetteville, NC 28305 • preppub@aol.com • (910) 483-6611

OBJECTIVE
To contribute to an organization that can use an experienced manager who offers proven decision-making and problem-solving skills along with a reputation as a resourceful, creative, well-organized professional with excellent written and oral communication skills.

EDUCATION
Bachelor of Arts in Sociology and **Business Administration**, the University of Nevada, Reno, NV, 1996.
Have excelled in numerous seminars and courses related to management.
Completed extensive training at the Nevada Justice Academy, Reno, NV.

EXPERIENCE
Have become known for my ability to communicate well with others and to assist others in developing realistic strategies for solving their life problems, finding suitable employment, developing career goals, and becoming productive members of society:
ADULT PAROLE SERVICES CASE MANAGER. Department of Corrections, Reno, NV (1998-present). Am extremely knowledgeable of how to network and "get things done" within the legal, law enforcement, business, and social services communities; apply that knowledge while managing a caseload of 150 clients comprised of offenders released from prison by the Parole Commission.

- Assist parolees in all aspects of life management including seeking help for substance abuse problems, prospecting for and obtaining suitable employment, managing personal finances as well as personal relationships, and generally finding a "focus" in life that is meaningful and motivating.
- Am known for my compassionate attitude as well as for my tough, creative, and practical approach to solving difficult problems.
- Work with law enforcement officials at all levels, from judges to police officers, while also performing liaison with attorneys, prison administrators, business managers and employers in the private sector, and federal assistance programs of every kind.
- Excel in a job which requires constant attention to detail as I supervise numerous conditions of parole including compliance with community service, debt and fee payment obligations, and other matters.
- Have acquired excellent "crisis management" skills while dealing routinely with incidents such as threatened suicides and other volatile, high-risk situations.

ADULT PROBATION SERVICES CASE MANAGER. Department of Corrections, Reno, NV (1994-98). Became skilled in the counseling and supervision of offenders placed on probation by the court system; enforced conditions of parole.

- Became known for my tact and diplomacy as well as for my excellent writing skills.
- Excelled in a profession generally regarded as very stressful and which has a very high turnover and "burnout" rate.
- Established an impressive track record of success in assisting dysfunctional people.

CERTIFICATIONS
Am Department of Corrections certified in unarmed self defense.
Am CPR certified; Certified in Arrest, Search, and Seizure.

SKILLS
Computer literate and experienced in working with various types of software.
Skilled in operating electronic house arrest equipment.

PERSONAL
Pride myself on my positive and cheerful attitude, and believe that a healthy mental attitude is the key to dealing with life's difficulties in a positive manner. Excellent references.

GOAL: "I'm changing fields and I have a pretty good idea what I'd like to do..."

Date

Exact Name of Person
Exact Title
Exact Name of Company
Address
City, State, Zip

It often takes more than wanting to make a career change. This experienced restaurant professional has been working nearly full time and going to school at night to obtain the degrees and training that will give her credibility in the field she is trying to enter--the computer industry.

Dear Exact Name of Person: (or Dear Sir or Madam if answering a blind ad):

With the enclosed resume, I would like to make you aware of my strong background in customer service, public relations, and business development and to acquaint you with the leadership, exceptional training skills, and education in business and computers that I could put to work for your company.

As you will see from my resume, I have completed an Associate's degree in Business Administration from University of Redlands, where I maintained a 3.5 GPA while working an average of 30 hours per week. While completing this program, I discovered a strong interest in computers, and I am now in the process of preparing to pursue the Microsoft Certified Systems Engineer certification.

Most recently, I have excelled as Head Server at DeLaFayette Café, Redlands' premiere fine dining establishment. In addition to ensuring an elegant and satisfying experience for patrons, I held additional responsibility for many important aspects of the restaurant's operation. I trained new service staff members, instructing them in all areas of providing the exemplary service expected by our customers. My ability to respond to rapidly shifting priorities was proven time and again, as I handled duties that ranged from ordering and maintaining the wine selection, to assisting patrons in planning and organizing special events, while consistently increasing profits through my exceptional sales ability.

Throughout my career in customer service and retail environments, I have consistently been placed in leadership roles, where my employers have benefited from my ability to train and motivate others to greater levels of efficiency and productivity. A native of Germany, my exceptional communication skills and flexibility have allowed me to adapt effectively to a new language and culture.

Although I was highly regarded by my previous employer and offered promotion into a management position, I have decided instead to explore other options where I can more fully utilize my growing education and further explore my interest in computers and technology. I hope you will welcome my call soon when I try to arrange a brief meeting to discuss your goals and how my background might serve your needs. I can provide outstanding references at the appropriate time.

Sincerely,

Susanna Jones

SUSANNA JONES

1110½ Hay Street, Fayetteville, NC 28305 • preppub@aol.com • (910) 483-6611

OBJECTIVE	To contribute to an organization that could benefit from an articulate and enthusiastic young professional with exceptional motivational, training, and organizational skills who offers a strong customer service background and an education in business and computers.
EDUCATION	**Associate's degree in Business Administration,** University of Redlands, Redlands, CA, 2001; maintained 3.67 while working 30 hours a week. Currently preparing to pursue Microsoft Certified Systems Engineer Certifications; course work begins in January 2001.
COMPUTERS	Proficient in operating many of the most popular computer operating systems and software, including Windows, Microsoft Word, Excel, PowerPoint, and others.
EXPERIENCE	**HEAD SERVER.** DeLaFayette Café, Redlands, CA (1996-1999). Coordinated and directed six servers, ensuring exceptional service to patrons of Redlands' finest dining establishment; provided instruction to new service staff members, training them in service techniques to ensure an elegant dining experience for customers.

- Maintained the restaurant's wine inventory, monitoring stock levels and ordering to satisfy customer demand while controlling costs.
- Assisted in planning events and parties for large groups, increasing sales by building the restaurant's reputation for providing the perfect atmosphere for special celebrations.
- Greeted patrons and effectively presented a number of special items and events, maximizing profit for the restaurant through my exceptional sales ability.
- Quickly built an excellent rapport with customers, generating repeat and referral business through my strong public relations skills and attentive service.
- Excelled in this fast-paced customer service environment through my strong problem-solving skills and ability to effectively respond to rapidly shifting priorities.

SHIFT MANAGER, TRAINER, and **HEAD SERVER.** Huggmugger's (Nelson Restaurant Enterprises), Redlands, CA (1994-1996). Provided leadership and training to the professional service and host staff at this innovative and successful local restaurant.

- Served as shift supervisor for the service staff, directing the completion of opening, ongoing, and end-of-day side-work and monitoring employee performance.
- Expertly trained a staff of 18 individuals in all aspects of restaurant operations and service; as a result of my efforts, guest service was maximized, food and beverage sales soared to record levels, customer base increased, and financial controls improved.
- Provided valuable input at monthly management meetings, to ensure the development of realistic objectives in both sales and customer satisfaction.
- Helped plan and organize special events and parties, including charitable events.

SERVER. Captain Jerry's Restaurant, Redlands, CA (1993-1994). Provided exceptional customer service to restaurant patrons at this busy local seafood restaurant; greeted guests, took customers' orders, and ensured a pleasant dining experience.

- Responsible for performing set-up and preparing the restaurant for the upcoming shift; supervised ongoing side-work and ensured guest satisfaction.

LANGUAGE	Bilingual and fully fluent in both written and spoken **Spanish.**
PERSONAL	Have a reputation as a self-motivated, hard working professional with the ability to develop effective relationships with customers. Excellent references are available upon request.

GOAL: "I'm changing fields and I have a pretty good idea what I'd like to do…"

Date

Exact Name of Person
Exact Title
Exact Name of Company
Address
City, State, Zip

**From Teaching to
Pharmaceutical Sales**

A few years of teaching
school has convinced
this outgoing young
professional that her
congenial personality
would be better suited to
a sales situation, and
she is approaching
pharmaceutical
companies.
Tip: Ms. McFarland has
teaching certifications
but, since she is trying to
leave the teaching
profession, she has not
included a
"Certifications" section
on her resume.

Dear Exact Name of Person: (or Dear Sir or Madam if answering a blind ad):

With the enclosed resume, I would like to make you aware of my interest in applying my talent for effectively presenting ideas and my exceptional communication skills for the benefit of an organization that can use an articulate young professional. I have been interested in pharmaceutical sales for some time, and I have decided to explore career opportunities within that field.

As you will see from my resume, I am currently a teacher and have made significant contributions to my school's growing success. I have excelled in every aspect of the teaching profession and have become an individual to whom other educators have turned in order to have their point of view expressed. For example, I was asked by the principal to serve as county representative to the Association for Accreditation of Schools and Colleges. I have also been named grade-level chairperson because of my leadership ability and proven skills in team management. Although I have enjoyed the challenge of educating young minds and have been told that I am one of the "best and brightest" members of the teaching profession, I have decided that I wish to embark on a career that will make better use of my sales, public relations, and marketing abilities.

I can assure you that I am held in the highest regard by my present employer and can provide outstanding personal and professional references at the appropriate time. However, I would appreciate your keeping my interest in your company confidential until after we have had the chance to meet in person.

I am hoping that you will give me an opportunity to meet with you briefly in person, because I am confident that you would find me to be a vivacious, congenial, and enthusiastic professional who could become a valuable member of your organization. I hope you will call or write me soon to suggest a time when we might meet to discuss your goals and how my background might serve your needs. I thank you in advance for your time and professional courtesies.

Sincerely yours,

Soraya McFarland

SOROYA MCFARLAND

1110½ Hay Street, Fayetteville, NC 28305　　•　　preppub@aol.com　　•　　(910) 483-6611

OBJECTIVE

To benefit an organization that can use an articulate, enthusiastic young professional with an outgoing personality and exceptional communication skills who offers a background of excellence in education as well as in community and civic activities.

EDUCATION

Bachelor of Arts, Butler University, Indianapolis, IN, 1990.
- Maintained a 3.2 GPA overall, 3.6 in my major.

Graduated from Baker High School, Indianapolis, IN, 1986; was a finalist in the Miss Indiana Beauty Pageant and was named **Miss Congeniality.**

EXPERIENCE

With Custer County Schools, have built a reputation as a loyal, enthusiastic and gifted educator, 1990-present:

TEACHER. Rockford Elementary, Indianapolis, IN (1996-present). Currently excelling in this position providing daily instruction to a diverse population of kindergarten students; implement lesson plans designed to foster individual learning styles and promote student mastery of basic skills and concepts.
- As grade-level chairperson, meet weekly with teachers to distribute information and develop lesson plans for use in all kindergarten classes; submit completed lesson plans to staff members.
- Played a key role in the school's achieving status as an **exemplary school** for the 1997-1998 school year, and an **exemplary school of distinction** for the 1998-1999 school year.
- Utilize my exceptional interpersonal and communication skills while interacting successfully with administrators, teachers, and parents, as well as with my students.

TEACHER. Howard Elementary, Indianapolis, IN (1990-1996). Excelled in this challenging position, providing motivation and effective instruction to children at a school in one of the most economically depressed areas of the county.
- Planned and executed instructional plans for the subjects which I taught, developing visual aides and other tools for use in the classroom.
- Served as **county representative** for Association for Accreditation of Schools.
- **Selected as one of only three teachers** who were rehired after the entire staff was displaced for a special project; passed a rigorous interview process to remain at Howard.
- Assisted the Superintendent and Principal as part of the interview committee that examined prospective staff members applying at the school.

ASSISTANT TEACHER. Elizabeth Elementary, Indianapolis, IN (1990). Worked with the exceptional children's program, quickly mastering time management and planning skills necessary to prepare lesson materials and run an organized, efficient classroom; developed a strong rapport with parents and other teachers.

AFFILIATIONS

Junior League of Indianapolis, active member since 1993; chaired the Training and Arrangements Committee in 1999 and the Yearbook Committee in 2000.

Victory Baptist Church, member since 1988; served on the Wedding Committee and the Preschool/Kindergarten Committee.

PERSONAL

A native and permanent resident of the Indianapolis area, have developed an extensive network of personal and professional contacts throughout the community. In my spare time, have modeled in local fashion shows. Excellent references are available upon request.

GOAL: "I'm changing fields and I have a pretty good idea what I'd like to do..."

Date

Exact Name of Person
Title or Position
Name of Company
Address (no., street)
Address (city, state, zip)

From Teaching to Public Relations

It didn't take more than a brief experience in student teaching to convince this young professional that she wasn't well suited to a long career in teaching. She has many talents, however, and will seek to transfer her excellent communication skills and outgoing personality to another type of work.

Dear Exact Name of Person: (or Dear Sir or Madam if answering a blind ad.)

Can you use an energetic and enthusiastic young professional who offers strong communication skills along with a persuasive professional style and sales experience?

As you will see from my enclosed resume, I recently received my Bachelor's degree from College of Atlanta, Atlanta, GA. While attending college, I refined my time management skills and displayed my adaptability in part-time and seasonal jobs requiring strong sales, communication, and instructional skills.

My experience as a student teacher was challenging and rewarding. I developed lesson plans which motivated and instructed the children while making learning fun. Among my greatest strengths are my tact and listening skills—I am able to hear both sides of an issue and diplomatically present my views. You would find me to be an optimistic and creative individual with a talent for "selling" ideas and effectively communicating concepts.

Although I love children and enjoyed my student teaching, I have decided that I wish to use my strong communication, organizational, and management skills in a business environment. I am certain that I will be able to apply my outgoing personality and multiple talents in a way that will help to enrich an organization's bottom line.

I hope you will welcome my call soon to arrange a brief meeting at your convenience to discuss your current and future needs and how I might serve them. Thank you in advance for your time.

Sincerely yours,

Annabelle Vines

ANNABELLE VINES

1110½ Hay Street, Fayetteville, NC 28305   •   preppub@aol.com   •   (910) 483-6611

OBJECTIVE

To apply my sales and communication abilities to an organization in need of a mature young professional who offers a talent for training and teaching others as well as a reputation as a creative thinker and good listener with a high level of enthusiasm and energy.

EDUCATION

Bachelor's degree, Elementary Education, the College of Atlanta, Atlanta, GA, 1997.

EXPERIENCE

STUDENT TEACHER. Macon Elementary School, Macon, GA (2000). After spending a short period of time observing the teacher's interactions with a class of third graders, took over all classroom activities including planning and carrying out daily activities for the children.
- Became skilled in planning lessons which called for a variety of learning styles and were interesting enough to motivate the students.
- Created a classroom management plan challenging enough to meet the standards of a very exacting supervisory teacher.
- Applied my creativity, optimism, and enthusiasm in making learning fun for children.
- Learned the importance of being patient and listening to the children's concerns.

Learned to manage my time while juggling the demands of attending college full time and excelling in often simultaneous part-time and seasonal jobs requiring strengths in the areas of sales, public relations, and providing instruction:
STOCKER. Talbot's, Washington, DC (1999). Applied my attention to detail while seeing that new merchandise was properly ticketed and also helped with unloading shipments and tagging merchandise for sale.

SALES REPRESENTATIVE. The Post and Courier, Charleston, SC (1996-98). Learned to use my persuasiveness and sales abilities while calling customers on the phone and letting them know the cost of subscriptions.
- Gained valuable experience in applying persistence and thoroughness when trying to sell a service.

HOSTESS/WAITRESS. The Captain's Restaurant, Myrtle Beach, SC (summers 1993-96). Contributed a cheerful attitude and patience while greeting customers and managing a waiting list that often stretched to two to three hours at this popular restaurant.
- Displayed the ability to work hard and still remain diplomatic and positive even when things were very hectic.
- Helped with daily activities including answering phone inquiries, serving drinks, and assisting in supporting other staff members to provide quality customer service.

SALES REPRESENTATIVE. The House of Hug'ems, Charleston, SC (1993). Refined my sales skills working independently by setting up a booth and making attractive displays and then demonstrating different puppets for sale.
- Displayed creative talents by finding interesting and new ways to make the puppets attractive to potential buyers.

COMPUTERS

Computer knowledge includes Word, Excel, Access, and PowerPoint.

PERSONAL

Offer proven ability to quickly grasp and apply new concepts. Excel in motivating others to learn and grow. Excellent references. Am known for my attention to detail in all matters.

GOAL: "I'm changing fields and I have a pretty good idea what I'd like to do..."

Date

Exact Name of Person
Title or Position
Name of Company
Address (no., street)
Address (city, state, zip)

From Teaching To Social Services

This teaching professional has a strong feeling that she would be best suited to the social services field, where she can utilize her strong motivational and counseling abilities.

Dear Exact Name of Person: (or Dear Sir or Madam if answering a blind ad.)

I would appreciate an opportunity to talk with you soon about how I could contribute to your organization through my experience and administrative skills related to the social services and mental health field.

As you will see from my resume, I have been involved since childhood in helping others as a role model and mentor. While earning my B.S. degree in Marketing and my A.A. in Business Administration, I worked with troubled youth and convinced many young people that hard work and a positive attitude combined with staying in school can overcome a bad start in life.

For the past two years after graduating from college, I have worked in classroom and camp environments with children who have varying disabilities including autism, mental retardation, cerebral palsy, and Down's Syndrome. As a teacher in a classroom of behaviorally disturbed children in Nebraska, I learned how to develop and implement effective lesson plans for disruptive students. As a teacher with the Perry County School System, I taught reading to autistic and mentally handicapped children and, on my own initiative, I learned sign language in order to help a child with Down's Syndrome learn to better communicate in his world. Most recently I was recruited by a classroom teacher for autistic students as one of seven staff members responsible for starting up a new summer program for autistic children and youth aged 4-20.

If we meet in person, you will see that I am an outgoing young professional with excellent communication skills and a very positive attitude. I truly believe that hard work and a positive attitude can help people overcome even the most disadvantaged childhood, and I take pride in the fact that I have helped many youth get off the wrong track and set high goals for themselves. I also offer excellent computer operations skills.

I hope you will write or call me soon to suggest a time when we might meet to discuss your goals and needs and how I might serve them. I feel certain that I could become a valuable and productive member of your team.

Sincerely yours,

Suzanne Justice

SUZANNE JUSTICE

1110½ Hay Street, Fayetteville, NC 28305　•　preppub@aol.com　•　(910) 483-6611

OBJECTIVE

To benefit an organization that can use a dynamic and articulate young professional who sincerely enjoys helping others while utilizing my strong organizational skills, computer knowledge, and thoroughly positive attitude.

EDUCATION

Bachelor of Science degree in **Marketing**, University of Nebraska—Lincoln, 1998.
Associate of Arts degree in **Business Administration**, University of Nebraska—Lincoln, 1996.

EXPERIENCE

ASSISTANT TO THE DIRECTOR & TEACHER. Camp Cloud Autistic Camp, Lincoln, NE (1998-present). Was specially recruited by a classroom teacher for autistic students as one of seven staff members to assist in starting up and implementing a new summer camp for autistic children which was funded by Lincoln County Mental Health, grants, and donations.
- Planned and implemented activities for children and youth aged 4-20.
- As the youngest member of the teaching/administrative team, have won the respect of my peers for my creativity, reliability, and willingness to always "go the extra mile."
- Helped children learn behavior skills while involving them in activities that promoted their academic, physical, and social development.
- Strongly expressed and implemented my belief that autistic children, like all children, need to learn and use good manners.

SUBSTITUTE TEACHER. Perry County Schools, Lincoln, NE (1997-98). Began as a substitute teacher with the Perry County System and taught reading skills to elementary children aged five to 11 years.
- On my own initiative, learned sign language in order to communicate with a monosyllabic child; taught him his colors and took pride in helping him gain communication tools which will help him throughout life.
- Earned widespread respect among teachers and administrators for my highly refined public speaking skills as well as my positive attitude.

SUBSTITUTE TEACHER. Muncie County Schools, Lincoln, NE (1997). For children aged kindergarten-grade 12, provided instruction based on daily lesson plans; learned to prepare and implement effective lesson plans for classrooms containing children with behavioral problems.
- Instilled in children the concept that hard work and a good attitude are the keys to success in life, and that you can overcome disadvantages in your background through initiative and attitude.

Other experience: While in college, worked as a mentor/counselor three days a week with troubled youth; taught them that one can overcome a poor beginning in life and that staying in school is essential to happiness and success.
- Believe I helped many youth discover hope and set new goals in life.
- Have a strong "helping instinct" which I have expressed through volunteer roles in programs including Feed the Homeless, Adopt a Family, All Sports Youth Program, and as Secretary and Teacher in my Sunday School program.

PERSONAL

Believe that my strong religious convictions are the foundation of my strong personal qualities which include determination to excel and persistence in achieving goals. Offer excellent computer skills with an ability to rapidly master new software.

GOAL: From Self-Employment to Something Totally Different

Date

Exact Name
Exact Title
Company Name
Address
City, state zip

**Cleaning Service
General Manager**

Establishing a company
"from scratch" and
managing it was just a
means to an end for this
hard-working individual
who used the business
she founded as a way of
paying for her education.
Now she is able to
pursue the career in
social services which she
has always dreamed
about!

Dear Sir or Madam:

I would appreciate an opportunity to talk with you soon about how I could contribute to your organization through my formal education in social work as well as my versatile experience in social services, business management, office operations, and transportation management.

As you will see from my resume, I recently completed the B.A. in Social Work degree which I started several years ago and was unable to complete quickly because my husband was being relocated worldwide as a military professional. I am especially proud that, through my persistence and determination, I was able to complete my degree even while managing a successful and fast-growing small business which I started "from scratch" and directed until recently, when we relocated to Washington.

In a previous job in the human services/social work field prior to receiving my degree, I worked as an Eligibility Specialist for the County of San Bernardino and was involved in interviewing clients and assessing their needs. I gained a reputation as a caring counselor and respected co-worker, and I was encouraged to apply for a social work position in the county if we were ever again residing in San Bernardino.

From my work experience in the Air Force and in office environments, I am accustomed to dealing graciously with the public while working under tight deadlines and solving difficult problems. I offer a naturally compassionate personality along with an ability to handle large volumes of work efficiently and accurately. I can provide outstanding personal and professional references.

I hope you will welcome my call soon to arrange a brief meeting at your convenience to discuss your current and future needs and how I might serve them. Thank you in advance for your time, and I will look forward to meeting you.

Sincerely yours,

Marlene Routhier

MARLENE ROUTHIER

1110½ Hay Street, Fayetteville, NC 28305 • preppub@aol.com • (910) 483-6611

OBJECTIVE	I want to contribute to an organization that can use a cheerful hard worker who offers an education related to social work and human services along with experience which includes proudly serving my country in the U.S. Air Force.
EDUCATION	**Bachelor of Arts (B.A.) degree in Social Work**, California State Polytechnic University, Pomona, CA, 2000; worked at night to finish this degree while managing a business during the day. Studied Social Work at Northwestern State University, Natchitoches, LA, 1980-82 and 1988. Excelled in supervisory and management training sponsored by the U.S. Air Force, 1982-87.
EXPERIENCE	**GENERAL MANAGER**. Marlene's Cleaning Service, Pomona, CA (1995-2000). On my own initiative and with only a fifty-dollar initial investment, set up "from scratch" a business which provided cleaning services for residential and commercial property; hired and supervised clerical and cleaning personnel while personally establishing the company's 18 major accounts. • Only two months after starting the business, generated monthly cash flow of $1,700 and personally handled the finances including accounts receivable/payable, financial reporting, tax preparation, and collections. • Was frequently commended for my gracious style of dealing with people. **ELIGIBILITY WORKER**. County of San Bernardino, San Bernardino, CA (1992-95). Performed assessments of clients to determine eligibility for medical assistance in the form of Medicaid. • Became acquainted with the vast interlocking network of social services organizations, and referred clients to those agencies and organizations as appropriate. • Assisted clients in preparing budgets and strengthened their ability to manage their finances. • Earned a reputation as a compassionate counselor and effective motivator while treating people from all walks of life with dignity and respect. • Became skilled in handling a heavy case load and large volumes of paperwork. **OFFICE MANAGER'S ASSISTANT**. M.T.S. Insurance Service, Brea, CA (1990-92). Worked as the "right arm" of a busy office manager in a fast-paced insurance office, and excelled in activities ranging from word processing, to invoicing, to customer service. **DATA ENTRY OPERATOR**. The Broadway, Los Angeles, CA (1988-90). Operated a computer in order to input data provided by sales associates; worked with customers in establishing delivery dates, and verified financial/accounting transactions. **PASSENGER & HOUSEHOLD GOODS SPECIALIST**. U.S. Air Force, McGuire AFB, NJ (1982-87). While serving my country in the Air Force, specialized in managing the transportation of people and property all over the globe. • Developed expertise in working with commercial airlines and shipping operations. • Expertly processed every kind of paperwork related to making reservations for domestic and international travel, issuing tickets, coordinating shipments of personal goods, and preparing monthly reports and bills of lading. • Learned to solve problems creatively and resourcefully in the process of locating "lost" people and property worldwide. • Received two prestigious medals for exceptional performance and exemplary service.
COMPUTERS	Have used Word and WordPerfect for word processing; can rapidly master new software.
PERSONAL	Am a patient, calm person who can handle a heavy work load and not get stressed out by tight deadlines. Have been told many times that I am a gifted counselor and communicator. Can provide outstanding personal and professional references upon request.

GOAL: From Self-Employment to Something Totally Different

Date

Exact Name
Exact Title
Company Name
Address
City, state zip

Dear Sir or Madam:

With the enclosed resume, I would like to introduce you to the sales expertise, leadership ability, and management skills which I could put to work for your organization.

Employers are *very* inquisitive about why an entrepreneur wants to make a change. This accomplished individual uses his cover letter to emphasize that he has worked in a big company as well as in the small company which he founded, and he makes it clear that he now wishes to be involved in sales. (Employers are looking for people who know what they want to do; entrepreneurs are usually definite in their preferences about what they want to do next.)

I am in the process of selling a company which I built "from scratch" and which, through my strong sales and management skills, I have grown into a profitable and respected small company in only two years. Although I have been successful in this entrepreneurial venture, I have decided that I wish to devote most of my energies to sales rather than to the day-to-day management details of a small business.

As you will see from my resume, I also offer a track record of proven results in managing a large company. In my first job after leaving the University of North Carolina at Chapel Hill, I went to work for a company in the oil industry and I advanced into the General Manager position. During the 20 years which I spent managing this large, diversified business with wholesale and retail operations, I took the initiative in building the first 10-minute oil change unit in VA. After acting as sales manager and developing the commercial fleet business, I sold the business to the Fast Lube franchise for a profit.

I can assure you that I am a tireless hard worker who thoroughly enjoys selling and developing a new marketing program as well as a great product/service. Although much of my experience has been in petroleum operations/sales and in automotive parts/sales with specialized knowledge of lubricants sales, I have proven my ability to sell products in other industries. As a Sales Representative of insurance products, I exceeded all quotas and was named a National Quick Start winner.

A naturally outgoing individual with a proven ability to lead and motivate others, I have been active in numerous leadership capacities in my community. I am a past president of the Rotary Club and former director of the Chamber of Commerce. If you can use my considerable sales and management abilities, I hope you will write or call me to suggest a time when we could meet in person.

Sincerely,

Wallace Jackson

WALLACE JACKSON

1110½ Hay Street, Fayetteville, NC 28305 • preppub@aol.com • (910) 483-6611

OBJECTIVE

To benefit an organization which can use a dynamic communicator and creative sales professional with outstanding negotiating and management skills along with a proven ability to transform ideas into operating realities while maximizing profit and market share.

EXPERIENCE

PRESIDENT & SALES MANAGER. Tidewater Sales & Rentals, Richmond, VA (1995-present). Utilized my entrepreneurial ability, aggressive sales orientation, strategic planning capabilities, and management skills to start a pre-owned car business "from scratch."
- Although I have been successful in starting up and managing a profitable business, I have decided to sell the company and seek a full-time sales situation.

SALES REPRESENTATIVE. State Farm Insurance, Richmond, VA (1993-1995). As a Property and Casualty Insurance Sales Professional for State Farm, handled "Family Insurance Check-ups" and personal lines.
- Excelled in my first sales experience outside the automotive and petroleum industry; was selected as a National Quick Start winner in 1993; received a company-paid excursion to Los Angeles, CA, for advanced training.
- Exceeded quotas and boosted insurance sales by introducing a unique insurance concept: a membership benefits package for independent business owners which provided clients with maximum insurance coverage through membership in the National Association for the Self-Employed (NASE) or other association programs.

GENERAL MANAGER. Jackson Oil Company Inc., Tidewater, VA (1973-1993). In my first job out of college, began with Mayfield Oil Company and advanced into the General Manager position; provided leadership in turning around a marginally profitable company and then helped it to achieve higher levels of sales and profitability each year; negotiated the buyout of key assets of Mayfield Oil Company by Jackson Oil Company in 1989 and continued as the corporation's chief executive officer.
- At the head of a diversified multiplex consisting of an oil company and a chain of convenience stores, worked at the wholesale buying level of the petroleum industry while gaining experience in managing a chain of retail convenience stores.
- Oversaw staffing, sales, purchasing, bookkeeping, financial management including accounts receivable/payable, vendor relations, and inventory control.
- Transformed a business with only 5 employees into a leading competitor in the region with a 40+ work force and profits which multiplied sevenfold.
- Took the initiative in building the first 10-minute oil change unit in VA and developed the operation from start-up to 35 cars a day; developed the commercial fleet accounts and then sold the business to the Fast Lube franchise for a profit in 1985!
- Established and managed a profitable automatic car wash business.

EDUCATION

Completed two years of college coursework, University of North Carolina at Chapel Hill, 1971-73.
Sales Training: Completed extensive sales and management seminars since 1973 including Dale Carnegie and A.L. Williams Management Seminars.
Technical Training: Completed numerous petroleum industry seminars and training programs sponsored by automotive and oil industry giants.

AFFILIATIONS

Former President, Rotary Club of the Tidewater Region. Membership Chairman, Social Chairman, and Chairman of the Board.
Other: Chairman of Miss Tidewater Pageant; Chairman of Tidewater Christmas Parade for five years; Chairman, Tidewater Centennial Parade; Co-Chairman of the Tidewater Heart Fund Drive; Member of Tidewater ABC Advisory Board for five years.

PERSONAL

Enjoy hunting, salt-water fishing, golf, and UVA athletic events. Outstanding references.

GOAL: From Self-Employment to Something Totally Different

Date

Exact Name of Person
Title or Position
Name of Company
Address (no., street)
Address (city, state, zip)

**Entrepreneur and
Business Manager**

This businessman offers experience in establishing a successful company and then selling it to a chain. He may attract the attention of a small or medium-size company that would like to be turned into a viable acquisition candidate. On the other hand, a large company may be attracted to his creativity and proven ability to "make it happen."

Dear Exact Name of Person: (or Dear Sir or Madam if answering a blind ad.)

I would appreciate an opportunity to talk with you soon about how I could contribute to your organization through my business management, sales, and communication skills.

As you will see from my resume, I have founded successful businesses, tripled the sales volume of an existing company, and directed projects which required someone who could take a concept and turn it into an operating reality. While excelling as a retailer and importer of products that included oriental rugs and English antiques, I have become accustomed to working with a discriminating customer base of people regionally who trust my taste and character. In addition to a proven "track record" of producing a profit, I have earned a reputation for honesty and reliability. I believe there is no substitute in business for a good reputation.

I am ready for a new challenge, and that is why I have, in the last several months, closed two of my business locations and turned over the management of the third operation to a family member. I want to apply my seasoned business judgement, along with my problem-solving and opportunity-finding skills, to new areas.

If you can use the expertise of a savvy and creative professional who is skilled at handling every aspect of business management, from sales and marketing to personnel and finance, I would enjoy talking with you informally about your needs and goals. A flexible and adaptable person who feels comfortable stepping into new situations, I am able to "size up" problems and opportunities quickly through the "lens" of experience. I pride myself on my ability to deal tactfully and effectively with everyone.

I hope you will welcome my call soon to arrange a brief meeting at your convenience to discuss your current and future needs and how I might serve them. Thank you in advance for your time.

Sincerely yours,

Desmond Vaughn

DESMOND VAUGHN

1110½ Hay Street, Fayetteville, NC 28305 • preppub@aol.com • (910) 483-6611

OBJECTIVE	To add value to an organization that can use a resourceful entrepreneur and manager who offers a proven ability to start up successful new ventures and transform ailing operations into profitable ones through applying my sales, communication, and administrative skills.
EDUCATION	Earned a **B.A. degree in Sociology**, University of Pennsylvania, Philadelphia, PA. Completed numerous executive development courses in business management and sales.
AFFILIATIONS & COMMUNITY LEADERSHIP	Have served by invitation on the Board of Directors of the following organizations:

Philadelphia Business Guild   Heart Association
Olde Philadelphia Association   Philadelphia Family Life Center
Philadelphia Hospital Pastoral Foundation New South River Association
City of Philadelphia Downtown Revitalization Commission

Have earned a reputation as a creative strategist with the ability to transform ideas into operating realities and with the communication and leadership skills necessary to instill enthusiasm in others.

EXPERIENCE	**FOUNDER & MANAGER.** The Captain's Den, Philadelphia, PA (1991-present). Established "from scratch" this business which grew to three locations with sales in seven figures; developed a product line which I bought from sources worldwide, and developed a customer base which included discriminating purchasers from all over the east coast.

- Refined my expertise in all aspects of business management, including financial planning and reporting, hiring and training personnel, designing advertising and marketing plans, selling products valued at up to thousands of dollars, and overseeing accounts payable and receivable.
- From 1991-95, simultaneously acted as an **Importer** and **Management Consultant** for an English antiques business; traveled to England three times a year as an importer.
- From 1993-95, after being recruited as **Development Director** by the Methodist State Convention, took on the paid job of coordinating the pledging and collection of $1.5 million to construct a dormitory and cafeteria for the Methodist State Convention; set up all systems and procedures and managed funds until construction was finished.
- Recently closed down the center city locations of The Captain's Den, and have turned over the midtown location to a family member.

ENTREPRENEUR. Desmond Vaughn, Inc., Philadelphia, PA (1990-95). While simultaneously managing the Captain's Den, was successful in this separate entrepreneurial venture; after extensive market research to determine the viability of establishing a business in the gifts and accessories niche, set up a store in the affluent midtown district which rapidly became successful through innovative promotions, vigorous marketing, and word of mouth.

- In less than two years, the business was producing sales in the low six figures.
- Sold the business to a large chain in the gifts and accessories industry.

SALES MANAGER. Solomon's Carpet Co., Inc., Philadelphia, PA (1981-89). Took over the management of an existing business and tripled the sales volume while increasing the staff from four to 11 employees.

- Used radio and newspaper in innovative ways which boosted traffic and sales.
- Supervised a five-person sales staff and trained them in techniques related to prospecting, closing the sale, overcoming objections, and solving customer concerns.

Other experience: **CAPTAIN & COMPANY COMMANDER.** U.S. Army. Was awarded the Bronze Star and Army Commendation Medal for service in Vietnam.

PERSONAL	Offer a proven ability to manage several functional areas and projects at the same time.

Date

Exact Name of Person
Exact Title
Exact Name of Company
Address
City, State, Zip

Financial Services Manager

After a successful stint as an entrepreneur, this professional has sold his insurance agency and part of the deal was a "noncompete" clause. Therefore, he has to seek employment outside the industry he knows best. His financial savvy and management skills are transferable to numerous types of organizations, including banking and financial services firms.

Dear Exact Name of Person (or Dear Sir or Madam if answering a blind ad):

With the enclosed resume, I would like to make you aware of my interest in exploring employment opportunities with your organization and introduce you to my background and credentials related to your business.

For the past ten years, I was involved in establishing and managing an independent insurance agency which I recently sold. The agency I founded grew to $10 million in revenue at its height and had relationships with most major carriers. Throughout my years of managing and growing the agency, I was a top sales producer. Every year I won an award from a major carrier based on my achievements in sales and profitability. Prior to founding my own company, I excelled as an Account Executive for Nationwide and handled all lines of personal insurance including health, auto, homeowners, life, and annuities. I am widely respected throughout the industry for my ability to resourcefully apply my expertise related to insurance, finance, and risk management, and I have established a vast network of contacts and relationships.

In prior experience outside the insurance industry, I worked in banking. For four years with Bank of America, I worked in the Finance Department and then as a Loan Officer for small commercial accounts and individual loans.

With an excellent personal and professional reputation, I hold licenses which include the Long-Term Care Medicare Supplement, Life and Health License, and Property and Casualty License. I have held the Series 6 license, and I am confident of my ability to obtain the Series 7 or any other license which I might require in order to meet an employer's needs.

I am now seeking to apply my considerable knowledge of finance, banking, and insurance within a larger organization which can benefit from my experience in sales, customer service, and accounts management. If my background and skills interest you, I hope you will contact me to suggest a time when we could meet in person to discuss your needs. Thank you.

Yours sincerely,

Nelson Zillini

NELSON ZILLINI

1110½ Hay Street, Fayetteville, NC 28305 • preppub@aol.com • (910) 483-6611

OBJECTIVE   To contribute to the growth and profitability of a company that can use a seasoned business executive with expertise related to insurance, financial consulting, and financial management as well as retail banking and commercial loan management.

EDUCATION   **Bachelor of Science (B.S.) degree in Business**, University of San Francisco, San Francisco, CA, 1985.
Completed extensive coursework sponsored by the **American Institute of Banking**, San Francisco Community College, San Francisco, CA.
• Later became an **Instructor of Banking** courses for the American Institute of Banking. Numerous training programs related to insurance, banking, finance, motivation, and sales.

LICENSES   Current Long-Term Care Medicare Supplement
Current Life and Health License
Current Property and Casualty License
Previously held Series 6 License

EXPERIENCE   **FORMER OWNER/FOUNDER & AGENCY MANAGER.** Zillini Insurance Group, San Francisco, CA (1991-2001). Recently sold the company that I founded which grew to $10 million in annual revenue with 20 employees and five agents licensed in property and casualty as well as life and health.
• Managed all aspects of the agency and was personally a major sales producer; every year since establishing the agency, I won an award, usually accompanied by a trip, from one of the major carriers based on my results in sales and profitability.
• Prospected for, secured, negotiated, and administered complex contracts.
• Handled risk management work for larger accounts; personally handled the agency's largest accounts.
• At one time, the agency handled the largest Workman's Comp premium in California.
• Became widely respected throughout the industry for my savvy insights and ability to resourcefully apply my expertise related to insurance, finance, and risk management.
• Recruited, trained, and developed a top-notch sales force; created and conducted training sessions to impart knowledge of insurance products.
• Played the key role in developing relationships with major companies such as CGU, Hartford, General Accident, California Casualty, and many others.

ACCOUNT EXECUTIVE. Nationwide Insurance Co., San Diego, CA (1988-91). Handled all lines of personal insurance: health, auto, homeowners, life, and annuities.
• Received numerous individual awards for exceptional productivity and profitability.

COMMERCIAL BANKER. Bank of America, San Diego, CA (1985-88). Began in the Finance Department and moved into retail banking as a Loan Officer.
• Handled small commercial and individual loans; actively recruited new commercial accounts while providing the highest level of customer service to established accounts.
• In my spare time, taught banking classes for the American Institute of Banking program.

AFFILIATION   Member, Independent Insurance Agents' Association and other industry associations

PERSONAL   Highly motivated individual who desires to work in a larger corporation and make a contribution to corporate goals, strategic planning, and profitability. Excellent references.

GOAL: From Self-Employment to Something Totally Different

Date

Exact Name of Person
Title or Position
Name of Company
Address (number and street)
Address (city, state, and ZIP)

**General Manager,
Industrial Supply Business**

After more than 18 years in his own business, this entrepreneur has diversified management and sales abilities which could enhance numerous organizations.

Dear Exact Name of Person: (or Dear Sir or Madam if answering a blind ad.)

With the enclosed resume, I would like to indicate my interest in your organization and my desire to explore employment opportunities.

As you will see from my enclosed resume, I recently sold a company which I built from a one-man operation into a thriving multimillion-dollar company serving a large base of commercial and industrial customers. I made the decision to sell the company to a large chain because it is my strong desire to utilize my background in sales and marketing for the benefit of a company such as yours.

I hope you will welcome my call soon to arrange a brief meeting at your convenience to discuss your current and future needs and how I might serve them. Thank you in advance for your time.

Sincerely yours.

Arthur Iles

Alternate last paragraph:
I hope you will call or write me soon to suggest a time convenient for us to meet and discuss your current and future needs and how I might serve them. Thank you in advance for your time.

ARTHUR ILES

1110½ Hay Street, Fayetteville, NC 28305 • preppub@aol.com • (910) 483-6611

OBJECTIVE	To benefit an organization that can use an experienced manager with proven entrepreneurial abilities along with a reputation as a dynamic individual with an ability to develop and maintain outstanding working relationships.
EDUCATION	**B.S. degree in Business,** University of Pennsylvania, Philadelphia, PA, 1978.
EXPERIENCE	**GENERAL MANAGER.** Iles Industrial, Inc., Malvern, PA (1979-present). Bought a company which was a one-man operation less than a year old and, after renaming it, transformed it into a highly successful industrial supply business with sales exceeding $2,500,000 and a customer base of 200 major companies; recently sold the company and am embarking on a career in sales.

Personnel Administration: Hired, trained, and motivated a staff of 14 employees, and was successful in maintaining a very low personnel turnover rate.

- **Financial Management**: Developed all internal accounting and financial management systems for accounts receivable, accountable payable, and other areas.
- **Purchasing and Inventory Control**: Handled all purchasing of equipment and supplies.
- **Vendor Relations**: Established and maintained an excellent credit reputation in the process of developing and maintaining effective working relationships with suppliers of equipment and materials; worked with suppliers from across the U.S.
- **Sales and Marketing**: In addition to hiring, training, and managing many inside and outside sales professionals, personally prospected for and obtained many clients through my personal contacts, referrals, and word-of-mouth from satisfied customers; became skilled in prospecting for high-volume corporate accounts and aggressively utilized all types of marketing tools including telemarketing and direct mail.
- **Shipping and Receiving**: Established and managed superior shipping and receiving operations which we continuously improved in order to assure customer satisfaction.
- **Total Quality Management**: Became known for my dedication to customer service and customer satisfaction through my hands-on management style, and continuously monitored the company's quality performance in all areas.

SENIOR BUYER. Pennsylvania Utility Co., Malvern, PA (1978-79). Excelled in a job which required me to handle responsibilities for purchasing various products for fossil and nuclear power plants.

- Became skilled in the bidding process including all aspects of examining extensive bids and evaluating vendors.
- Handled all aspects of purchase order placement, and oversaw the progress of bids including all follow-up; became skilled in solving problems from the initial bid phase to completion.
- Developed "instincts" for anticipating and avoiding problems before they occurred.
- In my first job out of college, began as a **Marketing/Customer Service Representative** and was rapidly promoted to Senior Buyer; learned how to market electric heat, became knowledgeable of new construction power hookups, and excelled in every aspect of customer service and problem solving.

PERSONAL	Can provide outstanding references. Exceptionally skilled communicator, motivator, sales professional. Would cheerfully relocate and travel extensively if needed.

GOAL: From Self-Employment to Something Totally Different

Date

Exact Name of Person
Title or Position
Name of Company
Address (no., street)
Address (city, state, zip)

General Manager, Service Business

Her husband's transfer to another city is what prompted this entrepreneur to seek employment with a company other than the one she started and managed.

Dear Sir or Madam:

With the enclosed resume, I would like to initiate the process of being considered for employment within your organization. A Rhode Island native, I have recently married and relocated with my husband to Cambridge, Massachusetts, which is now our permanent new home.

In my most recent job I actually founded and managed a successful small business which provided quality services to business and residential customers. I hired, trained, and managed four people and molded them into a hard-working team which helped the business earn a name for reliability, honesty, and quality work. I believe my outgoing personality and hard-working nature as well as my ability to deal graciously and tactfully with customers were the keys to my success in that business.

My previous jobs gave me the foundation which I needed to manage and grow a successful small business. Previously I excelled in jobs as a Hospital Supply Manager and as an Office Manager. In one job with a radio station as an Account Executive, I prospected for and landed the largest account in the station's history—a $100,000 account with Alaska Railroad. I have a knack for establishing and maintaining strong business relationships.

Now that my husband and I are making our permanent home in Cambridge, I am eager to find a company that I contribute to and grow with on a long-term basis. If you meet me in person, you will see that I have excellent public relations and customer service skills along with a proven ability to use tact and diplomacy in solving difficult customer problems. I can provide outstanding personal and professional references.

If you can use a hard worker with a strong bottom-line orientation, I hope you will contact me to suggest a time when I can make myself available for a personal interview at your convenience. Thank you in advance for your time.

Sincerely,

Elaine Cercone

ELAINE CERCONE

1110½ Hay Street, Fayetteville, NC 28305 • preppub@aol.com • (910) 483-6611

OBJECTIVE   To become a valuable member of an organization that can use an outgoing and highly motivated individual who offers a proven ability to produce a profit, control costs, satisfy customers, as well as coordinate billing and accounting.

EDUCATION   Studied **Computer Technology,** 1994-95; and studied **Medical Terminology,** Jamestown Vocational Technology, 1993-94; Jamestown, RI.
Completed numerous courses sponsored by Nissan related to product features, automobile financing, prospecting and selling techniques, and customer service.
Refined my public speaking skills in the Dale Carnegie Course, 1998.

EXPERIENCE   **GENERAL MANAGER.** Cleaning Solutions, Jamestown, RI (1993-00). Established "from scratch" and then managed the daily operations of a business which provided janitorial services; initially developed a base of residential customers and gradually phased out all residential accounts as I developed a customer base of business and industrial accounts with which I negotiated long-term contracts.
- Hired, trained, motivated, and managed four individuals who became a hard-working team of people which helped the business earn a reputation for reliability, honesty, and quality service.
- Designed and implemented all systems for billing, accounting, and payroll administration.
- Prospected for new accounts through telemarketing and through personal sales calls; after the first year, enjoyed a strong word-of-mouth business as well as loyal, repeat customers.
- Gained valuable experience in managing the operations of a busy office and in scheduling employees for maximum productivity.
- Believe that—in addition to hard work—my outgoing personality and my ability to deal with people and solve their problems in a tactful and gracious manner were the main keys to success in this entrepreneurial venture.

Excelled in simultaneously handling the following two positions at Jamestown Hospital, Jamestown, RI:
MEDICAL ASSISTANT/COMPUTER OPERATOR. (1992-93). Assisted doctors with minor medical procedures and diagnostic examinations.
- Was commended for my ability to put patients at ease and to explain their medical procedures in a way that lessened their anxiety.

HOSPITAL SUPPLY MANAGER. (1990-92). Was the first woman ever hired for this position and excelled in managing the ordering of hospital supplies.
- Negotiated with vendors; assured vendor compliance with contract terms.
- Became respected by hospital department heads for my outstanding customer service.
- Oversaw the shipping and receiving function; coordinated with accounting.

Highlights of other experience:
- **SALES ASSOCIATE/ACCOUNT EXECUTIVE.** Was Top Sales Associate several months at a car dealership.
- **OFFICE MANAGER.** For a business equipment company, excelled as a sales representative while also managing the office and eight employees.

PERSONAL   Am skilled at dealing with people and earning their confidence. Am a member, National Association of Female Executives. Excellent references.

GOAL: From Self-Employment to Something Totally Different

Date

Exact Name of Person
Exact Title
Name of Company
Address (no., street)
Address (city, state, zip)

General Manager, Small Business

Entrepreneurs often have established an excellent reputation within their communities, and this individual's active community leadership is one of his distinguishing features. A prospective employer likes an employee who comes with a substantial "network" of associates, because that could be a ready-made customer referral base.

Dear Sir or Madam:

With the enclosed resume, I would like to initiate the process of being considered for employment within your organization.

When you look at my resume, you will see that I have demonstrated a proven ability to transform ideas into operating realities and to improve the profitability and productivity of existing ventures. In my current position, I have developed "from scratch" a highly profitable business which now serves customers throughout Ohio.

With an outstanding personal and professional reputation, I am known as an excellent communicator and dedicated community leader. In Dayton County, I was elected to the Board of Education and then elected by my peers to act as Vice Chairman of the Board.

I am certain I could become a valuable asset to your organization, and if you can use my considerable talents please contact me to suggest a time when we might meet to discuss your needs and goals and how I might serve them.

Thank you in advance for your time.

Yours sincerely,

Jonathan Da Silva

JONATHAN DA SILVA

1110½ Hay Street, Fayetteville, NC 28305 • preppub@aol.com • (910) 483-6611

OBJECTIVE	To benefit an organization that can use an experienced manager with a proven ability to improve profitability while providing outstanding customer service, training and motivating employees, and transforming new ideas into operating realities.
HONORS	Active community leader, and have served Dayton County in these ways: Vice Chairman, Board of Education, 1996-present: Was elected by my fellow board members to serve in this leadership capacity.

- Member, Board of Education, 1994-present: Elected by the people of Dayton County because of my leadership ability and commitment to quality education.
- Am a trusted public official known for outstanding communication and leadership skills.

EDUCATION & LICENSES	Received a Bachelor of Science degree as an **Honor Graduate,** Turf Grass Management Program, Ohio State University, Columbus, OH, 1979.

- Completed professional development courses related to business management, personnel supervision, financial administration, and other areas.
- Obtained Ohio Department of Agriculture Pesticide **License** after extensive technical training by the N.C.D.A. related to the identification and control of insects, diseases, and weeds in ornamentals and turf.
- Received Ohio Registered Landscape Contractor License #348, February 1989.

EXPERIENCE	**GENERAL MANAGER.** Finescaping, Inc., Dayton, OH (1988-present). Have utilized my extensive technical expertise as well as my general management skills in building "from scratch" a business which employs up to five people while providing quality landscaping services to residential and commercial customers.

- *Financial Management*: Developed all internal accounting and financial management systems for accounts receivable, accountable payable, and financial control.
- *Purchasing and Inventory Control:* Handled all purchasing of equipment and supplies.
- *Vendor Relations*: Established and maintained an excellent credit reputation in the process of developing and maintaining effective working relationships with suppliers of equipment and materials; worked with suppliers from across the U.S.
- *Sales and Marketing*: Obtained many clients initially through my outstanding personal and professional reputation and then through referrals and word-of-mouth from satisfied customers; aggressively prospected for new customers through telemarketing, direct mail, and personal sales.
- *Safety Management:* Emphasized superior safety practices, and continuously trained equipment operators in safety procedures.
- *Personnel Administration*: Hired, trained, and motivated all employees including foremen and supervisors.
- *Total Quality Management:* Have a hands-on management style, and continuously monitor progress to assure the company's quality performance in all areas.
- *"Do it right the first time:"* Have learned that doing a job right the first time is often the key to customer satisfaction and repeat business, and try to instill this attitude in all employees.

SUPERINTENDENT. Garden & Lawn, Dayton, OH (1986-88). Supervised employees in all phases of installing landscape and irrigation systems, and managed projects ranging from $5,000 projects to $100,000 projects.

PERSONAL	Outstanding references can be provided. Adaptable individual with versatile skills.

ABOUT THE EDITOR

Anne McKinney holds an MBA from the Harvard Business School and a BA in English from the University of North Carolina at Chapel Hill. A noted public speaker, writer, and teacher, she is the senior editor for PREP's business and career imprint, which bears her name. Early titles in the Anne McKinney Career Series (now called the Real-Resumes Series) published by PREP include: *Resumes and Cover Letters That Have Worked, Resumes and Cover Letters That Have Worked for Military Professionals, Government Job Applications and Federal Resumes, Cover Letters That Blow Doors Open,* and *Letters for Special Situations.* Her career titles and how-to resume-and-cover-letter books are based on the expertise she has acquired in 20 years of working with job hunters. Her valuable career insights have appeared in publications of the "Wall Street Journal" and other prominent newspapers and magazines.

Judeo-Christian Ethics Series

BACK IN TIME
Patty Sleem
Published in large print hardcover by Simon & Schuster's Thorndike Press as a Thorndike Christian Mystery in November 1998.
(306 pages)
"An engrossing look at the discrimination faced by female ministers." – *Library Journal*
Trade paperback 1-885288-03-4—$16.00

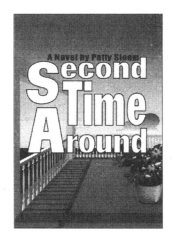

SECOND TIME AROUND
Patty Sleem
"Sleem explores the ugliness of suicide and murder, obsession and abuse, as well as Christian faith and values. An emotional and suspenseful read reflecting modern issues and concerns." – *Southern Book Trade*
(336 pages)
Foreign rights sold in Chinese.
Hardcover 1-885288-00-X—$25.00
Trade paperback 1-885288-05-0—$17.00

A GENTLE BREEZE FROM GOSSAMER WINGS
Gordon Beld
Pol Pot was the Khmer Rouge leader whose reign of terror caused the deaths of up to 2 million Cambodians in the mid-1970s. He masterminded an extreme, Maoist-inspired revolution in which those Cambodians died in mass executions, and from starvation and disease. This book of historical fiction shows the life of one refugee from this reign of genocide.
(320 pages)
"I'm pleased to recommend *A Gentle Breeze From Gossamer Wings*. Every Christian in America should read it. It's a story you won't want to miss – and it could change your life."
— Robert H. Schuller, Pastor, Crystal Cathedral
Trade paperback 1-885288-07-7—$18.00

BIBLE STORIES FROM THE OLD TESTAMENT
Katherine Whaley
Familiar and not-so-familiar Bible stories told by an engaging storyteller in a style guaranteed to delight and inform. Includes stories about Abraham, Cain and Abel, Jacob and David, Moses and the Exodus, Judges, Saul, David, and Solomon.
(272 pages)
"Whaley tells these tales in such a way that they will appeal to the young adult as well as the senior citizen."
– *Independent Publisher*
Trade paperback 1-885288-12-3—$18.00

WHAT THE BIBLE SAYS ABOUT… Words that can lead to success and happiness
Patty Sleem
A daily inspirational guide as well as a valuable reference when you want to see what the Bible says about Life and Living, Toil and Working, Problems and Suffering, Anger and Arguing, Self-Reliance and Peace of Mind, Justice and Wrong-Doing, Discipline and Self-Control, Wealth and Power, Knowledge and Wisdom, Pride and Honor, Gifts and Giving, Husbands and Wives, Friends and Neighbors, Children, Sinning and Repenting, Judgment and Mercy, Faith and Religion, and Love.
(192 pages)
Hardcover 1-885288-02-6—$20.00

RESUMES AND COVER LETTERS THAT HAVE WORKED

Anne McKinney, Editor

More than 100 resumes and cover letters written by the world's oldest resume-writing company. Resumes shown helped real people not only change jobs but also transfer their skills and experience to other industries and fields. An indispensable tool in an era of downsizing when research shows that most of us have not one but three distinctly different careers in our working lifetime. (272 pages)
"Distinguished by its highly readable samples…essential for library collections."
– *Library Journal*
Trade paperback 1-885288-04-2—$25.00

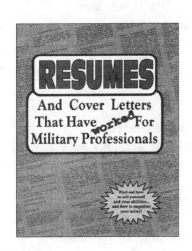

RESUMES AND COVER LETTERS THAT HAVE WORKED FOR MILITARY PROFESSIONALS

Anne McKinney, Editor

Military professionals from all branches of the service gain valuable experience while serving their country, but they need resumes and cover letters that translate their skills and background into "civilian language." This is a book showing more than 100 resumes and cover letters written by a resume-writing service in business for nearly 20 years which specializes in "military translation." (256 pages)
"A guide that significantly translates veterans' experience into viable repertoires of achievement." – *Booklist*
Trade paperback 1-885288-06-9—$25.00

RESUMES AND COVER LETTERS FOR MANAGERS

Anne McKinney, Editor

Destined to become the bible for managers who want to make sure their resumes and cover letters open the maximum number of doors while helping them maximize in the salary negotiation process. From office manager to CEO, managers trying to relocate to or from these and other industries and fields will find helpful examples: Banking, Agriculture, School Systems, Human Resources, Restaurants, Manufacturing, Hospitality Industry, Automotive, Retail, Telecommunications, Police Force, Dentistry, Social Work, Academic Affairs, Non-Profit Organizations,

Childcare, Sales, Sports, Municipalities, Rest Homes, Medicine and Healthcare, Business Operations, Landscaping, Customer Service, MIS, Quality Control, Teaching, the Arts, and Self-Employed. (288 pages)
Trade paperback 1-885288-10-7—$25.00

GOVERNMENT JOB APPLICATIONS AND FEDERAL RESUMES:
Federal Resumes, KSAs, Forms 171 and 612, and Postal Applications

Anne McKinney, Editor

Getting a government job can lead to job security and peace of mind. The problem is that getting a government job requires extensive and complex paperwork. Now, for the first time, this book reveals the secrets and shortcuts of professional writers in preparing job-winning government applications such as these:
The Standard Form 171 (SF 171) – several complete samples
The Optional Form 612 (OF 612) – several complete samples
KSAs – samples of KSAs tailored to jobs ranging from the GS-5 to GS-12
Ranking Factors – how-to samples
Postal Applications
Wage Grade paperwork
Federal Resumes – see the different formats required by various government agencies. (272 pages)
Trade paperback 1-885288-11-5—$25.00

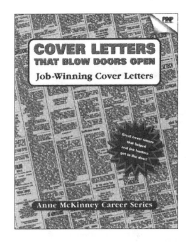

**COVER LETTERS THAT
BLOW DOORS OPEN**

Anne McKinney, Editor

Although a resume is important, the cover letter is the first impression. This book is a compilation of great cover letters that helped real people get in the door for job interviews against stiff competition. Included are letters that show how to approach employers when you're moving to a new area, how to write a cover letter when you're changing fields or industries, and how to arouse the employer's interest in dialing your number first from a stack of resumes. (272 pages)
Trade paperback 1-885288-13-1—$25.00

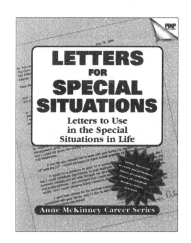

LETTERS FOR SPECIAL SITUATIONS

Anne McKinney, Editor

Sometimes it is necessary to write a special letter for a special situation in life. You will find great letters to use as models for business and personal reasons including: letters asking for a raise, letters of

resignation, letters of reference, letters notifying a vendor of a breach of contract, letter to a Congressman, letters of complaint, letters requesting reinstatement to an academic program, follow-up letters after an interview, letters requesting bill consolidation, letters of reprimand to marginal employees, letters requesting financial assistance or a grant, letters to professionals disputing their charges, collections letters, thank-you letters, and letters to accompany resumes in job-hunting. (256 pages)
Trade paperback 1-885288-09-3—$25.00

PREP Publishing Order Form

You may purchase any of our titles from your favorite bookseller! Or send a check or money order or your credit card number for the total amount*, plus $3.20 postage and handling, to PREP, Box 66, Fayetteville, NC 28302. If you have a question about any of our titles, feel free to e-mail us at preppub@aol.com and visit our website at http://www.prep-pub.com

Name: _____

Phone #: _____

Address: _____

_____

E-mail address: _____

Payment Type: ☐ Check/Money Order ☐ Visa ☐ MasterCard

Credit Card Number: _____ Expiration Date: _____

Check items you are ordering:

☐ $25.00—RESUMES AND COVER LETTERS THAT HAVE WORKED.

☐ $25.00—RESUMES AND COVER LETTERS THAT HAVE WORKED FOR MILITARY PROFESSIONALS.

☐ $25.00—RESUMES AND COVER LETTERS FOR MANAGERS.

☐ $25.00—GOVERNMENT JOB APPLICATIONS AND FEDERAL RESUMES: Federal Resumes, KSAs, Forms 171 and 612, and Postal Applications.

☐ $25.00—COVER LETTERS THAT BLOW DOORS OPEN.

☐ $25.00—LETTERS FOR SPECIAL SITUATIONS.

☐ $16.00—BACK IN TIME. Patty Sleem

☐ $17.00—(trade paperback) SECOND TIME AROUND. Patty Sleem

☐ $25.00—(hardcover) SECOND TIME AROUND. Patty Sleem

☐ $18.00—A GENTLE BREEZE FROM GOSSAMER WINGS. Gordon Beld

☐ $18.00—BIBLE STORIES FROM THE OLD TESTAMENT. Katherine Whaley

☐ $20.00—WHAT THE BIBLE SAYS ABOUT... *Words that can lead to success and happiness.* Patty Sleem

New titles!

☐ $16.95—REAL-RESUMES FOR SALES. Anne McKinney, Editor

☐ $16.95—REAL-RESUMES FOR TEACHERS. Anne McKinney, Editor

☐ $16.95—REAL-RESUMES FOR CAREER CHANGERS. Anne McKinney, Editor

☐ $16.95—REAL-RESUMES FOR STUDENTS. Anne McKinney, Editor

☐ $16.95—REAL ESSAYS FOR COLLEGE AND GRAD SCHOOL. Anne McKinney, Editor

☐ $10.95—KIJABE...An African Historical Saga. Pally Dhillon

_____ **TOTAL ORDERED (add $3.20 for postage and handling)**

Volume discounts on large orders. (910) 483-6611 for more information.

THE MISSION OF PREP PUBLISHING IS TO PUBLISH BOOKS AND OTHER PRODUCTS WHICH ENRICH PEOPLE'S LIVES AND HELP THEM OPTIMIZE THE HUMAN EXPERIENCE. OUR STRONGEST LINES ARE OUR JUDEO-CHRISTIAN ETHICS SERIES AND OUR BUSINESS & CAREER SERIES.

Would you like to explore the possibility of having PREP's writing team create a resume for you similar to the ones in this book?

For a brief free consultation, call 910-483-6611
or send $4.00 to receive our Job Change Packet to
PREP, ATTN: Career Change, Box 66, Fayetteville, NC 28302.

QUESTIONS OR COMMENTS? E-MAIL US AT PREPPUB@AOL.COM